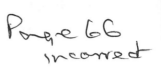

ROCK CLIMBS
IN
MALLORCA

ABOUT THE AUTHOR

Chris Craggs was born in Richmond, North Yorkshire, in 1950. He started rock climbing in 1965 on Yorkshire gritstone and in the Lake District. He moved to Sheffield in 1970 to train as a teacher and 'hit' the Peak District. He currently teaches in a special school for children with severe learning difficulties.

Chris has climbed extensively in the UK, from Jersey to northern Scotland and all stops in between. In Europe he has been to locations as far apart as northern Sweden and Gibraltar, including 40 trips to Spain. He has also made nine extended trips to the USA, where he visited spots as varied as Squamish Chief in British Colombia, the Devil's Tower in Wyoming and City of Rocks in Idaho, as well as the honey pots of Yosemite, Zion and the Grand Canyon.

Chris has written six books on UK and foreign climbing destinations, and writes regularly for the UK outdoor press. He has been the Peak Area correspondent for *Climber* for a number of years and wrote the latest BMC *Stanage Guide*.

Other Cicerone books by the author:

Costa Blanca Rock
Andalusian Rock Climbs
Selected Rock Climbs in Belgium and Luxembourg

ROCK CLIMBS
IN
MALLORCA

(including Ibiza, Tenerife, Gran Canaria and Lanzarote)

by
Chris Craggs

CICERONE PRESS
MILNTHORPE, CUMBRIA
www.cicerone.co.uk

© Chris Craggs 2000
2nd edition
ISBN 1 85284 319 5
A catalogue record for this book is available from the British Library

Acknowledgements

This book is dedicated to all the people I have climbed with on regular visits to these superb islands over the past twelve years: John and Oliver Addy, Colin Binks, Dave Gregory, Rory Gregory, Willie Jeffrey, Mike Riddings, Jim Rubery and Dave Spencer, and to Pete (POD) O'Donovan for dragging me up some of the islands harder routes. Also thanks to Mike Appleton; I have never climbed with him on Mallorca, but after many visits to the Costa Blanca together I missed him out of my most recent guide, and hope this redresses the balance a little. Thanks also to Terry Fletcher, Roger Briggs and Brian Evans who took the trouble to report back on grades, approaches, new routes, etc, from their visits. Cheers lads – it is much appreciated.

Also thanks to all the talented climbers who have offered advice about the grades of the harder routes, especially Andy Barker, Gary Gibson, George Haydon, Paul Harrison, Dave Musgrove, Mike Owen, Tony Mitchell and Karl Smith.

Special thanks as ever to my 'other half', Sherri Davy – fourteen years on and 40+ trips to all over Spain and we still love it!

Colin Binks and Dave Gregory deserve an extra mention this time around as they were happy to use up their holiday allowance following me round the island on that most unrewarding of activities, 'checking'!

And to Deborah Carter and Caroline Dickinson at Wrestler Foods who have provided us with Wayfarer's excellent provisions for the last couple of years. They have certainly made our catering a lot easier: Chicken Dopiaza followed by Spotted Dick and Custard – unbeatable! Also to Mrs Morrison and all the team at Premier Car Hire – thanks for ten years' good service!

Finally a special thanks must go to the small nucleus of climbers on Mallorca without whose talents and hard work the place would not be worth a visit by the serious sport climber. Where we have gone others will follow, those souls who visit the Costa Blanca year in and year out might well enjoy a trip to Mallorca.

Chris Craggs

Front cover: *Colin Binks on BT2.13 (6a) on the recently developed cliffs at Betlem, northern Mallorca*

CONTENTS

MALLORCA

GRAN CANARIA

LANZAROTE

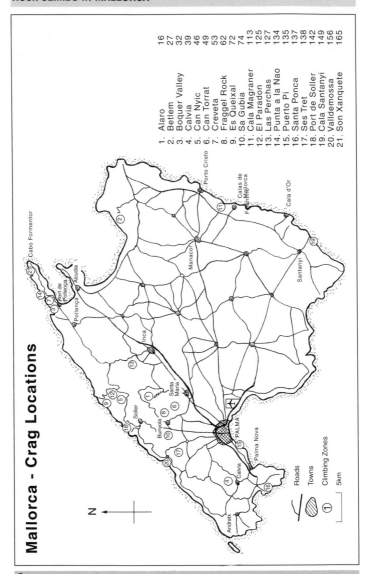

Mallorca - Crag Locations

1. Alaro	16
2. Betlem	27
3. Boquer Valley	32
4. Calvia	39
5. Can Nyic	46
6. Can Torrat	49
7. Creveta	53
8. Fraggel Rock	62
9. Es Queixal	72
10. Sa Gubia	74
11. Cala Magraner	113
12. El Paradon	125
13. Las Perchas	127
14. Punta a la Nao	134
15. Puerto Pi	135
16. Santa Ponca	137
17. Ses Tret	138
18. Port de Soller	142
19. Cala Santanyi	149
20. Valldemossa	156
21. Son Xanquete	165

N ←

Roads

Towns

① Climbing Zones

5km

MALLORCA

Introduction

I first visited Mallorca in 1988 after a series of excellent winter holidays in and around the Costa Blanca. As always when visiting somewhere new I had some reservations: chiefly because information on the climbing was hard to come by and I had heard that the weather could be less reliable than on the mainland. It was therefore with some trepidation we booked a trip; but then again, nothing ventured.... Flying in over the Sierra del Norte on that first afternoon dispelled all the doubts, and as we have got to know the island so our feelings for the place have continued to grow. It is a truly stunning place worth one visit by anybody, and a lot of visits by most folks. Whether you want a few easy routes to spice up a restful beach holiday, or you want to climb classics in superb surroundings or to spend a week climbing routes in the upper 7s, the place has lots to offer.

On that first trip to Mallorca I was impressed by several things. As expected the weather was pleasantly mild and the island was quiet, having its annual breather from the invading hordes. More surprising was the stunning beauty of much of the island, and perhaps of most significance was the amount of undeveloped rock scattered around the place.

In the back of my original 1990 guide to the Costa Blanca I included 30 pages on Mallorca as a brief introduction to the place. My 1995 guide included 120 pages on the island and still the expansion continues. My 1990 prediction that 'there is little doubt that Mallorca will become a major European centre for sports climbing in the years ahead' has already been realised, and it vies with the Costa Blanca for the accolade of premier European centre for winter rock climbing such is the wealth of rock, the ease of access from the UK and Germany, and the good weather.

Mallorca remains a premier foreign holiday destination for Brits abroad. Even with the emergence of Greece and Turkey, along with other more exotic summer venues, Mallorca stills sees in excess of seven million visitors a year. The chief attractions are the unending summer sunshine, fine beaches and crystal clear seas. To service this summer influx there is a massive infrastructure with the 'Costa de Concrete' stretching around the Bahia de Palma from Santa Ponca to El Arenal, and with various soulless outliers scattered up the eastern edge of the island. There are also much more traditional resort towns typified by the beautiful Puerto

Pollenca on the north of the island and Soller to the west.

The flights, the accommodation, the weather, the rock and even the bolts are already organised – the last little bit is up to you. See you out there!

Getting There

There are more flights to Mallorca from the UK than to any other holiday destination, and they leave from virtually every national airport. Prices vary from knock-down (less then £50 return) at quiet times to rather inflated (say £150+) during the school holidays. All inclusive packages can be good value, though self-catering accommodation of all classes abounds. Shop around! Some airlines have proved to be unreliable, especially when it comes to delays; we have had long waits with Peach, Spanair, Sabre and AirOps. You may not have problems, but at least you have been warned of the possibility.

On a much more positive note, EasyJet have started flying to Palma from both Liverpool and Luton, and they have rather upset the airline apple-cart. We recently got return flights for £17.50 each way, plus taxes, on a modern aircraft, with a daily scheduled service and no delays – what more could you want? Check out their web site and on-line booking (credit card or Switch required) at: www.easyjet.com. Go (British Airways) http://go-fly.com fly from Stansted to Palma. Although generally not as cheap as EasyJet, they are worth a look.

If all else fails it might worth considering flying scheduled with Iberian airlines, though they can be rather pricey. They fly direct from Heathrow, or from Manchester via Barcelona. At quiet times they do special 'two for the price of one' deals – just ask. Their central booking office can be reached on 0845 6012854.

Transport

A car is pretty much a necessity. Although the island has a reasonable transportation system a number of the cliffs are remote, and the distances involved between the various centres make for difficult commuting. It would be possible to stay at Gubia or Fraggel Rock and cope without a vehicle (once you were established), but then there are the problems of shopping, water and security. For car hire I have always used Premier Car Hire, who are based in Harlow. They have always proved reliable and they offer a range of vehicles with prices currently starting at about £75 a week in the winter, which is £10 less than it was five years ago! Phone 0279 641040 for a current brochure. A rep will meet you at the airport (don't forget your driving licence) and the car is normally delivered with a full tank of petrol. You leave it as empty as you dare at the end of the holiday. Mention that you are a frequent user and you will normally get a discount and/or an upgrade. Baby seats and roof racks can be fitted free.

A Base

Quite where you stop on the island depends in part upon the kind of holiday you envisage. Both Puerto Pollenca and Soller are exceptionally pleasant, but they are a touch remote from the mainstream climbing areas. However they are ideally situated for exploring the northern mountains and coasts and make perfect bases for family holidays. On the other hand the modern resorts, such as Magaluf or Palma Nova, have some positive points: they are quiet in the winter, accommodation is plentiful and most of the climbing is within a twenty to thirty minute drive. If you want comfortable, cheap accommodation, with easy shopping and some low-key night life, you could do worse!

It is probably best to avoid resorts such as Porto Cristo and Calla Millor on the eastern edge of the island unless you enjoy driving. If you book a package with accommodation allocated on arrival, beware; Murphy's Law ensures that you will end up as far from your favourite cliff as geographically possible!

A good percentage of the accommodation on the island is owned by Brits and it is usually possible to sort something out before you leave home. The Sunday papers and magazines such as *Dalton's Weekly* or *Private Villas* have plenty of places to rent, usually with UK contact numbers. Another alternative is simply to turn up and look for signs 'apartments to rent' in any of the resorts. Prices can be as low as £10 a night for basic accommodation for four (cheaper than camping back home or even than camping in Spain). Again the key is to shop around.

Our best deal to date was flight, five in a group A car (with a roof rack of course!) and five in an apartment (four in beds and Colin on the floor) for £98 plus spends, beat that!

Season

It goes without saying that the best time to visit Mallorca is in the depths of the northern winter, when the climate is usually pleasantly mild and the whole place is quiet. Unfortunately good weather is not guaranteed, but you would be unlucky not to get an adequate time on the rock any time between October and April. Despite this, I once heard of a team of Scots who had a week's holiday on Mallorca: it rained every day and they all had flu! It has to be said that their experience was exceptional.

Summers are hot, crowded, expensive and insect ridden, but if family commitments and other circumstances force you to visit the island throughout the hotter months of the year all is not lost. With a bit of foresight there is enough rock to be found that faces out of the sun at different times of the day, so some good sport should be available. The mountains are high enough to escape the worst of the heat, and of course the beaches are available once it becomes just too hot.

The Guide Book

This is the fifth guide book I have written to foreign rock climbing destinations, and the production of these guides has gone through a gradual evolution. Wherever possible I have tried to take on board the comments that people have made about the previous books, and the overriding aim behind this guide is to provide as much information as possible. It strikes me that once people have bought a guide, then the more information it contains the better! To this end I have included full description for as many climbs as possible, pitch lengths, star ratings and as much peripheral information as was available. Perhaps most importantly the approaches have been checked and rechecked and each crag now has a locator map.

As to the diagrams, they are drawn from original photographs of the cliff wherever possible, but cannot be completely accurate at this scale. The descriptions provide more detailed information.

The cliffs in the guide are of two broad types, the first and largest number are the well-known and well-publicised cliffs about which I have been able to accumulate detailed information from a variety of sources. The second type are cliffs (often more recently developed) where solid facts and even the route names have been harder to come by. The information on these has come from an amalgamation of personal experience, searches of Spanish magazines, conversations with both British and local climbers and a variety of rough topos. The first set of cliffs have been covered in detail, whereas the second have been described using a combination of topo format and brief descriptions. In the few cases where names are unavailable, I have simply numbered the routes. If no information has been available over a number of years, I have made the point of inserting the occasional 'made up' names in my guides. This perhaps a bit of a dubious tactic, but I feel it is better than lines of 'Unnamed's, and it also helps to keep an eye out for any plagiarism! I hope the information provided here gives an adequate basis for locating the cliffs and routes.

I have pondered long and hard whether to bother including any UK grades, but have decided to stick with the French (Spanish!) grade. I have done away with all UK grades except on routes that require the carrying of a rack, as this appears to adds an extra layer of confusion. A comparison table is included as a rough approximation of what to expect (see below), always remembering that Mallorcan grades have always been regarded as being a little (or a lot) on the harsh side.

Historically many (though not all) of the routes on Mallorca are graded rather stiffly when compared to their mainland counterparts; this can be up to one and a half grades difference. It means that some Gubia routes graded 6a+ would get 6c on the mainland and 6c+ at Buoux. Also there is the slight fly in the ointment that grade anomalies are more marked on some cliffs than others, depending – at least in part – on who developed the cliffs. To have upgraded every route on the island would have been a bit heavy-handed. In the end I have decided to use the currently accepted Mallorcan grades, and interestingly the most recent local guide has introduced plenty of upgrades, though some will still be perceived as a bit tough.

If you find the Spanish/Mallorcan grades rather (or very) tough, it is not that you are having an off day; don't get demoralised, just change the grade in your guide! The grades given are either in the form:

- 5 – indicating confirmed Mallorcan/Spanish grades, or
- 7a? – indicating suspected Mallorcan/Spanish grades.

It is probably worth mentioning that with bolt-protected routes most climbers find they can climb a grade or two harder when there is no imminent danger of death due to runners falling out. Climbers who operate at VS 4c might be daunted by the lack of lower grade climbs in the guide, but they should be able to battle up 5 and even 5+, which will open a whole new world.

Any comments on new routes, grading anomalies, descriptions and the like are always welcome, and can reach me via Cicerone Press or directly via e-mail at chris.craggs@which.net. Also check out my web site http://homepages.which.net/~chris.craggs for recent developments, new cliffs and so on.

Approximate grade comparisons

UK		Fr/Sp	USA
S	(4a)	4	5.6
VS	(4c)	4+	5.7
HVS	(5a)	5/5+	5.9
E1	(5b)	5+/6a	10a
E2	(5c)	6a/6b	10c
E3	(6a)	6b/6c	11a
E4	(6a)	6c/7a	11c
E5	(6b)	7a/7b	12a
E6	(6c)	7b/7c	12c
E7	(6c)	7c/8a	13a

The list below features the cliffs in the order they appear in this section; the brief notes should allow you to choose your poison.

Mallorca cliffs

Crag	Aspect	No of routes	Comments
Alaro	SE	50	Great tufas, varied routes, great outlook.
Betlem	W & N	22	Nice setting, great rock.
Boquer Valley	All	30	Generally short, superb setting.
Calvia	S	20	Mid-grade face climbing.
Can Nyic	NW	13	Cool face climbing.
Can Torrat	W	22	Excellent big 7s and one huge 6.
Creveta	SW	33	Sharp mid-grade classics
Fraggel Rock	E	52	Tough tufas.
Queixal	W	12	Short mid-grade walls.
Gubia	All	114	The best on the island. Classics galore.
Magraner	SE	76	Seaside mid grade outings + the Caves!
Paradon	S	4	Adventures, apply here.
Perchas	N	27	Steep or slabby, choose your crag.
Punta a la Nao	W	2	Recent seaside sport.
Port Pi	W		Scruffy bouldering
Santa Ponca	N	7	Short and sharp.
Ses Tret	N	18	Steep and shady
Soller	W	32	Steep stuff below the building site.
Santanyi	S	36	Majestic setting, though generally tough.
Valldemossa	W	34	Varied roadside cragging.
Son Xanquete	N	14	Very short and very steep.

A Plea

Despite the massive scale of the tourist industry on the island, much of Mallorca away from the coast remains unspoilt. This applies explicitly to many of the climbing areas; please treat them and the local inhabitants with due respect. More specifically (and I shouldn't need to say this): don't leave litter, don't block access routes, avoid crossing cultivated land and don't taint water supplies. If you cannot organise your bodily functions to use the resort facilities, get WELL away from footpaths and the climbing areas. A group trowel might not be an altogether bad idea – so you can bury it, paper and all. If in doubt treat Mallorca like your back garden at home, and you won't go too far wrong.

A Warning

Crime on Mallorca does not appear to occur on the same scale as parts of the mainland, where the popular parking areas are regularly 'checked out' by hooligans on scooters. Despite this it makes good sense not to leave any valuables in your car. As an extra precaution I always make a point of leaving the empty glove box open, the boot empty and the parcel shelf out of the car so as to discourage speculative break-ins; it makes sense to avoid any holiday hassles. A word of warning to the wise, your equipment is not completely safe even at the crag, so keep half an eye on it!

ALARO

Character

The cliffs that almost completely encircle the impressive mountain (822m) behind the small town of Alaro are amongst the most extensive on Mallorca, though development has been minimal up to the present date. There are enough climbs here for one or two visits at the moment, always depending on the grade you climb at, though most of the best routes here are pretty tough. These are spread along the face in three sectors. Extending rightwards from the developed areas the cliff swings round to face east; the rock is in the order of 250m high and it is manifestly magnificent. Climbers looking for a bit of traditional adventure climbing could do worse than to direct their attentions here. The cliffs at the Castillo de Alaro (and on Soncadena, 816m, directly across the valley) are approaching the scale of the Falaise d'Escales in the Verdon, but their development is still in its infancy; they will doubtless become major destinations in the fullness of time.

Access

From the town of Alaro follow the road northwards towards Orient. In a couple of kilometres signs are seen for the Castillo de Alaro; follow these! A tarmac road runs up the mountain, but then becomes unmetalled and rather rough. A considerate approach towards your car's underbody is probably a good idea. An impressive taverna is passed at about half-height with parking for the first two sectors. It is well worth checking out the place at the end of a day's sport. The road continues to wind its way up the hill until it pops over a col to arrive at an extensive parking area in the trees. From here a well-made path heads up rightwards towards the only gap in the cliffs about 10 minutes' hike away.

The buildings on the hill top are about another 10 minutes' walk from the climbing by the entrance. They include a bar, restaurant and cheap rooms, and they form a very popular destination for weekend walkers who troop up the path in their hundreds. The walkers are always politely intrigued by the climbers, though if you are not too keen on performing in a public arena it might be best to avoid weekend visits to the cliffs.

The Climbs

There are three developed areas on the huge west-facing wall below the cliff top dwellings. From right to left these are SECTOR CHORRERAS, SECTOR DEL

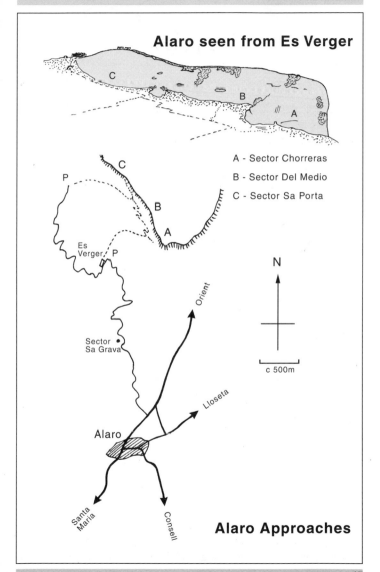

Alaro seen from Es Verger

A - Sector Chorreras
B - Sector Del Medio
C - Sector Sa Porta

N

c 500m

Alaro Approaches

MEDIO and the SECTOR SA PORTA (see diagram for location of these). There is also a small collection of hard routes on the boulder that is passed on the way to the cliff, just above the first sharp bend on the approach road, and they are included here for those who like that kind of thing. The routes here are on the:

SECTOR SA GRAVA (Gravel Sector)

NO ES FACIL SER DIOS * 7c 12m
The steep south-west arête.

SUCOT DE POMA * 8a 12m
The centre of the south face, left of the tree.

DIAL 'M' * 7b+ 12m
Right of the tree passing a large hole near the top.

RAMONES * 7b+ 12m
The blunt south-east arête.

CUATRO MEJOR QUE CINCO 6a 10m
The 'slabby' west face.

The three routes on the north face share a lower-off:

ESPIRITU SANTO 6c 10m
The left-hand side of the north face.

PADRE 7a 10m
The centre,

HIJO 6b 10m
and the right-hand side.

The rest of the climbs are spread along the huge west-facing wall. All of these are described from right to left.

SECTOR CHORRERAS (Sector of the Spouts)

Park at the Cafe Es Verger and follow the path rightwards in front of the buildings horizontally until it starts to rise following the conspicuous diagonal path easily seen from the parking. At the third bend (or second zig) cross the wall carefully, scramble down 10m then head horizontally right passing slabs until below a steeper 'black and tan' slab. There are a dozen or so routes here, a mixture of fairly good lower/middle-grade slab routes and some 'super-tufa' routes. There are also two more routes 100m further to the right just around the arête of the

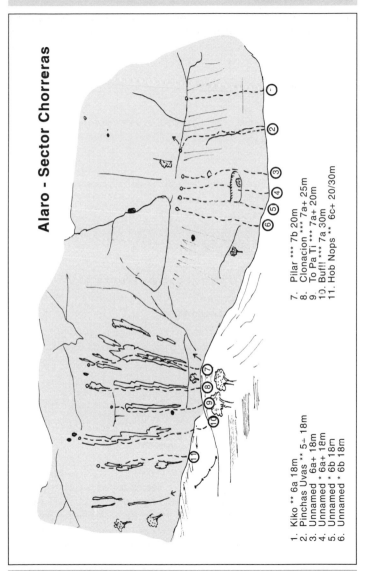

Alaro - Sector Chorreras

1. Kiko ** 6a 18m
2. Pinchas Uvas ** 5– 18m
3. Unnamed * 6a+ 18m
4. Unnamed * 6a+ 18m
5. Unnamed * 6b 18m
6. Unnamed * 6b 18m

7. Pilar *** 7b 20m
8. Clonacion *** 7a+ 25m
9. To Pa Ti *** 7a+ 20m
10. Bufl! *** 7a 30m
11. Hob Nops ** 6c+ 20/30m

mountain: XAVIER ** 7a+ 20m, up a wall, and UNNAMED *** 7b+ 17m, the leaning wall from a cave.

On the slabby apron is:

1. KIKO ** 6a 18m
The slab gives a good sustained pitch.

2. PINCHAS UVAS ** 5+ 18m
The thin crack has two peg runners and then five bolts. Move right to a lower-off. An upper pitch has a old frayed rope hanging down it and looks unlikely at the quoted 7b+.

3. UNNAMED 6a+ 18m
To the right of the hollow climb the steep slab on disconcertingly hollow rock, not one of the greatest routes on the island.

4. UNNAMED * 6a+ 18m
The right-hand side of the hollow and the slab above also feature the odd creaky flake.

5. UNNAMED * 6b 18m
From the bushy hollow pull steeply onto the slab and follow it direct.

6. UNNAMED * 6b 18m
The left-hand side of the slab is sharp fingery.

The remaining routes are up and left in a tufa-encrusted wonderland. The routes here are amongst the best of their style on the island. At either extremity of the wall are two projects, but the five routes between these should keep most mortals happy for an afternoon.

7. PILAR *** 7b 20m
The right-hand line with ten bolt runners.

8. CLONACION *** 7a+ 25m
The next one to the left, nine bolts and a stuck-on hold.

9. TO PA TI *** 7a+ 20m
The central line. Ten bolts and a tough finish.

10. BUF!! *** 7a 30m
Twelve bolt runners protect, the crux is right at the top and the route is brilliant.

11. HOB NOPS ** 6c+ 20/30m
The left-hand line, the grade is 'old Malloquin', the extension is even harder!

SECTOR DEL MEDIO

Follow the path from the parking (as for the previous sector) as it rises gradually to the right, then ascends two zig-zags and heads resolutely back towards the castle. Fifty metres after the last of these bends a narrow track (tiny cairn) heads steeply up into the undergrowth. A steep, strenuous and overgrown 10 minutes (if you don't get lost) leads to the base of the wall. A pair of orange caves at 20m should help identify your position.

12. MAGNUM *** 7a,6c,6b 75m

Start on the right at a tufa system and climb to the right-hand edge of a cave (25m). Step right and follow the steep crack to the major ledge system (25m). Then take the steep wall and crack to the cliff top (25m). A left-hand version to the second pitch is:

13. SANCHEZ 22m grade unknown.

14. THERAPY *** 7b 25m

Start up SUPERCHORRERA (see below) but move out right to a stance between the two caves. Gain the right-trending crack, follow it to its termination then continue up the wall to a lower-off just below the ledge system.

15. X.T.R. *** 7b+ 25m

From the stance (as above) power through the bulges then continue up the leaning wall above.

16. SUPERCHORRERA *** 6a,7b 45m

Climb the wall to a stance in the left-hand cave (a pleasant pitch at the grade 20m). Move left and climb the spectacular twinned sharks fins, 25m.

17. LUTE ** 7a 18m

Start by climbing past the 'sheep's head' at 8m and continue through the bulges above.

18. UNNAMED *** 6c,6c,6b 70m

Start up the hanging dong in a cave, 22m. Move right then climb the wall, 24m. Finish up the wall above, 24m.

19. UNNAMED * 6b 14m

The short wall to the left.

20. UNNAMED * 5+ 14m

The shallow scoop, then trend right to join the previous climb.

Sector Del Medio

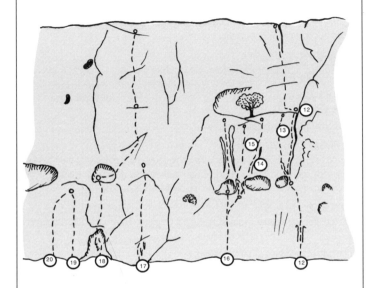

12. Magnum *** 7a,6c,6b 75m
13. Sanchez ? ? 22m
14. Therapy *** 7b 25m
15. X.R.T. *** 7b+ 25m
16. Superchorrera *** 6a,7b 45m
17. Lute ** 7a 18m
18. Unnamed *** 6c,6c,6b 70m
19. Unnamed * 6b 14m
20. Unnamed * 5+ 14m

SECTOR SA PORTA (Sector of the Doorway)

This can be reached from the Cafe Es Verger by following the previous approach for 20–25 minutes. It is easier to continue up the track (a bit rough in places) to parking on the col, then follow the tracks rightwards towards the castle until it meets the rock.

The first routes are on rather shrubby rock right above the bend. Most of these have been extended upwards and are now well worthwhile.

21. HOLA QUE TAL ** 6a 28m
The right-hand and toughest line.

22. LAS MALLAS DE CRISTO ** 5 28m
The centre of the slab.

23. VAGON ROL * 5 26m
The left-hand line, trending left.

To the left are two newer climbs (either side of a tree on the wall). The grade and names of these are not known, though they look much the same as those just to the right.

24. ? ? 22m
Just right of (and almost in) the tree.

25. ? ? 22m
Immediately left of the tree.

26. FIDO-DIDO * 6a 14m
A line up the cleaner rock to the left.

27. SNOWBOARD * 5+ 14m
Left again, climb the right-hand side of an open scoop.

The next route climb a clean slab to left and just to the right of a large tree growing at the foot of the slab, close to the path.

28. UNNAMED *** 6a 28m
The pleasant slab leads to steeper rock and then a series of bulges which are passed using undercuts to reach a flake. From here swing briefly right into a groove and then back left to a steep pull to gain the belays. A fine sustained pitch.

To the left of the tree is an easy slab leading to a line of overhangs 10m up the face. Two short and rather inconsequential 'quick ticks' climb through these. The ledge at the base of the climbs is most easily reached by a short scramble from the left, where a red ladder is painted on the rock. It is possible to belay on the first bolt runner.

29. SOBRASSADA * 5 14m

Climb through the centre of the bulges by a right-trending groove. An exceptionally well-bolted pitch and a safe introduction to 'sport' climbing.

30. FRIT! * 6a 14m

A line up the left edge of the bulges following a vague crack-line to a couple of taxing layback moves to reach the belays.

Directly above the slab with the ladder painted on it is a steep orange wall where there are three routes of rather more substance than those just to the right, and also a couple of 'half-routes' for those looking for something a little gentler.

31. NO RES ** 7a+ 23m

The right-hand line is good and hard. It contains several blind moves and some mighty sharp rock. It is 5+ 15m, to the half-height lower-off.

32. MATA GUIRIS ** 7a+ 25m

The central line is another tough cookie with the crux passing the bulge and the top wall proving to be on worryingly 'crunchy' rock. Again it is 5+ 15m, to the half-height lower-off.

33. A FERRA EL TUL ** 6c 20m

The left-hand of the trio trends leftwards up the wall. The lower wall gives pleasant sustained climbing to a rest below a bulge. Passing this proves to be the crux, with a difficult pull on poor holds being required to gain the easy angled hollow above.

To the left is a project (old bolts) and then a bush on the slab, and left again is an odd brick construction that may be of religious significance. On the wall behind the construction is:

34. ZATROPECK *** 7c 20m

A line between the prominent grey tufas is marked by old bolt-heads and more recent bolts.

To the left of the construction on old bolt ladder (project?) and then a large orange recess 10m up. Two tough routes climb either edge of this, making strenuous use of tufas and uniting at a common belay directly above the niche. These are:

35. 'MUERTA YA' *** 7c 20m

SECTOR SA PORTA (Sector of the Doorway)

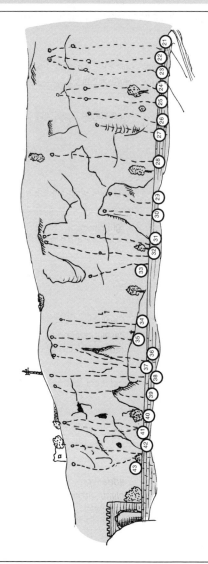

21. Hola Que Tal ** 6a 28m
22. Las Mallas De Cristo ** 5 28m
23. Vagon Rol * 5 26m
24. Unknown ? ? 22m
25. Unknown ? ? 22m
26. Fido-Dido * 6a 14m
27. Snowboard * 5+ 14m
28. Unnamed *** 6a 28m

29. Sobrassada * 5 * 4m
30. Frit! * 6a 4m
31. No Res ** 7a+ 23m
32. Mata Guiris ** 7a+ 25m
33. A Ferra El Tul ** 6c 20m
34. Zatropeck *** 7c 20m
35. 'Muerta Ya' *** 7c 20m
36. Foam Party *** 7b+ 20m

37. Amigos Para Siempre? *** 7c+ 20m
38. Esteban ** 7b? 20m
39. Project ? 7b? 20m
40. Unnamed ** 6a 16m
41. Unnamed ** 6a+ 15m
42. Unnamed *** 6c+ 15m
43. Unnamed ** 7a+ 16m

Excellent climbing just to the right of the recess to a lower-off where the angle eases.

36. FOAM PARTY *** 7b+ 20m
Just left of the recess to a lower-off above its rim.

To the left of the orange recess is a wall with two more routes.

37. AMIGOS PARA SIEMPRE? *** 7c+ 20m
This first line climbs a prominent thin tufa and continues up the steep pockets and bulging orange head wall to a move right to a lower-off in a niche.

Left again and directly under the electric cables is:

38. ESTEBAN ** 7b? 20m
Climb easily over a right-facing flake then continue up the steep wall by fingery moves on a motley assortment of sharp pockets.

39. PROJECT ? 7b? 20m
An uncompleted line just to the left.

Further to the left is the final collection of routes, hidden in a hollow by a collection of bushes and situated directly below part of the castle walls. There are four worthwhile climbs in this nicely secluded setting. The rightmost line starting from the bay is:

40. UNNAMED ** 6a 16m
The juggy bulging rib is protected by white bolts. It is followed steeply on generous holds, trending generally leftwards.

41. UNNAMED ** 6a+ 15m
The bulging white rock to the left is climbed directly. The 'blank' section is overcome by judicious use of the hidden drilled mono-doigt (if you can find it). Steep jug-pulling up the rib above remains. Hard at the Mallorcan grade.

42. UNNAMED *** 6c+ 15m
Gain and climb the right-trending orange tufas to the left of the cave 5m up, until these fizzle out. From here powerful moves can be made left across the bulging rib to regain the line which continues with sustained 'interest'.

43. UNNAMED ** 7a+ 16m
The final route offers more steep climbing starting from the cave at the left edge of this section of the cliff, and trending leftwards up the steep wall into the final groove.

BETLEM

A newly developed cliff in the far north of the island. The setting is quite sublime, though there are perhaps too few routes to make the place worth a visit from afar. Climbers operating in the 6b/7a range could fill a day on Betlem 2, those keen on monkeying about could pass a few hours on the excessively steep (and short) Betlem 1. Without exception the rock is sharp. As is the norm with newly developed areas the names of the routes have not been forthcoming. I have used occasional scratched inscriptions on the rock to aid identification.

Access

Drive west from Alcudia for 24km to a left turn to Colonia de San Pedro/Pere. Where the road turns sharp left continue straight on the bumpy road to the end of the tarmac just beyond the collection of villas that is Betlem. It is possible to park here, leaving a 15 minute walk to Betlem 1 and a 25 minute walk to Betlem 2, though it makes more sense to drive down the track (rough but not excessively so). There is parking just after Betlem 1 (the unmistakable 'cornice' on the right), and 100m or so before Betlem 2 (just after the road crosses a dry valley). It is also possible to continue out to the headland that is another of those Mallorcan paradises.

BETLEM 1

A small set of very steep routes right above the track. Perhaps an ideal venue for climbers who have trained on short, steep indoor walls. It is worth pointing out that there is stacks of scope here for more of the same. The routes are listed from right to left, as this is the easiest approach. All lengths are approximate, though rest assured you will not run out of rope.

BT1.1 ? ? 10m
Just to the right of the right-hand arête of the cliff.

BT1.2 * 7a 10m
The overhangs and pocketed wall out of the right-hand side of the cave.

BT1.3 ? ? 10m
A line starting from the back of the left-hand cave, steeper than most.

BT1.4 ? ? 10m

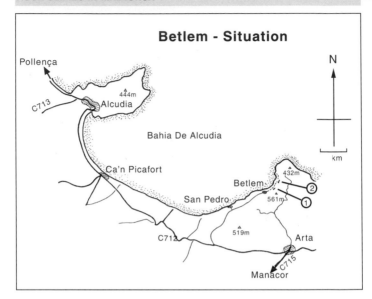

The hanging tufa starting from a convenient block.

BT1.5 * 7a+ 10m

Start up a hanging tufa shield and trend left up the wall. Keeping right makes the route harder (7b+).

BT1.6 * 6c 10m

Start in the same place but step out left onto the 'dong' and then climb the wall leftwards.

There may be another route to the left starting at twinned tufas.

BETLEM 2

A pleasant buttress a little further down the track and only minutes from the sea. The routes described from right to left. A 5 minute scramble up and right from the main cliff is a slab with a single bolt runner and a lower-off 15m up. It looks to be about grade 4.

The first route on the main buttress starts up and right, reached by a short scramble.

Betlem 1

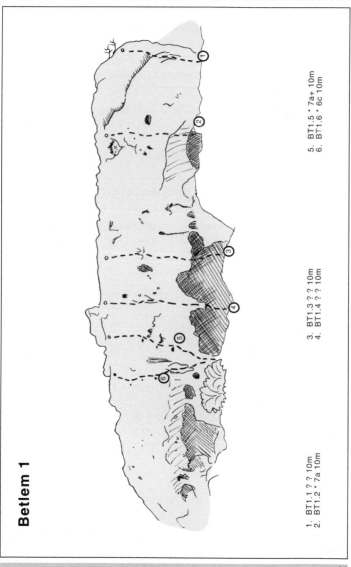

1. BT1.1 ? ? 10m
2. BT1.2 * 7a 10m

3. BT1.3 ? ? 10m
4. BT1.4 ? ? 10m

5. BT1.5 * 7a+ 10m
6. BT1.6 * 6c 10m

BT2.1 * 6c+ 16m
The thin right-trending seam is tough for the grade and is no slab! At the end of the seam jig left and climb the wall.

BT2.2 ? ? 18m
The smooth wall between the two diverging cracks looks completely impossible.

BT2.3 * 6c 10m
The left-trending seam is also very thin for the grade – touches of old Mallorca here.

BT2.4 ? ? 14m
The pale wall to the left is apparently a project.

BT2.5 6a 12m
The short blocky rib to the left gives an unsatisfying struggle.

BT2.6 ** 5+ 18m
The twisting groove gives a much more pleasant and juggy pitch.

BT2.7 ** 6b 18m
The rib and spiky wall just to the left of the groove is sharp, fun and photogenic.

BT2.8 ** 6b+ 15m
The deep crack, pocket roof and rib above is also sharp, fun and photogenic.

BT2.9 (IMEZ) ** 7a+ 24m
The right-hand side of the barrel-shaped buttress is taxing, especially reaching and leaving the drilled pocket. The scabby thread and old bolt near the top can be ignored.

BT2.10 * 6b+ 24m**
The route of the cliff and worth the drive. Start to the left of 'the shepherd and his dog' and step right off a flake, then climb the steep sustained slab on sharp pockets and 'dinks' until things ease. Sprint to the lower-off.

BT2.11 (JESUS SEBAS CHON) * 7a 10m
The steep and hard slab just to the left leads to a poor lower-off below steeper rock.

BT2.12 * 7a 10m
The steep wall just to the left (not all of the pockets are natural) leads to the runnel and a short sprint to the belay.

Around to the left and up the slope is a fine grey wall that faces north, a good summer venue and a cool winter one. There are four good routes here.

Betlem 2

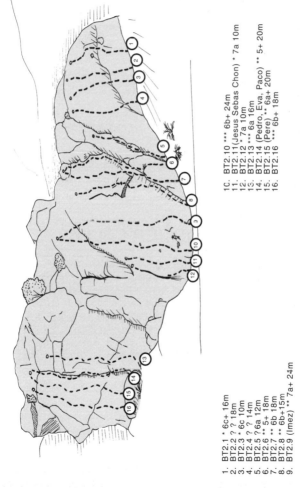

1. BT2.1 * 6c+ 16m
2. BT2.2 ? ? 18m
3. BT2.3 * 6c 10m
4. BT2.4 ? ? 14m
5. BT2.5 ?6a 12m
6. BT2.6 ** 5+ 18m
7. BT2.7 ** 6b 18m
8. BT2.8 ** 6b+15m
9. BT2.9 (Imez) ** 7a+ 24m

10. BT2.10 *** 6b+ 24m
11. BT2.11(Jesus Sebas Chon) * 7a 10m
12. BT2.12 * 7a 10m
13. BT2.13 *** 6a 16m
14. BT2.14 (Pedro, Eva, Paco) ** 5+ 20m
15. BT2.15 (Pere) ** 6a+ 20m
16. BT2.16 *** 6b+ 18m

BT2.13 *** 6a 16m
After an awkward start the wall to the right of the crack gives superb sustained climbing.

BT2.14 (PEDRO, EVA, PACO) ** 5+ 20m
The long crack gives good climbing on rock that is sharp with a capital OUCH. The 'interesting' block at 4m is best passed with care. At the top step left to the lower-offs. A three-star outing for refugees from Pembroke's finest.

BT2.15 (PERE) ** 6a+ 20m
The wall just left of the crack is tricky at one-third height (staying out of the crack is especially tough) and juggy above.

BT2.16 *** 6b+ 18m
The fine grey wall just to the left offers a pitch of gradually escalating difficulty and sharpness.

A line just to the left (6a+) has been debolted. Across the gully is a steep rib capped by a bulge, name and grade unknown. It looks like mid 7.

BOQUER VALLEY

Note: Recently there have been access problems in the valley, with the owner of the large house threatening climbers (with a gun!), despite the sign on his gate saying no biking or rappelling! I don't want to encourage confrontations, but the classic route on the Shark's Fin is well away from the house! All the routes in the valley are described briefly here in the hope that the situation can be resolved in the future.

Character
A superb wild valley running out to the sea from just north of the beautiful town of Puerto Pollença, from where it can easily be reached. There is a wealth of rock in the valley, and up to the present day the development of the considerable potential of the area has been rather sporadic, concentrated mainly on the boulder field at the entrance to the valley and the prominent ridge of L'AGUILA (the Eagle) above these. The path that runs out through the valley towards the sea is an immensely popular walk and is much used by 'twitchers' in search of rare Mediterranean species. The northern side of the valley is bound by the Caval Bernat ridge, a fine

Colin Binks on BT2.7 (6b) on the recently developed cliffs at Betlem

rocky scramble which is Mallorca's best known answer to Crib Goch. It is exceptionally exposed on its 'other side', where it overlooks the dramatic setting of the small resort of Cala San Vincent.

Access

The entrance to the Boquer Valley (see section 'Creveta', Situation & Access map on page 54) is easily reached from Puerto Pollença via the prominent tan-coloured castellated farmhouse on the hill behind the town. Drive though Puerto Pollença towards Formentor until the farmhouse can be seen on the left. Running up towards this is an avenue of trees, and just past these a left turn leads into the 'Urbanisation Boquer' – a grid-iron road pattern with the street lights in place but no houses as yet (early 2000). Drive to the top left corner of this then follow the track up past the front door of the farm, cats galore! Go through the gate on the left then bear right to reach the good track that runs up through the valley. In less than 10 minutes from the car the first of the boulders is reached; they are big enough to ensure that you are unlikely to miss them.

The routes are listed as they are passed walking up the valley, on the boulders first and then on the ridge above the boulders. See map and diagram in this section to aid route location. As I have been unable to find names for most of the routes I have simply numbered them. Arriving at the boulders, the first one to the left of the track has a low wall and entrance built under it offering a possible bivouac site for the terminally destitute. To the right of the track, opposite this potential doss, is a taller boulder with a very steep north face.

1. 7a? 10m
The underside of the boulder is protected by a selection of new 'glue-in' bolts.

2. 6b? 10m
There is also a short hand traverse from the left to the same belay.

Continuing a short distance further the path passes through a narrowing, almost a ravine, between two high boulders. The one on the right side of the track, LA CREU, has three routes:

3. 4 20m
At the narrowest point of the ravine the rib on the right is approached steeply and then followed on the left or right to the easier upper section. Rather sparingly bolted at present, take a few slings and/or nuts.

Around to the right is a steep north-east-facing wall with two short routes on its left side.

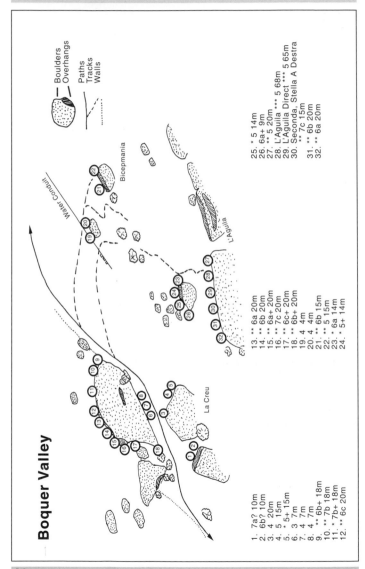

Boquer Valley

1. 7a? 10m
2. 6b? 10m
3. 4 20m
4. 5 15m
5. * 5+ 15m
6. 3 7m
7. 4 7m
8. 4 7m
9. ** 6b+ 18m
10. * 7b 18m
11. * 7b+ 18m
12. ** 6c 20m

13. ** 6a 20m
14. ** 6b 20m
15. ** 6a+ 20m
16. ** 7c 20m
17. ** 6c+ 20m
18. ** 6b+ 20m
19. 4 4m
20. 4 4m
21. ** 6b 15m
22. ** 5 15m
23. * 6a 14m
24. * 5+ 14m

25. * 5 14m
26. 6a+ 9m
27. ** 5 20m
28. L'Aguila *** 5 68m
29. L'Aguila Direct *** 5 65m
30. Seconda, Stella A Destra
    ** 7c 15m
31. ** 6b 20m
32. ** 6a 20m

4. 5 15m
The right hand line is rather artificial.

5. * 5+ 15m
The left line is slightly steeper, rather more sustained, and more worthwhile.

On the opposite (left when walking up the valley) side of the path through the 'ravine' is the southern side of the biggest boulder in the area, the ROCA DU TRAMPO. On this major monolith is a good and varied selection of a dozen routes. The attractive sharp arête that faces you as you approach the boulder looks like it could be a classic VS; carry a rack. The first three bolted routes are located in the left-hand side wall of the ravine, to the right of the sharp arête just mentioned. These are short offerings, though they are not without interest. They share a conspicuous and substantial mutual belay, and offer a pleasant introduction to the attractions of sport climbing.

6. 3 7m
The red groove and its right rib lead to a move out right.

7. 4 7m
The wall just to the right leads directly to the chains.

8. 4 7m
The wall just right again trending leftwards to the chains.

Continuing through the ravine there is some scope on the same wall, notably a tough-looking roof and an easy-looking blocky staircase. The side wall of the boulder then swings round to face north, above a pleasant grassy field which is reached by climbing, with great care, over the stone wall. The rock here gets the sun late in the day, or provides cool shade at other times.

9. ** 6b+ 18m
The steeply leaning flake system immediately to the right of the stone wall offers a fine piece of thuggery. Above the termination of the flake continue rightwards up the still steep wall.

10. ** 7b 18m
The rebolted wall (paired old and new bolts) to the right is thin, sharp and technical. It leads directly to the belay of the previous route.

11. * 7b+ 18m
The drilled wall to the right starts from a block, and at the moment it awaits the attention of the rebolting crew. Once they have given the route an overhaul it may be worth **.

The attractive right side of this face is home to three new offerings:

12. ** 6c 20m
The first of the new routes pulls over a small overlap then climbs the fine wall to the right of a grey streak to finish over the overhang just below the top of the wall.

13. ** 6a 20m
The next route to the right is more amenable. It trends right up a vague scoop and crack-line before heading away to the left to a pull over the capping overhang. Good.

14. ** 6b 20m
Just left of the right arête is a route trending slightly to the left until it almost joins the previous route then back to the right; finish over the bulges above.

15. ** 6a+ 20m
The right arête of the face is climbed on its right and then on its left. Worthwhile.

To the right the cliff swings round to form a fine west-facing wall, easily seen from the path.

16. ** 7c 20m
The obvious 'impossible' line up the fiercely leaning prow.

17. ** 6c+ 20m
Round the arête, climb the flat wall and then the flake.

18. ** 6b+ 20m
The thin crack in the face reserves its crux for the final section.

The next routes to be described are to be found on the other (uphill) side of the main path. On exiting from the 'canyon' there are several tracks that branch off diagonally to the right and run up the hillside. At the point where the paths cross a water conduit at some small troughs is a small boulder with two 'one-bolt wonders' that both lead rapidly to a single-bolt lower-off.

19. 4 4m
The wall a short distance right of the arête.

20. 4 4m
The arête on its right side.

Continuing in the same direction is a much more impressive boulder, easily recognised by its leaning valley face and sharply pointed summit. This is BICEPMANIA and there are two worthwhile routes here.

21. ** 6b 15m

Climb easily into a hollow in the left side of the overhanging face, then climb through the roof and on up the tilted arête using occasional holds around to the left until it is possible to lean across to the right to reach the chains. Steep!

22. ** 5 15m

Around to the left is a fine wall facing out to sea. Climb steeply onto a ledge at the foot of the face then continue straight up its centre on excellent rock to a lower-off just below the top.

The final boulder that contains routes is the egg-shaped one capped with conspicuous plants and standing in front of the right side of the tower of the Eagle, which towers over this area. Various vague paths lead through the exotic (and sharp) scrub to the boulder. The routes are described from left to right and it is worth pointing out that the upper sections of the first three climbs, though not too difficult, are not overly bolted.

23. * 6a 14m

The left-hand route starts (for most mortals) from a pile of stones and trends left through the bevy of bulges to easier-angled rock above. The lower section is hard work.

24. * 5+ 14m

Gain a good flake then trend slightly leftwards through the bulges to reach the foot of the thin crack in the upper slab. Climb direct from here.

25. * 5 14m

Climb steeply past mouldering threads (best backed up with your own if you are carrying a sling) to gain access to the more amenable face above. Romp on up the thin crack-line.

26. 6a+ 9m

The right arête of the front face leads steeply to a swing right to chains at the top of the groove on the right. The groove makes a good candidate for a quick top-roping session.

The final routes that are described are all found on the line of cliffs that tower over the right side of valley. There are six climbs here at present, all are worth doing and all are located on the prominent fin of the Eagle. I have also had a report of a traditional route called SOBRASADA 5 which climbs 'the corner groove on the left side of the central buttress, crossing from right to left where it narrows'. I have not been able to identify this with certainty, though it may be the chimney system that splits the left side of the buttress to the left of the Eagle.

The routes on the main tower are described from left to right. These are:

27. ** 5 20m

Start at the left edge of the face by an old bolt and pull rightwards onto the slab. Trend left up the gradually steepening face on superb rock following the line of speckled bolts to a tricky bulging section. This is most easily tackled from left to right, above which a couple more ticklish moves lead to easier terrain and a rather tatty belay.

28. L'AGUILA *** 5 68m

The original route up this section of cliff is a venerable classic following a continuously interesting line. The first pitch may be fully bolted though a few wires, and slings will be required for the rest of the route.

1. 5 22m Climb onto the slab from the left (by an old bolt-head) and traverse right to the foot of the crack. This is steeper than it looks and is also quite slippery. It eases after 12m, then easier climbing leads to the belay on the previous route.
2. 4 24m Traverse to the right and make an awkward move out right below a bulging wall to gain the base of an easier groove line. Climb this past fixed gear at one possible stance to a better one at the top of the groove.
3. 4 22m Climb the slab trending slightly rightwards until it rears up and a tricky little wall is climbed past an antiquated bolt runner to a belay in a notch on the crest of the ridge. Enjoy the view before thinking about the descent.

Descent: Either abseil back down the line of the climb or, perhaps safer, traverse the crest of the ridge eastwards for a short distance to the better belays at the top of the L'AGUILA DIRECT and abseil back down this.

29. L'AGUILA DIRECT *** 5 65m

A great route, as undeviating as the name suggests, on stunning rock and which was fully bolted, though rumours suggest that at least some of these have been removed. Well worth the trip to the valley to do.

1. 20m 5+ Climb onto the slab from the left (by an old bolt-head) and traverse right to the foot of the crack of the regular route. Lean right to clip the first bolt to the right then climb the wall, awkwardly at first but generally on good holds, to where the angle drops back and a twin-bolt belay and comfortable stance are found.
2. 20m 4 Climb straight up the slab to a steepening which is tackled by moving right then back left to reach the rib above. Up this to a small stance and very substantial belay.

3. 25m 4+ Climb straight up the slab to reach the left edge of a vegetated break (loose block in the grass on the right, beware), then continue up the fine sustained 'shark's skin' slab above to a stance astride the very crest of the ridge. Abseil descent.

30. SECONDA, STELLA A DESTRA ** 7c 15m
Start at the large painted name and climb the bulging wall on very sharp holds.

31. ** 6b 20m
Towards the right side of the front face are two bolt lines, the left-hand one has the newer bolts. A tough start leads to a shallow ramp that leads up leftwards until it is possible to trend back to the right to the lower-off.

32. ** 6a 20m
The right-hand line has rather older bolts. Climb easily to white ledges then continue up the steep, sustained wall above on a collection of razors, knife edges and broken glass.

CALVIA

Character
An excellent small cliff of perfect grey limestone tucked away in a narrow valley in the rolling hills, a short distance inland from Palma Nova. The cliff faces south and so makes an ideal venue throughout the winter and offers an excellent introduction to the climbing on Mallorca. The sheltered position of the crag means that it can get oppressively hot in the summer, when an early start with a midday break for the beach may be called for. Generally speaking the climbs are not too steep and they are well protected by frequent and substantial bolts; climbing here is chiefly concerned with enjoyment. A competent party can tick all the routes hereabouts in a couple of visits, though in reality that is not what the place is about.

From the ground the upward view of many of the climbs can be rather daunting because of the compact nature of the rock. Fortunately once you rub noses with the raw material it becomes apparent that it is covered in a mosaic of tiny flakes and solution pockets, making for elegant though often rather fingery face-dancing. Many of the routes have their names painted in neat black lettering at their foot, thus aiding identification. Without exception all climbs here can be done to the lowering points and back to the ground on a single 50m rope.

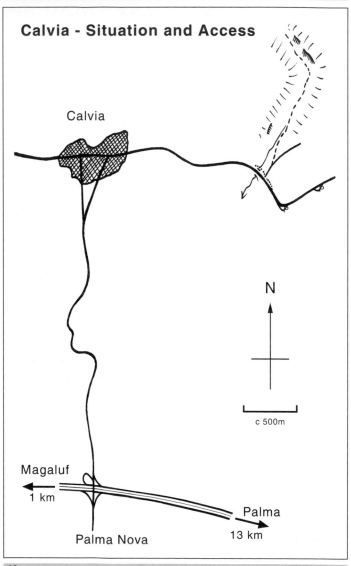

Calvia - Situation and Access

Calvia

N

c 500m

Magaluf

1 km

Palma

13 km

Palma Nova

Unfortunately on some of the routes the bolts are becoming a bit tired and the rock is getting polished.

Access

From the centre of Palma follow the main coastal motorway eastwards towards the port of Andratx for 13km to a junction signed Palma Nova (towards the sea) and Calvia (inland). Turn uphill here and follow the road as it winds up away from the coast to reach the old town of Calvia after 6km. The town contains an impressive church and a number of very pleasant bars, though the latter are perhaps best left until later in the day. In the centre of the village take a right turn that is signed to Puigpunyent. (An unsigned branch road runs past the local school and cuts out the need to travel through the centre of the town, see map.) The narrow road is followed for 2.5km until the stone wall on the right side of the road ends at a right-hand bend. It is possible to park on the right side of the road just a little further on at a small projecting lay-by. The number of cars here is normally a good indicator of how busy the crag will be. Leave no valuables in the car.

Return to the bend and enter the field (on the left coming from Calvia) at a rickety gate. Follow the track up to the right for 100m and then bear left along terraces making for the prominent valley that lies dead ahead. The main cliff is a rough ten minute scramble up this and it is hidden until the very last moment.

Note: The main track to the cliff currently (Jan 2000) has a 'no entry' sign and is chained shut. It is possible to cross the fence 50m before the gate (where the fence is low) or 100m after it (where the fence meets the wall). Please keep a low profile and stay well off cultivated land. Apparently there have been problems at weekends but not in the week; time your visit accordingly.

Opposite the point where the path to the crag leaves the main track there is a small crag, partly hidden in the trees on the opposite side of the valley. To approach this please keep off any cultivated land. There are four climbs here: three short, tough, well-chiselled pitches on the left side based around an arch, and an innocuous looking slab, 5+, that rises behind a large pine tree and looks worthwhile.

SECTOR PRINCIPAL

This is the main section of the cliff; all the climbs here are well worth doing. These are described from right to left, as this is the normal approach route. To the right of the first route is a slabby area of rock that could provide a few lower grade climbs.

1. PRIMERA EXPERIENCA *** 4 18m

This is the well-named bolt line at the very right edge of the main section of the cliff, passing just left of a large bush at 8m. It provides a great pitch with excellent holds and exemplary protection. A tricky couple of moves at half-height from a massive hold provide the main entertainment. A perfect introduction to the cliff and the style of climbing.

2. CALENTURA INVERNAL ** 4+ 18m

The name means 'winter heat'. Start below a substantial thread at 5m and follow the sustained rib and wall on generally excellent holds to the lower-off. Hard for the grade.

3. EL ULTIMO DE LA FILA ** 6a 18m

The central line on this section of wall gives excellent climbing, well worth doing, offering pleasant climbing with a tricky couple of moves. Start from a ledge at 3m and head straight up the wall to a small red bulge that is passed slightly right then back left.

4. PINCHITO MORUNO ** 5+ 18m

Follow the line of bolts immediately to the right of the big tree that grows miraculously out of solid rock. Predominantly large holds lead to a shallow scoop, entering and leaving, which requires just a touch of technical application. Just a little higher good holds lead out right to the belay of the previous climb.

The wall above the three previous climbs has a bolt ladder up its centre. This provides a rather tougher extension to the climbs below and is the delectable:

5. FLIPAS PIPAS *** 6a 18m

Large holds are followed to a 'blank' scoop which is crossed leftwards by a couple of slippery and technical moves to reach the belays just above. Excellent sport.

6. 9.2.92 ** 5+ 18m

Immediately to the left of the big tree is a bolt line that is followed directly to the crux moves; an awkward bulge just above the final bolt. Lower off the same belay as EXTRAFINA.

7. EXTRAFINA ** 6a 18m

A line of bolts (the second one to the left of the big tree and just left of a tufa topped with a flower garden) trends slightly rightwards and passes below a patch of vegetation before reaching ledges and the belay of the previous climb. A sustained and fingery pitch.

8. CAGUERA PERPETUA ** 5+ 20m

Ten metres to the left of the prominent tree growing from the rock is a steep slab with two bolt lines running straight up it. This route follows the right-hand line, which gives fine sustained climbing with plenty of *in situ* protection.

Calvia

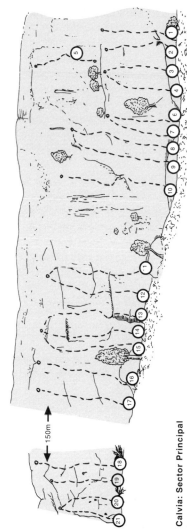

150m

Calvia: Sector Principal

1. Primera Experienca *** 4 18m
2. Calentura Invernal ** 4+ 18m
3. El Ultimo De La Fila ** 6a 18m
4. Pinchito Moruno ** 5+ 18m
5. Flipas Pipas *** 6a 18m
6. 9.2.92 ** 5+ 18m
7. Extrafina ** 6a 18m
8. Caguera Perpetua ** 5+ 20m
9. Batakalofis * 5+ 21m
10. Tu Polla Me Enrolla *** 6a 25m
11. Jota Jota *** 6a+ 24m
12. Saque Mate *** 6b+ 24m
13. Tirili ** 6b 22m
14. Perona ** 6b 22m

Calvia: Sector Buoux

15. Chanco *** 6a 22m
16. Nc Al Senyor Fiscal *** 5+ 20m
17. Windjammer ** 6a 15m

18. Buoux * 6a 14m
19. Sector * 5+ 14m
20. Semen Semidesnatado * 6a+ 14m
21. Vuelo Sin Moto ** 6c 20m

9. BATAKALOFIS * 5+ 21m

The left-hand line starts at a small scratched arrow by a right-facing white flake. Climb straight up the slab towards a conspicuous flake system 20m off the ground. On reaching this, move up and right to cross over to the lowering point of the previous climb.

10. TU POLLA ME ENROLLA *** 6a 25m

A superb pitch up the steepening wall immediately to the right of a prominent area of grey flowstone high on the cliff. The lower wall is quite tricky and leads to a diagonal steepening. Cross this leftwards and then head up the steep wall using a series of large wart-like protuberances to reach a gradual easing in the angle above. Continue up the sustained wall with moderately spaced bolts to the lower-off. Superb.

To the left the base of the cliff rises up and a huge fallen flake is reached. The collection of climbs above this area is hardest on the cliff due to the steeper nature of the rock. Fortunately the bolt protection remains as good as ever. The next two routes start from on top of the flake.

11. JOTA JOTA *** 6a+ 24m

One of the finest pitches on the cliff, giving sustained and involved climbing that is never desperate but is always interesting. Step off the flake and climb the easy slab to steeper rock. Pull over the overlap leftwards on hidden holds, then head directly up the steep wall by awkward and sustained climbing.

12. SAQUE MATE *** 6b+ 24m

Another great and fingery climb. From the flake climb the unprotected but straightforward slab to the steep rock to a bolt just to the left of yellow marks, or follow the previous climb to its second bolt and then step left. Cross the bulge by a tough sequence on small finger-holds, then continue straight up the wall on spaced sharp holds.

The next feature to the left is a shallow corner crack formed by a right-facing flake. Starting here is:

13. TIRILI ** 6b 22m

Climb the corner to the bulge and cross it awkwardly rightwards to gain a blunt, hanging rib. From here head up the steep wall on good holds to a second bulge, which is passed to the right of the bolt line by a strenuous sequence of moves. Continue up the still steep face before strength evaporates and it becomes possible to head left to the belays.

Between the right-facing flake and a large tree there are two climbs that start up a smooth-looking slab and then climb steeper rock above.

14. PERONA ** 6b 22m

Up the right side of the slab by thin move to reach the steeper wall. Step right, almost onto the previous climb, then trend slightly leftwards on small holds to a final steepening, which is crossed with difficulty to better holds and then a lower-off as for the previous climb.

15. CHANCO *** 6a 22m

A fine pitch: steep, sustained and unlikely. Climb the left-hand line on the slab, passing the first bolt with difficulty to reach easier rock and then a good pocket containing an interesting collection of herbage. The steep wall above is sustained and requires occasional blind moves until relief arrives in the form of some large holds. Swing right to the lower-off of the previous two climbs.

16. NO AL SENYOR FISCAL *** 5+ 20m

The penultimate route on the main section of the cliff is well worth seeking out and gives climbing that is easier than it looks. Start 3m left of the big tree and climb a flake to the left of the initial bolt until it is possible to swing right to gain the line of the route. This gives superb sustained climbing.

17. WINDJAMMER ** 6a 15m

A pleasant recent addition 6m to the left of NO AL SENYOR FISCAL. An easy slab above a block leads to the start of the route at the name in pink writing. A pleasant pitch with the best gear on the cliff, and a couple of thin moves passing the fourth bolt, just before the angle eases.

A couple of hundred metres further up the valley, on the same side as the main cliff, is a dome-shaped buttress, the SECTOR BUOUX.

SECTOR BUOUX

This section of rock has four worthwhile pitches that are useful when you have 'ticked' the main cliff, or if it proves to be a bit too busy. The grades here appear to be a touch of old Mallorcan, if you know what I mean. The area is most easily reached by following a vague path along the dried-up stream bed until the buttress appears on the right, though a vague track from the left edge of the main cliff can also be used. To the right of the routes described below is a clean slab that could provide half a dozen lower-grade routes with just a little expenditure of time and energy. The routes are described from left to right.

The first climb starts at the left edge of the front face of the buttress below three hollows in the rock 3m off the ground.

18. BUOUX * 6a 14m
Climb into the scoops then step right and continue by sustained fingery and blind moves straight up the face until it is possible to swing right to the large but solitary belay bolt.

19. SECTOR * 5+ 14m
Start between two clumps of bushes at a flat block on the ground directly below a red roof at 15m. Climb the centre of the face on good but spaced holds until a long reach gains good holds in the hollow below the red roof. Swing left to the belay of the last climb.

20. SEMEN SEMIDESNATADO * 6a+ 14m
Start to the right of the bushes and climb a floral slab to steeper rock. This is climbed up a red streak on small but generally good finger-holds to a belay in the right side of the hollow.

21. VUELO SIN MOTO ** 6c 20m
The rightmost line climbs the slab and then continues up the steep and technical wall, passing just to the left of a prominent orange streak to gain a shake-out at a large flaky pocket. A final difficult sequence leads from here up and right to the belay. The hardest pitch in the valley.

CAN NYIC

Set at over 1000m and facing north-east, Can Nyic (also known as Torrella) is definitely not a winter venue. There are only a dozen or so routes here at present – on fine grey sheets of limestone in a very grand setting. Climbers looking for something a little more traditional could well spend some time exploring the impressive cliffs that surround this area, or head through the tunnel for a look at the impressive buttress on the side of the Puig Major. The sport routes here currently number only 13 in total and consist of quality face climbs up to 28m in height. The crag is an ideal venue for those who find themselves on the island in high summer.

Access
The cliff is most easily reached from Soller by taking the C710 road towards the monastery at Lluc. This climbs steadily for 10km until just before the entrance to a long tunnel (where the road disappears straight into the mountain), and there is

Can Nyic and El Paradon - Access and Routes

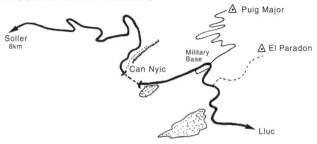

1. Agent Orange *** 8b 25m
2. Max Cady ** 7c 15m
3. S'Horabaixa *** 7b+ 28m
4. Na Faresta *** 7b 25m
5. Tutup *** 6c 20m
6. Molins De Paper *** 6b+ 20m
7. Bona Nyic *** 6a+ 18m
8. Ho Passam Pillo *** 7a 16m
9. Sa Fosca ? ? 16m
10. Sa Fura ? ? 16m
11. Borinot ** 6c 16m
12. Nyicnyatos * 5 12m
13. Bernadi Company ** 6c 20m

parking on the left and an excellent viewpoint on the right. Scramble up the bank and follow the base of the cliff leftwards. The first route is on an orange wall a short distance beyond where a cable lies on the ground, the next is just past a stone wall, and all the rest are 5 minutes further up the hill (see diagram).

1. AGENT ORANGE *** 8b 25m
Just beyond the cable on the ground is a long streak. Climb this if you can!

2. MAX CADY ** 7c 15m
Just past the stone wall is the shallow left-facing groove which is both hard and sustained.

Further up the hill past some boulders and fencing, the next routes are just left of some large ivy patches:

3. S'HORABAIXA *** 7b+ 28m
High in the grade for 7c and even more so for 7b+!

4. NA FARESTA *** 7b 25m
Excellent climbing, though the start is often wet.

5. TUTUP *** 6c 20m
A great route with the fingery start and bolder moves towards the top.

6. MOLINS DE PAPER *** 6b+ 20m
Also excellent, being sustained and strenuous.

7. BONA NYIC *** 6a+ 18m
The most popular pitch here gives a great sustained route up the wall left of the flake at the base of the cliff.

8. HO PASSAM PILLO *** 7a 16m
The bulging wall just left again sees less traffic.

The wall to the left has two projects.

9. SA FOSCA ? ? 16m

10. SA FURA ? ? 16m

Almost at the end of the face is a shallow groove:

11. BORINOT ** 6c 16m
The blank groove, tricky and technical.

12. NYICNYATOS * 5 12m
An unspectacular outing whose main recommendation is that it is the easiest route

on the face.

13. BERNADI COMPANY ** ** 6c 20m
Across the gully is a slender tower with this route on its front face.

CAN TORRAT

A fine cliff suitable for those who are not quite up to the mega-challenges of Fraggel but who find most of the stuff at Gubia a bit too easy. The cliff contains an excellent collection of fine face routes, with many of the pitches being 30m long or more. Sustained and sharp big pitches are the main attraction of the place, with most of the routes being in the 7a to 7c category. The crag is in the shade in the morning and full sun in the afternoon, which is very convenient.

Access
Follow the road from Bunyola towards Santa Maria as far as the 3.2km marker stone. Turn left here (towards the hills) into a wide gateway with red and green 'target' painted on the gatepost. Drive up the dirt road for 3.3km to the point where the track forks by a house on the left. Take the right-hand branch which zig-zags up into the hills (sections of concrete) for .5km (check the odometer). Limited parking is available where a track doubles back to a house on the left and another track forks to the right. Follow this right-hand track as its climbs steeply, passing a pair of rock houses on the right and a small steep crag (Sector des Cami) on the left to eventually reach the spectacular gates that guard access to the house in the valley. Continue up this track past the house until it is possible to double back to the right and ascend to the base of the cliff, 15 to 20 minutes from the car. Quality ratings and gradings are taken from the local guide to the cliff – so be warned.

Note: Last time we climbed here there was a new landowner who was in the process of reclaiming the section of the valley below the cliff. He was happy for us to follow the track through the valley but didn't want us climbing on 'his' cliff. Talking with the locals at Gubia suggested that this was only a problem at weekends, and that they visit the cliff during the week.

SECTOR DES CAMI
The small, steep cliff that overhangs the bend on the road, on the way to the main cliff, has four bolt lines. All are very short and very steep.

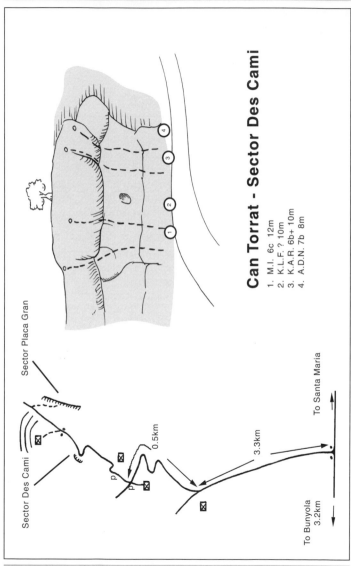

Can Torrat - Sector Des Cami

1. M.I. 6c 12m
2. K.L.F. ? 10m
3. K.A.R. 6b+ 10m
4. A.D.N. 7b 8m

Sector Placa Gran

Sector Des Cami

0.5km

3.3km

To Santa Maria

To Bunyola
3.2km

1. M.I. 6c 12m
The left-hand line through a notch in the roof.

2. K.L.F. ? ? 10m
The impossible-looking leaning rib in the centre of the cliff is a project. No surprises there then.

3. K.A.R. 6b+ 10m
The wall and crack to the right of centre.

4. A.D.N. 7b 8m
The tiny right-hand line.

SECTOR PLACA GRAN

All the routes on the main wall are well worth the effort of the approach. These are listed from left to right (see diagram).

5. AUTE * 7b+ 14m
The left-hand side of the short leaning and pocketed wall at the left side of the cliff.

6. PAYO ** 7b+ 14m
A similar line up the centre of the short wall.

7. PROJECT ? 7a? 22m
The right-hand side of the wall and the bulges above.

8. DIEDRE *** 6b 45m
The huge soaring groove line is the best lower-grade route on the cliff.

9. SIROQUET ** 24m
The leaning wall to the right of the groove.

10. PROJECT ? ? 24m
Right again.

11. KACTUS *** 7a 30m
The first of the mega-pitches, starting from the left-hand side of a recess.

12. FELA LUGOSI *** 7b 30m
And another, from the centre of the recess.

13. SEX MACHINE ** 7b+ 25m
The leaning wall starting between the recess at the foot of the cliff.

14. NO TE EXTRANES QUE TE EXTRINA ** 7a+ 25m

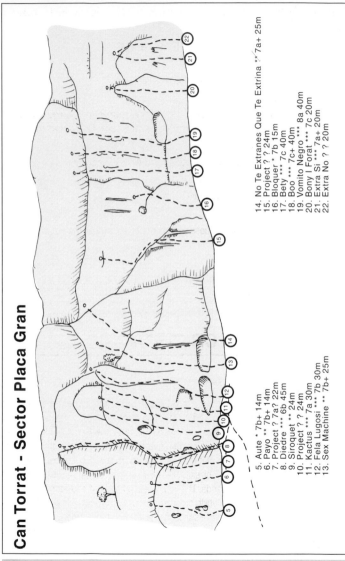

Can Torrat - Sector Placa Gran

5. Aute * 7b+ 14m
6. Payo ** 7b+ 14m
7. Project ?, 7a? 22m
8. Diedre *** 6b 45m
9. Siroquet ** 24m
10. Project ?, ? 24m
11. Kactus *** 7a 30m
12. Fela Lugosi *** 7b 30m
13. Sex Machine ** 7b+ 25m

14. No Te Extranes Que Te Extrina ** 7a+ 25m
15. Project ?, ? 24m
16. Bloquer * 7b 15m
17. Bety *** 7c 40m
18. Boo *** 7c+ 40m
19. Vomito Negro *** 8a 40m
20. Bony I Forat *** 7c 20m
21. Extra Si *** 7a+ 20m
22. Extra No ?, ? 20m

From the right-hand side of the recess climb the long tufa and the wall above.

15. PROJECT ? ? 24m
The impressive leaning wall and tufas 15m to the right.

16. BLOQUER * 7b 15m
Rightwards up the leaning wall – the name says it all.

17. BETY * 7c 40m**
The first of a trio of 'super routes' up the slightly more amenable angled wall to the right. These would provide a good morning's work for a suitably talented individual.

18. BOO * 7c+ 40m**
The middle one of the trio is a touch harder and is very sustained.

19. VOMITO NEGRO * 8a 40m**
The final one of the trio is the hardest.

20. BONY I FORAT * 7c 20m**
The wall to the right of a cave/recess at 8m.

21. EXTRA SI * 7a+ 20m**
The tufa wall.

22. EXTRA NO ? ? 20m
The last line on the cliff.

CREVETA

Character

A fine cliff that has a lot to offer: a broad range of grades, perfect if somewhat rough rock, plentiful protection and an idyllic outlook. In some ways the crag is complementary to the popular Calvia, which is situated towards the other corner of the island, though the setting of Creveta is rather grander. The climbing tends to be less than vertical and much of it is on very sharp holds – a couple of days here requires a high pain resistance or skin like a pachyderm. A stiff pair of boots and good foot work may pay dividends. The cliff faces south-west and so is in the sun from about 1pm onwards. It is worth organising your day around this event, always taking due regard to the time of year and prevailing temperatures. Much of the vegetation around the foot of the cliff is very wiry; take care if lightly clad or you will get lacerated.

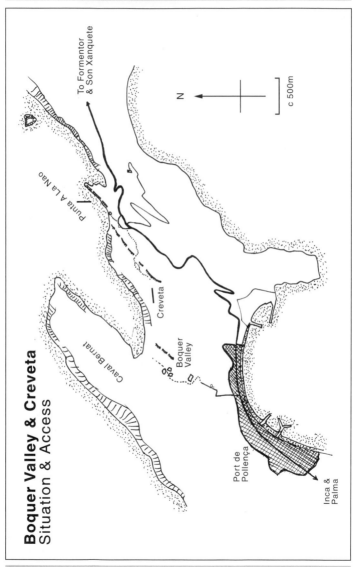

Boquer Valley & Creveta
Situation & Access

To Formentor
& Son Xanquete

N

c 500m

Punta A La Nao

Creveta

Caval Bernal

Boquer Valley

Port de
Pollença

Inca &
Palma

Access

The cliff is reached in about 15 minutes from the first mirador (view point) on the road that eventually runs out to reach the Formentor lighthouse. From the town of Puerto Pollença follow the road that runs north-east out towards the peninsula of Formentor. Soon after leaving the built-up area (from where the cliff can be seen if you know where to look) the road climbs rapidly via a couple of long zig-zags, and then as it levels out there is an extensive and usually busy parking area on the left for the mirador. A quick walk out to the end of this offers an excellent photo opportunity. When done clicking, walk back towards Puerto Pollença following a partly buried pipeline that runs away at a tangent from the road. Two hundred metres down this, and just before a warning sign, a very vague track heads uphill to pass beneath a series of rocky bluffs and arrive at a col with a large cairn. More direct routes usually end up in wiry vegetation and blocky outcrops. Cross the ridge at the lowest point of the col (on the left) and then either: descend awkward slabs and terraces right then left for 50m until a cairned track is picked up heading horizontally in a south-west direction (to the left looking out); or (shorter but trickier) descend for 10m then follow a sloping terrace leftwards to a tricky descent right under the cliff face. Follow vague tracks and occasional cairns for a couple of hundred metres until just round the headland, at which point both Puerto Pollença and the cliff come into view. The routes are all described from left to right throughout.

Note 1: On the way from the parking area to the col described above an earlier col is seen. DO NOT try to descend here. If you are not sure why, feel free to take a look over it. There is now a route below the first col; the lower-off and top few bolts can be seen from above, but no details are known.

Note 2: Returning to the car by continuing round below the cliff or descending direct to Puerto Pollença is not recommended unless you have full body armour and a machete!

After the descent the path towards the cliff passes under steep rock, and then an impressive barrel-shaped buttress with a left to right rising ramp at its base. There are four excellent routes here, usually in the shade, all the work of Rab Anderson. It shows what a little imagination (and a drill) can do.

1. GRINGO STAR *** 6c 30m
Start left of the ramp and climb the spiky black streak and sustained blunt rib on great (but very sharp) rock to chains on the crest of the wall.

2. PAMMI – A *** 6b+ 30m
From the ramp and climb the soaring crack, passing a bulge early on (crux) then trending slightly rightwards when the crack finally fades to ring-bolt lower-offs.

3. COOL MAX *** 7a 30m
The centre of the pillar is steep, sustained and fingery, and quite superb. The lower-off is as for the previous climb.

4. FRANK TAPAS *** 7a 30m
The right arête of the pillar and the discontinuous crack-line gives the final offering of this great quartet.

Shortly before the main cliff is reached there is a long north-facing corner. The corner itself looks like a traditional classic, and its right wall has two steep bolt lines; no grades known, though they look harder than most of the other climbs on the cliff. The bolts look ready for replacement.

Just before the main section of the crag (and 100m from the previously described routes) is an open slabby groove, and to the left of this is a 4m high cave entrance. Between the two is a pair of steeper open grooves. The right-hand one is:

5. LION RAMPANT *** 7a 25m
Enter the groove and cross a series of bulges to a resting ledge. Climb the leaning brown wall (crux) and more bulges to a lower-off on the crest of the wall.

Stood in front of the left edge of the main cliff is a tall flake/block. The front face of this has one route:

6. BOULDERING 5+ 10m
Use the cairn to reach the first holds (and second bolt) then sprint on to the lower-off. Hard and pretty poor.

Behind the boulder a route starts in the spiky vegetation:

7. NORDKAP * (for the upper three-quarters) 6a/6b+ 25m
Mantle onto the ledge then clip the first 'glue-in' bolt, then extemporise past this (6b+) or step left and use the small tufa to reach better holds (6a); pass the bulge then press on up the 'duff' slab to the lower-offs. A hopelessly unbalanced route, with both starts under-graded and the rest a path by comparison.

8. SUDKAP ** 5 25m
Starting up the next route and traversing the yellow handrail leftwards to join the climb makes much more sense and is well worth doing.

The next routes start on top of a pile of white blocks and below a smart grey slab forming the left side of the continuous section of the cliff face.

9. SUDWAND *** 4+ 25m

Creveta

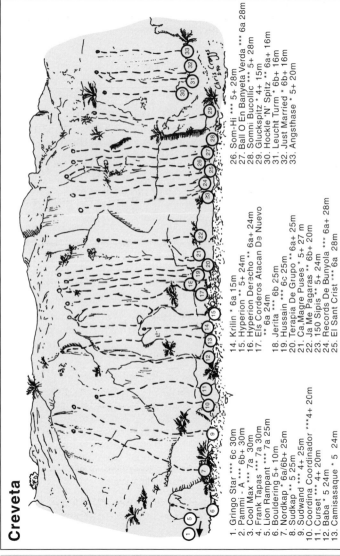

1. Gringo Star *** 6c 30m
2. Pammi - A *** 6b+ 30m
3. Cool Max *** 7a 30m
4. Frank Tapas *** 7a 30m
5. Lion Rampant *** 7a 25m
6. Bouldering 5+ 10m
7. Nordkap * 6a/6b+ 25m
8. Sudkap * 5 25m
9. Sudwand * 4+ 25m
10. Coordina Coordinador *** 4+ 20m
11. Curset *** 4+ 20m
12. Baba * 5 24m 20m
13. Camisasaque * 5 24m

14. Krilin * 6a 15m
15. Hyperion *** 5+ 24m
16. Hyperion Derecho ** 6a+ 24m
17. Els Corderos Atacan De Nuevo ** 6a 24m
18. Jerita *** 6b 25m
19. Hussain *** 6c 25m
20. Terapia De Grupo ** 6a+ 25m
21. Ca. Magre Puses * 5+ 27 m
22. Ja Me Pagaras ** 6b+ 20m
23. 150 Sipis ** 5+ 24m
24. Records De Bunyola *** 6a+ 28m
25. El Sant Crist ** 6a 28m

26. Som-Hi *** 5+ 28m
27. Ball O En Banyeta Verda *** 6a 28m
28. Somni Bucollic *** 5+ 28m
29. Gluckspitz * 4+ 15m
30. Hockle 'N' Spitz ** 6a+ 16m
31. Leucht Turm * 6b+ 16m
32. Just Married * 6b+ 16m
33. Angsthase * 5+ 20m

The first of three excellent lower-grade offerings, arguably the best such selection on the island. Climb to the first ring bolt using the loose flake and some goutte-d'eaux, then up juggy rock to the slab. Follow this, trickier to the right, all the way to easy ground and twin rings.

10. COORDINA COORDINADOR *** 4+ 20m
Starting below the centre of the slab climb the tricky initial section slightly leftwards to a steeper area which is passed on a excellent selection of holds to reach a lower-off above the highest point of the slab. Wonderful stuff.

11. CURSET *** 4+ 20m
Start just to the right of the centre point of the slab and trend slightly right until it is possible to step back left over a bulge into a shallow groove. Climb this to steeper rock, which is crossed on good holds to reach the same lower-off as the previous climb. Oddly named considering how pleasant it is!

To the right of the slab is a rather scruffy-looking left-trending groove to the left of a gorse bush and with a prominent peg runner low down.

12. BABA * 5 24m
A worthwhile climb that is better than it looks. Climb the initial groove past a bolt to the peg then continue up the sustained right-hand branch until it curves over to the right. Make a dainty traverse below the overlap then pull back leftwards over the bulges to a padlocked belay below the crest of the wall.

To the right is a clean triangular slab, 15m high, with twin white perched flakes on its summit. The next four routes start up this. The first route climbs the left side of lower the slab and the shallow groove above, and is pleasant if somewhat unbalanced.

13. CAMISASAQUE * 5 24m
Climb the left side of the slab to its apex (quite tough but very short) and continue passing the perched flakes to enter the pale shallow groove above. Up this pleasantly to join and finish as for the previous climb.

14. KRILIN * 6a 15m
The centre of the triangular slab gives a pleasant 'quick-tick' protected by four bolts. Absolutely no deviations are allowed at the grade!

The next two climbs share a common start up the right side of the triangular slab and then find their different ways up the rock above to a shared belay below the bulges that cap the wall.

15. HYPERION ** 5+ 24m

Climb the tricky right side of the triangular slab (maybe just a move of 6a) then follow the easy ramp line to its tip. From the flakes here step right, then continue straight up the wall until it is possible to move right to reach the belay.

16. HYPERION DERECHO ** 6a+ 24m

The initial section is the same as the regular route to the ramp. From here (bolt above on the left) step out to the right just above the overlap and make a difficult couple of pulls to get established just to the right of a bubbly grey streak. Continue first right then back left to the same lower-offs as the regular route.

The next four climbs all start from a domed ledge system 5m from the ground. This is most easily reached from the left. A direct approach involves crossing some highly abrasive vegetation, and if your second does not fancy an involuntary trip through this it might be worth considering taking a belay on the ledge system. The left-hand route above the ledge is:

17. ELS CORDEROS ATACAN DE NUEVO ** 6a 24m

From the left edge on the ledge climb the awkward slab to a thin ledge occupied by some shrubs, then make baffling moves up and left, using small pockets, to enter the diagonal scoop. An entry from further left is a bit of a cop-out and risks a prickly landing in the event of a miscalculation. Once established in the scoop, climb to its top before stepping left onto the wall and following good holds to the lower-off.

The next three routes are amongst the most difficult on the cliff, offering fine sustained and fingery climbing.

18. JERITA *** 6b 25m

The left-hand line starts just to left of the centre of the curving ledge and climbs direct past a small but prominent semi-circular scar. Above this sustained moves and plenty of protection combine to guarantee a classic outing. From the lower-off it is possible to check out the rather harder route to the right, and even place the quick-draws (if that's allowed).

19. HUSSAIN *** 6c 25m

The central line climbs directly up the steepening slab into a shallow scoop and makes thin steep moves out of this (try a left-facing 'rock over') to thankfully reach an easier crack line and the lower-off some distance above. The climb is rather easier if you stray to the right of the 'true path'.

20. TERAPIA DE GRUPO ** 6a+ 25m

The right-hand line is thought by some to be the best of bunch, though the grade is just a touch tight-fisted! More thin sustained climbing following the thin white streak on razor-sharp flakes and pockets. If you are really keen to do this one it is probably best not to leave it to the last route of the day!

The right side of the steep slab is bounded by an open black scoop. This is most easily reached from the right and is climbed by:

21. CA, MAGRE PUSES * 5+ 27m

A pleasant route with short-lived difficulties. Climb to ledges then continue easily up the white slab into the scoop. Make technical moves up the steepening groove, and continue past broken flakes and up the scoop on poor holds to a flaky section where it is possible to step out left to reach the belays.

To the right of the black scoop is a steep barrel-shaped buttress climb by the oh so painful:

22. JA ME PAGARAS ** 6b+ 20m

Climb to a ledge then up a blunt rib to more ledges and the start of the difficulties. Head up the steep buttress with a short jig out to the right at the third bolt on some of the sharpest holds in the world. Single-bolt belay. A route for real masochists or those with skin like chain-mail.

Ten metres right is a clean lower slab with a palm tree growing at its bottom left corner, close to the rock. Four metres to the right of a 3m high white perched flake is the excellent:

23. 150 SIPIS ** 5+ 24m

Climb the straightforward lower slab to the prominent horizontal break, then continue more steeply to a move using an insubstantial 'razor' to reach better holds. Continue up the right side of a corner then step right to the belays.

24. RECORDS DE BUNYOLA *** 6a+ 28m

Three metres right climb past a detached-looking flake at 3m to the base of this superb 'blank' face. Gain the base of the wall using an undercut two-finger pocket and continue by sustained moves to the left edge of a large curving hole/pocket. Make a long reach then continue up the centre of the upper wall (still sustained but on surprising holds) to a lower-off just to the left of a bush in the centre of the upper slab. If you are using a 50m rope take note of the length of this pitch!

25. EL SANT CRIST *** 6a 28m

Great climbing with a sudden transition from 'jugs to razors'. Climb the lower slab above two large blocks, past the horizontal break to a position below the left side of the horizontal cave halfway up the face. Pull steeply rightwards out of this to gain the upper wall then trend right to the lower-offs.

26. SOM-HI *** 5+ 28m

Start just to the right of the blocks at the foot of the face and climb the sustained slab past an obvious horizontal orange-stained overlap. Smoother rock leads to the bulging wall, above which is best climbed quickly before the whole affair becomes too painful.

27. BALL O'EN BANYETA VERDA *** 6a 28m

An excellent route marked by alternating black and white bolts. The technical lower slab gives fine sustained climbing past a constriction in the horizontal break. Continue (crux) to the bulges that are best crossed by a tricky move left followed by a romp back to the right past a huge 'ringing' flake. Easier rock remains.

28. SOMNI BUCOLLIC *** 5+ 28m

The last route on the main face has a tough crux and plenty of good climbing as well. Climb the slab just to the right of a thin crack to reach the bulges that cross the face. Step left and make a couple of unlikely thin moves (especially so for the short) to reach better pockets, which gives sustained but easier moves until it is possible to step left to reach the huge 'ringing' flake of the previous route. Finish rightwards up easier rock.

At the right-hand side of the cliff there are five newer offerings. Though shorter than those on the main cliff they are worth doing.

29. GLUCKSPITZ * 4+ 15m

Start by scrambling up to the tip of some white flakes. Follow 'glue-ins' up the steep slab to a lower-off on ledges above. Six bolts.

To the right is a smooth grey wall rising above ledges and reached by a diagonal scramble. A belay here is a sound idea in view of the drop.

30. HOCKLE 'N' SPITZ ** 6a+ 16m

Climb the sharp water streak then the more amenable white scoop right and back left. Seven bolts protect.

31. LEUCHT TURM * 6b+ 16m

Climb just to the left of (and occasionally in) the thin ragged cracks using a series of sharp holds. Six bolts protect.

32. JUST MARRIED * 6b+ 16m

Similar moves just to the right of the crack.

33. ANGSTHASE * 5+ 20m

Climb just left of the white flake (using it if you must) and the better wall above trending right.

FRAGGEL ROCK

Character

A glowing golden bowl of truly 'tufatastic' routes and a genuine Mecca for those in search of high-standard, high-quality climbing. For a while Fraggel was the best kept secret of the Mallorcan climbing scene. Only a short distance from the town of Bunyola and the well-known cliff of Gubia, the locals, accompanied by French visitors, found a valley stuffed with rock and set about developing one of the more impressive cliffs in it, producing some stunning and very tough climbs in the process. Originally the intention was to keep the place hush-hush from visiting climbers, but inevitably (considering the quality of the climbing) the crag has gradually become known to a wider audience and now it is firmly on the island's regular climbing circuit.

At present there are over 50 routes here and most of them are hard to very hard. There are also a few more moderate offerings scattered around the edges of the cliff, and so the place is worth at least one visit by most parties. People training for the harder routes on British limestone could spend all week here and then still come back for more.

Almost all the routes are steep and involve either pocket-pulling or doing powerful battle with impressive hanging tufa systems. The cliff faces south-east and goes out of the sun shortly after midday. Sun worshippers will need to arrive early, and of course the place makes an excellent after-lunch venue when it is too hot to climb full in the sun.

Note: After prolonged rain many of the tufas weep for extended periods. This is especially a problem after the autumn (October) and spring (March) rains.

All the routes are fully equipped with 10mm bolt runners, and almost all can be done to the lower-off and back to the ground on a 60m rope. The few that are longer are mentioned in the text.

Access

The cliff (see section 'Sa Gubia', Situation & Access map, page 75) is quite difficult to locate on first acquaintance. On the south-eastern side of Bunyola (on the road running towards Santa Maria), immediately before the town sign, is a rough road running towards the hills. This is followed past houses and around a small valley, and it then begins to climb rapidly. The road is quite rough in places, and is followed for a bum-numbing 5km. An unexpected 900m section of tarmac arrives and just past the end of this, and the 5km marker, is parking space on the right by a 'respect the mountains' sign on a tree. A good track leads down into the woods here and is followed for 100m (passing camp fire rings) to a charcoal-burning circle hidden in the trees 5m to the left of the track. (The circle is unmistakable, being about 4m across and covered in bright green moss.) At this point the cliff top is dead ahead and can be approached by a long abseil if you are carrying a spare rope. The base of the wall is reached by a long loop to the left. Pass round the left side of the circle to locate a narrow track running off into the trees. This is followed gently downhill past one zig-zag to a large block (and occasional cairn) by the track, where a slabby rock band and then an awkward 10m groove can be descended to reach the base of the cliff. (If this proves too steep for non-climbing members of the party, it is possible to continue along the main track to an easy scramble down and then double back along the cliff base.) From the foot of the rock band turn right (facing out) and follow various indistinct trails to where the cliff becomes more impressive; 15 minutes from the car. The final section of the approach passes some rock that could be developed to produce less intimidating climbing than on most of the rest of the cliff.

The routes are described from right to left, as this is the usual direction of approach.

The first climbs start off a narrow ledge where the approach path to the cliff climbs up a short rise.

1. CHRIS LINE * 4 14m
Closely-spaced red bolts up the rib starting from the ledge system at end of the approach path. A pleasant but very untypical pitch which is obviously on the wrong cliff.

2. CHURROPINO ** 5+ 16m
The steep groove with *in situ* tree and gold-coloured bolts. A tricky start over the bulge gains the right wall of the groove, which is followed with interest.

To the left is a steep orange tower capped by a tilted prow, home to three lines.

3. TOFOL *** 6b+ 16m
The right-hand line has a sharp start. Pass left of the tree and tackle the upper section on a continually surprising set of holds.

4. MARMADE ** 7a+ 16m
The central line on small (chipped) holds leads to a belay in common with the previous climb.

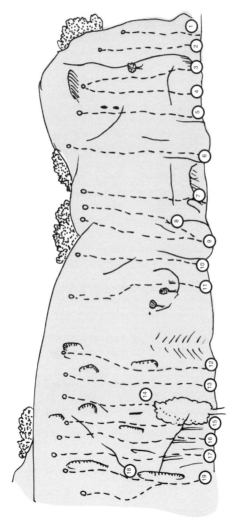

Fraggel Rock - Right

1. Chris Line * 4 14m
2. Churropino ** 5+ 16m
3. Tofol *** 6b+ 16m
4. Marmade ** 7a+ 16m
5. Peep Show's Garriga ** 7b+ 16m
6. Nameless ** 6b+ 16m
7. Comando Rasta ** 6a 16m
8. Sementir ** 6a+ 16m
9. Esto No Es Calvia.** 6b+ 16m
10. Cous Cous *** 6c 20m
11. Cotorrot ** 7c+ 18m
12. 7b El Plumero ** 7b 18m
13. Pastanaga Punyetera *** 8a 20m
14. On Es L'Avi ***7b 24m
15. Cuencamelo *** 7b+ 28m
16. Rock Punk *** 7c 26m
17. El Ultimo Vals.*** 7c+ 24m
18. Tete De Pen *** 7c+ 26m
19. Glasnost ** 7b+ 16m

Dave Gregory proves it isn't always red hot on Mallorca

Coordina Coordinador (4+), Creveta

Football Fan (8a): one of Fraggel's finest

5. PEEP SHOW'S GARRIGA ** 7b+ 16m
The left-hand line has even smaller (chipped) holds. To the left is a slabbier section of cliff, and towards its left side a 4m high club-shaped flake leans against the rock.

To the right of the flake is an easy angled slab.

6. NAMELESS ** 6b+ 16m
The easy slab is climbed to pockets, then steeper orange rock leads with escalating difficulty into an open finishing groove.

7. COMANDO RASTA ** 6a 16m
Climb over the flake with care and head up the sustained and interesting pocketed wall above.

To the left is a rounded rib before the cliff becomes much more spectacular. Two routes start up this, past a prominent peg runner.

8. SEMENTIR ** 6a+ 16m
Pass the peg then move out right to the line of gold bolts. The midway bulge proves troublesome.

9. ESTO NO ES CALVIA ** 6b+ 16m
Up the rounded rib past the peg runner, then follow the line of oldish bolts up the gradually steepening wall.

Around to the left of the rib is a shallow groove running out into steeper rock.

10. COUS COUS *** 6c 20m
Up the groove then step right and climb the steep wall with the crux around bolts number 5 and 6 and a slightly run-out finish. The first of the real belters.

To the left is a small tree in an orange hollow 7m up the cliff.

11. COTORROT ** 7c+ 18m
The bolt line rising from the right side of the tree in the hollow and forging on up the steep wall.

12. 7b EL PLUMERO ** 7b 18m
Five metres left of the tree in the hollow is a hole 8m up the cliff. Enter this easily then step left and do battle with the next section until it is possible to pull right to gain a respite in another hole. Step out left and make a precarious couple of moves to easier ground.

13. PASTANAGA PUNYETERA *** 8a 20m

Fraggel Rock - Right

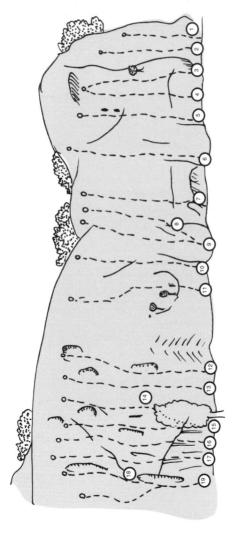

1. Chris Line * 4 14m
2. Churropino ** 5+ 16m
3. Tofol *** 6b+ 16m
4. Marmade ** 7a+ 16m
5. Peep Show's Garriga ** 7b+ 16m
6. Nameless ** 6b+ 16m
7. Comando Rasta ** 6a 16m
8. Sementir ** 6a+ 16m
9. Esto No Es Calvia ** 6b+ 16m
10. Cous Cous *** 6c 20m
11. Cotorrot ** 7c+ 18m
12. 7b El Plumero ** 7b 18m
13. Pastanaga Punyetera *** 8a 20m
14. On Es L'Avi *** 7b 24m
15. Cuencamelo *** 7b+ 28m
16. Rock Punk *** 7c 26m
17. El Ultimo Vals *** 7c+ 24m
18. Tete De Pen *** 7c+ 26m
19. Glasnost ** 7b+ 16m

The steep orange rib immediately to the left and just right of a pine tree standing close to the rock. Sustained and on tiny holds and unhelpful tufas.

Left of and behind the pine tree is a tufa-covered lower wall 7m high and capped by a leaning, ginger section of cliff. There are four tough routes on this section of wall.

14. ON ES L'AVI *** 7b 24m
The right-hand line keeping to the edge of the ginger wall reserves its crux for the upper wall.

15. CUENCAMELO *** 7b+ 28m
The next line left follows the edge of the tufa directly behind the tree and then forges straight up the wall.

16. ROCK PUNK *** 7c 26m
The next offering lies just left again and makes manful use of an array of tufas.

17. EL ULTIMO VALS *** 7c+ 24m
The final route here is located just to the right of the large groove system.

Left again is a major overhanging groove leading to an elongated cave halfway up the cliff. Off-width and chimney freaks please note that this feature is unclimbed at the time of writing. Left of the groove is a prominent triple tufa, and left of this is an innocuous-looking open orange scoop running up the cliff to fade out into steeper rock.

18. TETE DE PEN *** 7c+ 26m
The open scoop system leads to the bulging rib where things turn tough. The first of a host of very hard on the central section of the cliff.

Starting in the same place and initially trending left is a line up a leaning wall passing a prominent and permanently chalked up mono-doigt. This is the first of five routes that have lower-offs on the large ledge in the centre of the cliff.

19. GLASNOST ** 7b+ 16m
Gaining and passing the 'mono' both prove problematical, especially the latter. The loss of a pinch-grip has not helped.

20. ALOHA FROM HELL *** 7b 20m
Just to the left a white wall leading to line of unhelpful pockets marks the line of this butch piece of exercise. Improvise up these then exit leftwards with difficulty.

To the left, the cliff becomes ever steeper.

21. MIGUELINE Y LOS PROBETAS *** 7c+ 20m
A lower leaning section leads to a large orifice above which the wall is climbed rightwards. The difficulties are continuous and excessive. Also known by its English translation of MIGUELINE AND THE TEST-TUBE BABIES.

To the left the wall is steeply tilted and it runs into another major (and steep) groove system. There are four lines on this section of wall, all of which utilise impressive tufa formations.

22. PANTANO BOAS *** 7c+ 20m
Follows the large, thick, flanged tufa to its top.

23. NO NAME *** 8b+ 20m
The steepest part of the wall utilising a sporadic tufa system is a contender for the hardest route here.

24. HUMANOIDE *** 8a+ 30m
The rather larger tufas just to the left again (two systems out from the deep groove). To the first lower-off is 7c+.

25. BODO DODO *** 7b+ 20/30m
The set of tufas before the deep groove with a short jig left at half-height. The climbing is 7b to the fifth bolt (maillon in place). The extension is harder.

The big groove itself is:

26. MISS PALMA *** 7b+ 20m
Steep bridging is the order of the day, easier for long-legged chimps and just a little run-out.

27. FES EL QUE PUGUIS ** 7a+ 20m
In the left wall of the groove is a set of twinned tufas which are followed (crux low down) until a traverse can be made to the right to the lower-off of the previous climb. One of the easiest climbs in the central section of the cliff and much used as a 'warm-up', hence it is now rather spoilt by the polish.

28. TERRE D'AVENTURE *** 7b+,8a 30m
The second line left of the big groove is tough to a stance on top of the tufa, and tougher again above this.

29. FRENCH KISS *** 8b 30m
A huge pitch up smooth wall just left again is (almost) interminable.

30. RAMADAN *** 8b+ 28m

The steeply tilted wall just left again is the other contender for the cliff's hardest route. As far as the fixed karabiner on the fifth bolt is the warm-up for this area at * 6b and involves the use of a rather rickety tufa. Above this the angle increases and the difficulties escalate dramatically.

31. SHABADA *** 8a+ 28m
Just above the step down in the base of the cliff is a line up prominent tufas. It gives a ** 7a to the first lower-off.

To the left, the foot of the cliff drops down a 7m step. Just above the foot of this is a route starting out of an orange cave:

32. FOOTBALL FAN *** 8a 28m
One of Fraggel's finest and low in the grade. Climb leftwards out of the hollow following a line of jazzy purple bolts. From a rest in another hollow, battle the leaning wall above with the crux just short of the lower-offs.

To the left a slabby section of rock leads to two separate tufa pillars. The belay for these routes is bolts linked by a long sling high above:

33. AMNESIA *** 8b 28m
The right-hand and shorter tufa.

34. LA GORILLE E UNE BONE MINE *** 7c 28m
Another major classic. The left-hand tufa leads to an open groove high on the face and the route requires two dynos from most mortals, one at half-height and one to grab the lower-offs.

35. GOO GOO MUCK *** 8a 25m
To the left of the slab at the foot of the face is a small hollow with a line of blue bolts rising from its left side and climbing through a zone of short tufas and small pockets.

Left again is a 15m high alcove of unsavoury-looking orange rock. The right-hand side of this is (not) climbed by a project, No 36.

Climbing out of the back left-hand side of the cave is:

37. SOLO SEX *** 8a+ 28m
Either a project or a superb route!

38. SALPICON DE MENISCO *** 8a 25m
The left-hand rib of the cave has a line of pinky/purple bolts and is the last of the 'big boys' offerings.

39. JUNGLE HOP ** 7a 30m

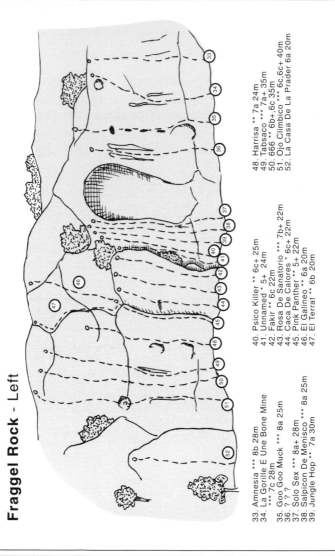

Fraggel Rock - Left

33. Amnesia *** 8b 28m
34. La Gorille E Une Bone Mine *** 7c 28m
35. Goo Goo Muck *** 8a 25m
36. ? ? ?
37. Solo Sex *** 8a+ 28m
38. Salpicon De Menisco *** 8a 25m
39. Jungle Hop ** 7a 30m

40. Psico Killer ** 6c+ 25m
41. Unnamed * 5+ 24m
42. Fakir ** 6c 22m
43. Rosa De Sanatorio *** 7b+ 22m
44. Caca De Calores * 6c+ 22m
45. Pink Panther ** 5+ 22m
46. El Galineo ** 6a 20m
47. El Terrat ** 6b 20m

48. Harrisa ** 7a 24m
49. Tabsaco *** 7a+ 35m
50. 666 ** 6b+,6c 35m
51. Ojo Climbico *** 6c,6c+ 40m
52. La Casa De La Prader 6a 20m

The white slab and steepening wall passing between two grey streaks, and climbing into and out of a niche.

40. PSICO KILLER ** 6c+ 25m
Climb the slab trending left to a broken flake and then on directly up easier-angled rock above.

To the left is a grotty-looking open chimney with in-situ bush, and beyond this the cliff juts forwards as a steep grey pillar with three bolt lines on its front face. The right wall of the open chimney and its upper section is:

41. UNNAMED * 5+ 24m
Not very inspiring but adds a little to the cliff's collection of easier outings.

42. FAKIR ** 6c 22m
The right-hand line on the front of the pillar passing over an overlap.

43. ROSA DE SANATORIO *** 7b+ 22m
The sharp central line on slightly overhanging rock.

44. CACA DE COLORES * 6c+ 22m
The left-hand line is (a bit) better that the name suggests. It is a slightly more amenable angle, but is still very spiky.

45. PINK PANTHER ** 5+ 22m
The left side of the pillar is bounded by a steep twisting bridging groove which offers a good pitch. From the ledge at the top of the route there are two ways on.

46. EL GALINEO ** 6a 20m
The right-hand line off the belay ledge is more in keeping with the lower groove, being pleasantly juggy.

47. EL TERRAT ** 6b 20m
From the lower-off above PINK PANTHER step left and finish up the steep wall and hanging rib above. Sharp!

Left of the pillar is an area of steep rock rising from a yellow bay, with two bolt lines above it.

48. HARRISA ** 7a 24m
The right-hand line, using pockets and some 'bottle'.

49. TABSACO *** 7a+ 35m
The left-hand line exits from the scoop and heads up a tufa to give a spicy pitch. Be aware of its length when lowering off.

50. 666 ** 6b+,6c 35m
Just before the crag becomes slabbier is this worthwhile beast.

51. OJO CLIMBICO *** 6c,6c+ 40m
The last route on the slab steepens as it rises to a stance in a hollow and then bears away leftwards. The start is marked by blue bolts.

52. LA CASA DE LA PRADERA 6a 20m
The last line on the cliff is not really worth the effort of walking all this way.

The cliff continues leftwards but not on the grand scale already passed. It awaits a devotee.

ES QUEIXAL

A relatively recently developed cliff in a superbly isolated setting. Unfortunately this means it is difficult to get at from almost anywhere on the island. It can also be difficult to reach from the parking! The name means 'tooth', and the reason for this can be seen when the crag first appears.

Access
From Soller or Lluc (or even Pollença) take the twisting road to where the side branch to Sa Calobra heads down towards the sea. Follow this down the hill (watching for coaches) until there is a left turn to Cala Tuent. The road climbs over the col and down in to the next bay. Park where a dirt road branches off to the left and walk to the small cluster of buildings of Fra Puig (see map). From here the crag is clearly visible, though the path is difficult to find. There are many overgrown terraces between the parking and the cliff which can make for a rather scratchy approach, though as ever the path is much easier to find on the return journey. The routes are listed from left to right.

The first three pitches are on the far left-hand side of the cliff reached by the short scramble:

1. ES MIRADOR ** 5+ 15m

2. IDO A QUE ESPERES ** 6a+ 15m
To the same lower-off.

Es Queixal - Access & Routes

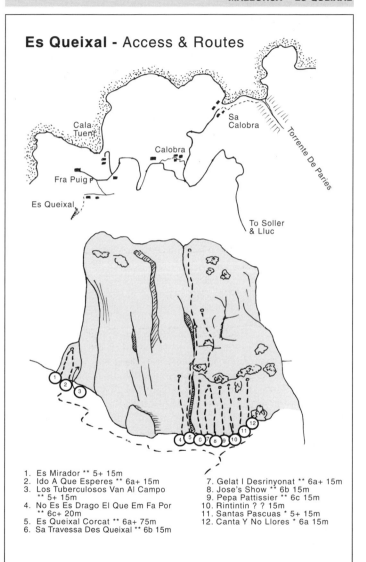

1. Es Mirador ** 5+ 15m
2. Ido A Que Esperes ** 6a+ 15m
3. Los Tuberculosos Van Al Campo
   ** 5+ 15m
4. No Es Es Drago El Que Em Fa Por
   ** 6c+ 20m
5. Es Queixal Corcat ** 6a+ 75m
6. Sa Travessa Des Queixal ** 6b 15m

7. Gelat I Desrinyonat ** 6a+ 15m
8. Jose's Show ** 6b 15m
9. Pepa Pattissier ** 6c 15m
10. Rintintin ? ? 15m
11. Santas Pascuas * 5+ 15m
12. Canta Y No Llores * 6a 15m

3. LOS TUBERCULOSOS VAN AL CAMPO ** 5+ 15m
Around to the right.

The rest of the climbs are found on the walls to either side of the long central groove of ES QUEIXAL CORCAT.

4. NO ES ES DRAGO EL QUE EM FA POR ** 6c+ 20m
To the left of the groove.

5. ES QUEIXAL CORCAT ** 6a+ 75m
The long groove is climbed in three sustained pitches (all 6a+); carry a full rack.

The remainder of the climbs are on the fine wall to the right of the central groove, and all can be ticked in a steady couple of hours' climbing. Above them is the extension pitch of LA PAZ DE ANDY SHERIDAN (no grade known).

6. SA TRAVESSA DES QUEIXAL ** 6b 15m
Just to the right of the groove.

7. GELAT I DESRINYONAT ** 6a+ 15m

8. JOSE'S SHOW ** 6b 15m

9. PEPA PATTISSIER ** 6c 15m

10. RINTINTIN ? ? 15m

11. SANTAS PASCUAS * 5+ 15m

12. CANTA Y NO LLORES * 6a 15m

SA GUBIA

Character
Despite the development of other cliffs Sa Gubia remains the premier rock climbing location on Mallorca with over 100 offerings. It is the best developed crag, has the widest range of routes and remains the most popular climbing destination on the island. The name Sa Gubia means 'his trowel' and at certain times of the day the shadowy hollow in the centre of cliff bears a passing resemblance to a huge gardening implement. The extensive cliffs here consist of ten separate 'sectors' spread around the entrance to an open ravine that cuts deep into the Sierra de

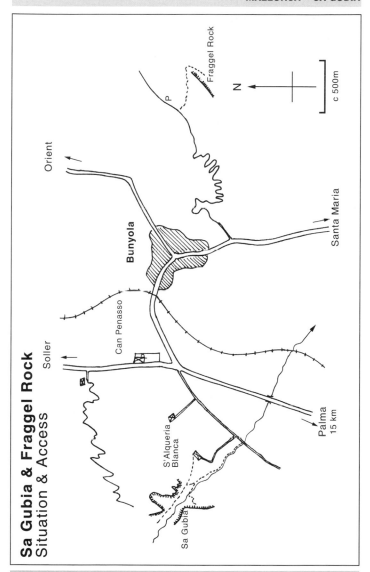

Sa Gubia & Fraggel Rock
Situation & Access

Soller

Can Penasso

Orient

Bunyola

Santa Maria

Fraggel Rock

P

N

c 500m

S'Alqueria
Blanca

Sa Gubia

Palma
15 km

Alfabia. This is located close to the small and pleasant town of Bunyola, 15km to the north of Palma. Each sector has its own atmosphere, and as they face almost all points of the compass it is usually possible to choose whether to climb in the sun or the shade. Routes extend from two-bolt 'quickies' to eight-pitch expeditions, and in grade from 4 to 'Mallorcan' 7b+. There really is something here for everyone, including the person who just wants to get away from it all. The rock ranges from perfect fluted grey sheets, through pocketed walls to incredible tufa pillars, and is impeccable almost without exception. Bolt protection is the norm and is usually frequent and substantial, as are the belays and lower-offs. The whole ambience of the area is quite magical, with vultures high overhead, the blossoms on the almond and olive trees in the fields below the gorge and in the far distance the blue waters of the Mediterranean. If you think the crag is worked out just take a 5 minute walk past the base of the Gubia Normal and get a look at the cliff high on the right – impressive or what?

If you have visited the crag in the past the new developments to the right of the Sector Polla Boba might be of passing interest.

The sectors are described in anti-clockwise fashion (right to left as the cliff is approached). The short pen-portrait of each one given below should give you a good idea where to head for first depending on how you like your sport.

The first seven sectors are all situated on the eastern side (right looking up the gorge) of the dried-up stream bed and are reached from the narrow path that cuts right through the gorge.

The sectors are as follows.

1. The SECTOR SILICONA is up to 22m high, faces due south and is generally slabby in nature. The routes have become rather polished. It contains a dozen routes from 4 to 6b+, most of which are 5+ and 6a.

2. The SECTOR EXCALIBUR runs up the side of a steep gully and is a south-facing wall up to 45m high. It contains 10 routes from 5+ to 7b+, with a spread across the grades and climbing that is mostly steep.

3. The SECTOR WHY is the steep, red west-facing tower directly above the path at the first narrowing in the gorge. It is up to 80m high and contains 10 routes from 5+ to 7b+, with a spread of grades. Most of the climbs are strenuous, following strong natural lines.

4. The SECTOR FINA Y SEGURA is a north-facing area based around a deep water-worn groove. There are 15 routes from 4 to 7b+. The routes here are generally short and shady, except for the longer classics of SEXO DEBIL and LA ISLA BONITA.

5. The SECTOR PRINCESA is the 160m high west-facing wall that towers above

Sa Gubia - Access & Sectors

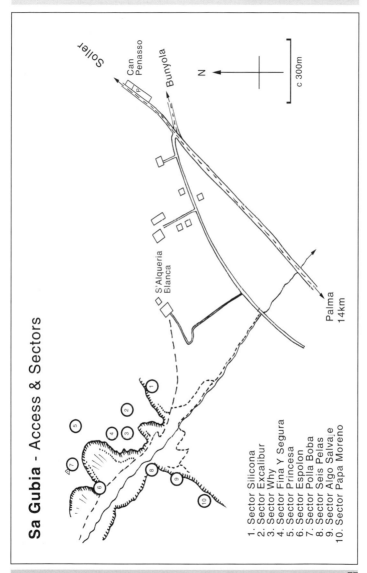

1. Sector Silicona
2. Sector Excalibur
3. Sector Why
4. Sector Fina Y Segura
5. Sector Princesa
6. Sector Espolon
7. Sector Polla Boba
8. Sector Seis Pelas
9. Sector Algo Salvaje
10. Sector Papa Moreno

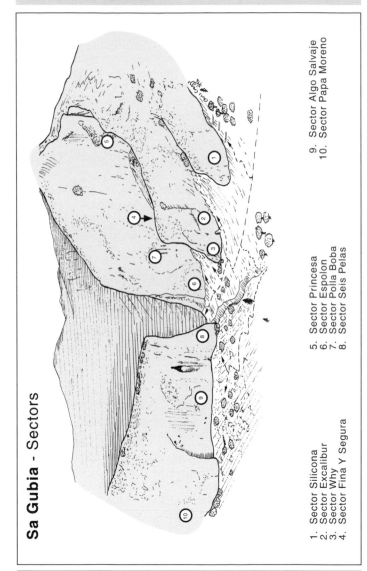

Sa Gubia - Sectors

1. Sector Silicona
2. Sector Excalibur
3. Sector Why
4. Sector Fina Y Segura

5. Sector Princesa
6. Sector Espolon
7. Sector Polla Boba
8. Sector Seis Pelas

9. Sector Algo Salvaje
10. Sector Papa Moreno

the bay in the centre of the cliffs. There is one great classic here and nine routes of (slightly) lesser stature.

6. The SECTOR ESPOLON is the massive ridge that stabs skywards at the narrowing of the ravine. It faces south and west and is home to a set short routes – most of which are quite tough, the great eight-pitch classic of GUBIA NORMAL and the more recently bolted gem of QUAN ES FA FOSC.

7. The SECTOR POLLA BOBA is the attractive south-facing wall of excellent rock situated below the ridge climbed by GUBIA NORMAL. It is 45m high and is home to a dozen good routes in the 5 to 6a+ category plus the long classics of LA LEY DEL DESEO and LOS BOMBEROS.

    The final three sectors are located on the western side of the dry steam bed and are known collectively as the PARET DES COLOMS (the Wall of Pillars). The cliff generally faces south-east.

8. The SECTOR SEIS PELAS is the right side of the wall, to the left and right of where a strange black hole disappears up into the cliff. There are 16 routes on this face, with the longest a huge 90m. Grades vary from 5+ to 7b, with many of these climbs being major classics.

9. The SECTOR ALGO SALVAJE is the impressive central section of the PARET DES COLOMS. There are 11 routes here graded from 6b to 7b. The routes are steep to very steep, and some are even steeper than that! Many involve climbing strange tufa features and formations.

10. The SECTOR PAPA MORENO is situated around to the left side of the PARET DES COLOMS. It is largely undeveloped, and at the moment contains only four routes, 5+ to 6b. A leaning orange wall some distance up the hillside might repay a visit from a suitably armed team.

Access

Note: Please follow the directions closely, park sensibly and avoid crossing cultivated land at all costs.

From Palma follow the main road (the C711) northwards towards Bunyola and Soller for 15km. The crag becomes visible on the left after about 12km with the striking arête of GUBIA NORMAL being particularly conspicuous. Immediately before the junction that provides a right turn into Bunyola is a small track on the left that doubles back towards the cliff; this is the route to the cliff. Drive another 150m or so along the main road and park on the right in the car park of the taverna Can Penasso (well worth checking out at the end of the day). Please park sensibly.

Walk back 160m towards Palma and then take the right turn. Where the tarmac ends (old parking on the right, still much used by the locals despite the signs), continue down the track through two rickety gates. Just beyond the second, walk up the stream bed, or the field to the left, for a couple of hundred metres to a gate across the stream. For the PARET DES COLOMS continue up the stream bed to the last large pine tree then head up and left. For the rest of the cliff climb out of the stream bed a short distance after the gate, keep left of the ploughed land and the miniature football field until steep tacks lead up and right to the path from the big house to the gorge (20 minutes from the car).

Note: There has been considerable development around the big house S'Alqueria Blanca on the old approach. A quick look revealed the presence of new fences and several dogs, one of which was the stuff of nightmares. It is probably best to stick with the above approach.

A direct link between opposite side of the gorge is best avoided because of the incised nature of the stream bed and the dense and thorny vegetation.

SECTOR SILICONA

A good place to start your Gubia apprenticeship, with a fine collection of pitches that are full in the sun for most of the day and are on superb rock. They are described from left to right up the bank.

1. HAWAI 5-0 ** 4+ 14m
The left edge of the wall is formed by a clean rib that starts from a bent-over tree. The rib is followed on great rock past six bolt runners to a final juggy steepening and a substantial lowering chain. Not surprisingly the route is becoming polished.

2. SILICONA * 6b 12m
The smooth wall 6m right of the arête has been rebolted, though the climbing is as thin and fingery as it ever was. It is possible to continue up the wall from the initial lowering point following a line of older bolts to reach the belay of the next climb (* 20m).

3. LULU ** 6a 18m
Start just right of bushes where a red groove leads to a flat roof at 7m with a conspicuous bolt above its lip. Climb the groove and trend left over the roof to reach the base of a thin crack. Climb this with difficulty then continue up the steeper wall on a surprising set of holds.

4. PROTEINA VEGETAL ** 5+ 16m
Start left of the large tree and climb up the tricky slab to steeper rock. Step left (or do it direct, 6a) and follow pockets to a belay in a hollow.

Directly above the large tree is a prominent white scar at 15m. The next climb reaches this from immediately behind the tree. It is:

Sa Gubia - Sector Silicona

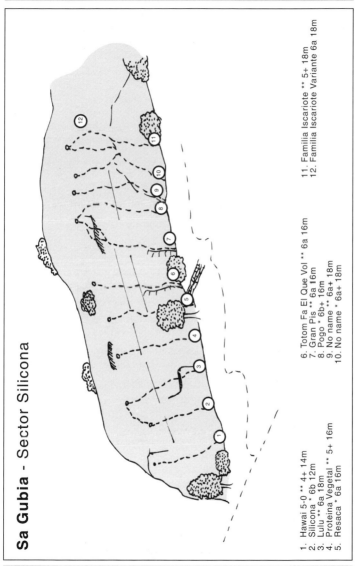

1. Hawai 5-0 ** 4+ 14m
2. Silicona * 6b 12m
3. Lulu ** 6a 18m
4. Proteina Vegetal ** 5+ 16m
5. Resaca * 6a 16m

6. Totom Fa El Que Vol ** 6a 16m
7. Gran Pis ** 6a 16m
8. Pogo * 6b+ 16m
9. No name ** 6a+ 18m
10. No name * 6a+ 18m

11. Familia Iscariote ** 5+ 18m
12. Familia Iscariote Variante 6a 18m

5. RESACA * 6a 16m

A sustained and interesting lower wall (very thin if you are totally puritanical about it) reaches the base of the scar. Clip a high bolt then step right and climb the centre of the scar on holds that keep appearing.

To the right is a section of walling/terracing, and above where this meets the rock is an open groove taken by:

6. TOTOM FA EL QUE VOL ** 6a 16m

The lower groove is straightforward, but just when you thought the route was in the bag it turns nasty. A very thin sequence leads to pockets and then the belay.

Three metres right of the walling is a broad, clean rib leading to steeper rock.

7. GRAN PIS ** 6a 16m

Climb straight up the broad rib then either pull straight over the overhangs and swing right or trend right through the bulges to reach the belays. Failure to clip the bolt in the centre of the crux moves may result in a grand pisser.

8. POGO * 6b+ 16m

A route with a short fierce crux section: try bouncing. Climb the scoop to the right of the previous climb then step right to the foot of a steep wall. A layaway is used to get established on this, and then a series of powerful moves leads right and then back left to better holds and an easing in the angle. Upgraded from a tough 6a+.

Just to the right is a slabby apron of rock, and climbing the left edge of this is a new route:

9. NAMELESS ** 6a+ 18m

The slab and steeper rock above.

Just to the right is an attractive slabby apron leading to steeper rock. This is climbed by three routes that share a common start.

10. NAMELESS * 6a+ 18m

The slab and left-hand line on the wall.

11. FAMILIA ISCARIOTE ** 5+ 18m

The pleasant slab leads to a large hold at a flowstone pillar. A thin section leads up the steeper wall, with a pull leftwards on razor blades gaining easier rock. Quite excellent and not too high in the grade.

To the right of the crux section of the last route is another line of rather older-looking bolts.

12. FAMILIA ISCARIOTE VARIANTE 6a 18m

Either start as for the previous climb or approach the bolt ladder from directly below via an easy but unprotected and somewhat shrubby slab. The steep wall gives thin and rather unsatisfying climbing until it is possible to swing left to the belays of the previous route.

SECTOR EXCALIBUR

The steep side wall of the gully behind the SECTOR SILICONA provides a good collection of pitches on excellent rock. The area is rarely crowded and gets the sun all day. The routes are described from left to right and the first offering starts at the left edge of the wall, where a 3m high 'tombstone'-like finger of rock gesticulates arrogantly skywards.

13. NA GUARRA * 6a 22m

From behind the 'tombstone' step left and climb the smooth-looking rib on well-hidden holds until a steeper pull gains easy ledges. Climb the sharp crack in the right wall of the groove (no bridging out left at the grade) to a lower-off above.

14. HORRIBLE BELLEZA *** 7a 16m

The flat orange wall directly above the lower-off of the previous climb gives a fingery test piece. Trend right up the lower section then head back left using a poor series of shallow pockets to reach a lower-off above the final difficulties.

Immediately to the right of the 'tombstone' is an attractive slabby ramp that cuts diagonally rightwards across the face to eventually fizzle out below a deep groove. This is the line of the original route of this section of cliff, the excellent:

15. EXCALIBUR *** 5+ 45m

1. 20m 5+ Follow the ramp rightwards into an increasingly dramatic position sandwiched between overhangs until below an orange groove. Climb this (crux) to a restricted stance and three-bolt belay by a tree.
2. 25m 5+ Climb the sustained groove behind the stance until it bends to the left and then fizzles out. Cross the bulge directly above to gain entry to an exposed crack-line, which is followed in a dramatic situation to the cliff top, where a lower-off (or tree belay) will be found. Descend by one long (45m) or two short abseils.

Starting in the same place as EXCALIBUR is another worthwhile route at a reasonable grade, and if you fancy something just a little tougher, then that is catered for too.

16. OPERA PRIMA * 5+/6a 15/20m

Climb onto the slab as for EXCALIBUR and continue straight up the wall and rib

Sa Gubia - Sector Why & Sector Excalibur

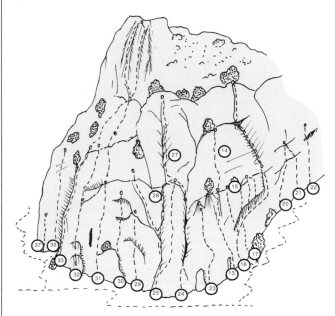

Sector Excalibur

13. Na Guarra * 6a 22m
14. Horrible Belleza *** 7a 16m
15. Excalibur *** 5+ 45m
16. Opera Prima * 5+/6a 15/20m
17. No Haces Mas Grado Porque
    Eres Enano ** 6b+ 18m
18. Trampera Matinera * 6b 18m
19. Il Panzeroto * 6a+ 18m
20. Bofetadas De Placer * 7c 18m
21. Carismatics ** 6c 16m
22. Hot Consuela (aka Ingleses) * 6c 16m

Sector Why

23. KGB ** 6c 16m
24. Zaraguay * 5+ 18m

25. Cortocircuito *** 6b 20m
26. Why ** 6b+ 20m
27. Agarrate Maldito *** 7b+ 20m
28. Gigolo ** 7a+ 20m
29. Bongo Bongo *** 7a 20m
30. Phantasmagoria ** 7b+ 20m
31. Franceses *** 6a 78m
32. Climber Gay ** 5,6b 32m

Sector Fina Y Segura

33. Unnamed * 6b 22m
34. La Isla Bonita ** 6c 66m
35. Pringa En El Metideco 6b 10m
36. Fina Y Segura ** 6b 22m
37. To Kiski'M'Toca 6c+ 12m

past an orange flake to a swing right onto steeper rock. This is all quite tough if climbed direct, so use a bit of lateral thinking! Just above the steep section is a lower-off; thus far the route is a pleasant one-star 5+. If you have had enough, lower-off; if you fancy a challenge use pockets to swing right onto the steep wall and make a quick pull on a razor blade (ouch that smarts) to reach easier rock and another lower-off, 6a.

The next three routes climb through the bulges that run above the ramp line of EXCALIBUR. All are worth doing, though the oldest is the best because it offers rather more balanced climbing than the other two. They all share a lower-off.

17. NO HACES MAS GRADO PORQUE ERES ENANO ** 6b+ 18m
Pull easily over the bulges to the right of the start of EXCALIBUR, then climb the slab, and follow the left-hand line of bolts up the thin technical wall which is climbed using three tiny layaway flakes to a final difficult (crux) stretch for the break. The steeper rock above has good – though spaced – holds. Just keep cranking. The name suggests that the originator of the climb found it tough because he is a dwarf, though maybe it is tough anyway!

18. TRAMPERA MATINERA * 6b 18m
Start as for the previous climb and cross the bulge on the left easily. Follow the big new bolts up the slab then make tricky moves up the steep wall to a battling pull over onto the slab above.

19. IL PANZEROTO * 6a+ 18m
Start as for the previous two climbs but trend right up the pleasant slab to enter and climb the steep shallow groove to the left of the scoop of EXCALIBUR. Pull left onto the rib then climb the final steepening by a couple of beefy pulls on good but spaced holds.

The final three routes in this area are harder offerings located further up the gully; pass round the back of a tree and climb a slippery scoop to a hollow beneath some impressive bulges, where there is an ancient three-bolt belay.

20. BOFETADAS DE PLACER * 7c 18m
Step left onto the leaning grey rib and climb past paired bolts (clip the newer ones!) using fiddly tufas and sharp pockets to a shake-out on a large flake/jug. When recovered press on to the lower-offs. Tough!

21. CARISMATICS ** 6c 16m
Fine strenuous climbing up the scoops and hollows directly above the flat area. Bridge up and out right, crossing a series of roofs to a well-chalked (and well-glued) flake. From this pull onto the wall above, crux, and continue up the leaning

wall on a series of juggy tufas to easier-angled rock.

To the right is an orange pillar and beyond this is:

22. HOT CONSUELA (aka INGLESES) * 6c 16m

The last route on the wall climbs an open scoop in grey rock to a large hole. Head up and right past a large *in situ* (and well-irradiated) thread and continue up the wall. Good technical climbing rather spoilt by the difficulty of clipping some of the bolt runners.

SECTOR WHY

The steep, red barrel-shaped tower that overlooks the open, flat section of the path (good picnic or base camp site) has a fine collection of steep, powerful lines. The area generally faces west and so is in the sun from midday onwards. The most conspicuous feature of this area is the bulging central crack-line which does not quite reach the ground. This is climbed by ZARAGUAY. The climbs are described from right to left, and the first route is located to the right of the easy-angle skirt of rock that runs around the lower section of this wall, and just around to the left of the tombstone-shaped flake at the left edge of the SECTOR EXCALIBUR.

23. KGB ** 6c 16m

Start just to the right of an easy right-facing corner below a smooth grey face leading to steeper rock. The lower wall is climbed on sharp holds until it steepens and a traverse to the left is required. This involves highly technical laybacking until some large pockets are reached. Follow the holes steeply to where they end, leaving a final sprint to the belay.

24. ZARAGUAY * 5+ 18m

The central crack system is approached up easier rock. Reaching the base of the crack is the crux of the climb. The crack gives a good old-fashioned thrash, combining mainly jamming and bridging moves until it is possible to step left to gain a multiple bolt belay.

To the left of the crack of ZARAGUAY is an impressive bubbly arête tackled by the dramatically exposed pitch of:

25. CORTOCIRCUITO *** 6b 20m

Approach the arête direct or from the base of the crack on ZARAGUAY and head up it with an increasing sense of apprehension using good but well-spaced holds. The prominent hole through the arête is best passed on the left lest you get inextricably stuck out in space. Easier climbing leads to the ledges above.

26. WHY ** 6b+ 20m

The steep open corner to the left of the flying arête gives an excellent and unusual piece of climbing. Straightforward rock leads to the base of the corner, and more awkward moves gain a final obstacle in the form of a smooth section of corner containing a solitary hold. The tall will find no difficulty; the short will. Why, oh why?

Above and left of the lowering point used by the previous routes is a stunning leaning prow:

27. AGARRATE MALDITO *** 7b+ 20m

The magnificent flowstone-festooned prow that hangs in space above the corner of the previous climb is a well-bolted beckoning piece of rock architecture. The prow gives a superb route requiring muscular thumbs for all that tufa pinch-gripping.

28. GIGOLO ** 7a+ 20m

The slanting crack that forks leftwards out of WHY gives a sustained and admirably protected tussle.

To the left of the open corner of WHY and before the cliff swings round to face north is an zone of red bulges approached by a short bushwhack through shrubbery and blocks. There are four climbs that pierce these bulges.

29. BONGO BONGO *** 7a 20m

The right-hand line is steep and is followed using a series of pockets. Once round the lip a crimpy crux sequence leads to the belay.

30. PHANTASMAGORIA ** 7b+ 20m

The line through the centre of the bulges is a couple of notches harder.

The next line leftwards on the bulging red wall is the start of the extended and classical:

31. FRANCESES *** 6a 78m

Start at a gap in the vegetation where easy angled rock leads to steeper terrain about 6m right of the point at which the cliff swings round to face north. The start of the route is marked by a bolt on the lip of a small overhang 3m off the ground.

1. 20m 6a Climb the easy rib to a steepening and make a short series of powerful moves to a narrow ledge and possible stance, or continue.
2. 18m 5 Starting just left of the belays a couple of tricky moves gain good holds then continue steeply up a bulging crack until forced to swing left to easy ground. Belay above.
3. 16m 5 Climb the slab directly above the belay to its apex then saunter up

easy rock (beware of occasional loose blocks) to a stance in a shrubby niche below a superbly fluted grey wall.

4. 24m 5+ Trend left past a thread to gain the left-hand bolt line and follow this up the fluted razors by bridging and jamming until it is possible to move right to a belay. This most unusual pitch is actually the finish of LA ISLA BONITA (see below). Descend by abseil.

32. CLIMBER GAY ** 5,6b 32m

A well-bolted new route with a pleasant first pitch and a finely positioned second one that is much harder.

1. 16m 5 From clearing a short distance to the right of the arête of the cliff slant slightly leftwards up awkward slabby rock to steeper moves up a rib on the left side of a recess. After a tricky start jug-pulling leads to a good ledge and belays.

2. 14m 6b Climb the steep sustained and fingery wall that hangs over the stance to easier rock and, some distance higher, a belay. Descend by abseil.

SECTOR FINA Y SEGURA

Immediately after the path passes under the steep red tower of the SECTOR WHY the cliff opens out into an immense bowl. On the right here is a curious water-worn groove whose back wall sprouts an unsightly growth. This is the base for a small number of climbs of very varying worth. The climbs here tend to face north, so the area makes for a suitable venue in high summer, always assuming you can cope with the walk in. In keeping with the approach the routes are described from right to left.

Starting on the right side of the scoop is the first pitch of the long and very worthwhile LA ISLA BONITA.

33. UNNAMED * 6b 22m

Start just down and right of ISLA BONITA and climb a steep crack and the rib to a fluted pillar. Crux moves follow up the broad rib, then easier rock leads to the old lower-off of ISLA BONITA. Graded 5+ elsewhere.

34. LA ISLA BONITA ** 6c 66m

Unfortunately the bolts in the first pitch are looking tired, and now the grade is pretty tough for the 6a given in the local guide. The route to the right (see above) is an alternative.

1. 22m 6b A painful start on 'razor edges' reaches better holds which are followed directly up the wall until it is possible to move right to a stance below a well-bolted, easy-angled slab.

Sector Fina Y Segura & Princesa

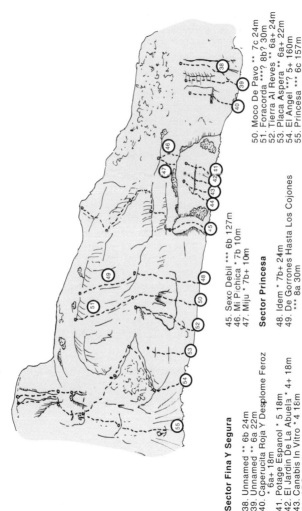

Sector Fina Y Segura

38. Unnamed ** 6b 24m
39. Unnamed ** 6a 22m
40. Caperucita Roja Y Desplome Feroz
    * 6a+ 18m
41. Potage Espanol * 5 18m
42. El Jardin De La Abuela * 4+ 18m
43. Canabis In Vitro * 4 18m
44. ABC 4 18m

45. Sexo Debil *** 6b 127m
46. Mi P'chica * 7b 10m
47. Miju * 7b+ 10m

Sector Princesa

48. Idem * 7b+ 24m
49. De Gorrones Hasta Los Cojones
    *** 8a 30m

50. Moco De Pavo ** 7c 24m
51. Foracorda ***? 8b? 30m
52. Tierra Al Reves ** 6a+ 24m
53. Placa Aspera ** 6a+ 22m
54. El Angel **? 5+ 160m
55. Princesa *** 6c 157m

2. 20m 4 Climb the over-protected slab then easy rock to a belay in a floral niche at the foot of the grey fluted wall.

3. 24m 6c Follow the right-hand bolt line with increasing interest until the rock becomes 'blank' and a short, desperate sequence is made up a blunt rib and then out left to better holds. Falling off the lower part of this pitch would be akin to sliding down a bread knife – don't even consider it! This pitch is actually the finish of FRANCESES (see above). Descend by abseil.

35. PRINGA EN EL METIDECO 6b 10m
The short route up the tufa in the back of the groove has been rebolted; two clips lead to single ring bolt just over the bulge.

On the left side of the scoop and just to the right of an easy groove is the rebolted line of the route that gave its name to the whole sector:

36. FINA Y SEGURA ** 6b 22m
The new bolts are nice and close together in the lower wall, which is straightforward until a couple of thin moves are required to reach a rest out on the right. The upper wall is just as hard as the lower section, and the bolts are rather further apart. Step back left, take a big breath and go for it. Excellent.

The left edge of the scoop has a short and fingery three-bolt exercise that is:

37. TO KISKI'M'TOCA 6c+ 12m
A short pitch, spoilt by the fact that the hardest thing about the route is trying to follow the line of bolts.

Up the slope to the left are three new routes, starting at a trampled area behind trees.

38. UNNAMED ** 6b 24m
The steep sharp rib on the right is worthwhile.

39. UNNAMED ** 6a 22m
The central scoop and shallow corner crack is good, but avoid being tempted out leftwards.

40. CAPERUCITA ROJA Y DESPLOME FEROZ * 6a+ 18m
The wall and roof starting from blocks is quite tough.

Up the slope is a slabby section of wall with some low-grade offerings, useful for escaping the midday heat or for using as a pleasant introduction to the sport.

41. POTAGE ESPANOL * 5 18m

The right-hand line has a thin flaky start and tricky bulge which is avoidable on the right. Above this head straight up the wall to lower-offs on the lip of a bulge.

42. EL JARDIN DE LA ABUELA * 4+ 18m
This also has a tricky central bulge which is passed by a slight jig to the right.

43. CANABIS IN VITRO * 4 18m
A tricky start and leads to easier ground above.

44. ABC 4 18m
A new route on the edge of the slab clipping the upper bolts on the last route, though keeping left and eventually sharing its lower-off.

Left again is a slabby and rather shrubby groove, that is 4 leading to three steep new pitches of unknown grade on the wall below the traverse of SEXO DEBIL.

Up the slope to the left of the scoop, and before the cliff swings round to face west again, is a magnificent wall. Here is the superb and alluring SEXO DEBIL. Start where a low-profile 'bent' pillar leans against the slabby lower section of the face about 20m off the ground.

45. SEXO DEBIL *** 6b 127m
A titillating brute that leads you on to the point of no return, then drops you right in it! Described as the best of its grade on the island; maybe, just maybe.

1. 35m 5 The gentle introduction. Climb the easy slab to steeper rock and continue on good holds to belays at the foot of the steep wall. This pitch is well worthwhile on its own as a ** 5, followed by an abseil descent.

2. 22m 6b The come-on. Trend right up the wall following the bolts and make one hard move to gain access to a hanging corner. Above this, easier but incredibly rough rock leads to belays in a bay with *in situ* chimp!

3. 24m 6b Walk along the scoop to a line of tufas supplemented with bolt-on holds – honest! These are so far apart that the integrity of the pitch has not been spoilt too much. Power up the wall (just to add a touch of spice one of the 'bolt-ons' is loose), then traverse left with more delicacy to a cramped stance in a dramatic position.

4. 24m 6b The trap is sprung. Make a thin traverse left then follow better holds up and left to the foot of a scoop. Swing left and climb the steep rib to belays but no stance. It is probably better to continue.

5. 22m 6b The climax. Trend right to regain the scoop by an exciting swing (stay low) to reach the easy groove that leads to the cliff top and the end of an admirable route.

Descent: The let-down. Either drop off the back of the ridge and keep bearing left (facing out) until is possible to head down right to the foot of the first wall

(SECTOR SILICONA) on the cliff. Or, much faster and much more scary, abseil 40m to a tufa foot-hold and triple-bolt belay, then make another 45m abseil, free hanging, back to the ground.

According to the local topo there are also two short routes located on the steeply tilted wall to the right of the third pitch of SEXO DEBIL. These are:

46. MI PICHICA * 7b 10m

47. MIJU * 7b+ 10m

These are probably worth seeking out if you really want to get away from the crowds. I can guarantee you will be alone up there.

SECTOR PRINCESA

As the path through the gorge passes the red tower of the SECTOR WHY, the cliff falls back into a huge bay with a soaring south-facing back wall riddled with caves and festooned with tufa pillars and other geological oddities. There are just two routes that tackle the full length of this impressive wall and only one of these is fully equipped at the time of writing, the magnificent PRINCESA. There are also a couple of excellent shorter routes and some tough tufa trips. The area is most easily reached by scrambling up towards SEXO DEBIL and continuing to the top of the bay. The most prominent feature of the right-hand side of the area is a large tufa that resembles an elephant's backside protruding from the rock. There are three lines to the right of this. On the far right is an unknown quantity. In the centre is:

48. IDEM * 7b+ 24m

A short pitch leading to:

49. DE GORRONES HASTA LOS COJONES *** 8a 30m

One of the most impressive pitches on the island.

50. MOCO DE PAVO ** 7c 24m

On the left (just right of the elephant) a scoop and bulges lead to:

51. FORACORDA ***? 8b? 30m

This one may still be a project.

52. TIERRA AL REVES ** 6a+ 24m

A fine pitch and a great counterpoint to the pussyfooting on the next route, climbing the scoop and bulges to the left of the elephant's arse-end protruding from the rock. Scramble up and right into a bay with twin trees. Climb the rib on the left then the orange tufa to the bulges. Butch a way rightwards though the bulges to mega-pockets on the tip where a delicate (at last) move gains easy ground. Where lowering off, don't kick the elephant's legs in case he kicks back!

53. PLACA ASPERA ** 6a+ 22m

The gradually steepening slab gives sustained climbing on wonderfully rough rock. It feels quite run-out (six bolts) and has a final pocketed section that reaches the lower-off just to the right of the line.

54. EL ANGEL **? 5+ 160m

This expedition of six pitches utilises the huge right-to-left diagonal system of hollows that cuts across the right side of the face. Through binoculars it is apparent that the route does not contain a lot of fixed gear, though some of the belay stations are in place. It climbs into the base of the hollow in two pitches by following a grey ramp that runs across the lowest section of the face leftwards to a belay and then trending back right on red rock to enter the caves. It then climbs to the apex of the cave before tackling a steep wall (crux 5+) to gain a crack system and following this to the cliff top. The route looks well worth doing. A descent is possible by abseiling back down PRINCESA, providing you can locate the belays.

To the left a good-looking newer route runs up the steep yellow wall and on up grey rock above, at least two pitches long, and possibly a direct start to PRINCESA. Anybody done it?

Continuing around the head of the bay, the next route is PRINCESA. Look for a scratched arrow on the slab 30m left of the grey ramp at the foot of EL ANGEL. The arrow points the way up slabby rock to a small bush and discreet belay bolts.

55. PRINCESA *** 6c 157m

A right regal outing up the highest part of the face offering one of the finest climbs on the island. The difficulties are limited to a few thin and well-protected moves three-quarters of the way up the first pitch, and the use of a couple of aid bolts (wash my mouth out) gives access to the great climbing above.

1. 48m 6c Climb up and left to reach the line of bolts and follow them, on good holds, straight up the steep impressive wall until things turn nasty (at an ominous trio of bolts). A thin sequence, perhaps slightly easier on the left, leads to good holds and, just a little higher, a small stance.
2. 36m 5 Trend left past a solitary bolt and then climb directly up easier rock until it is possible to move right to a good ledge, complete with shady trees, below a steep wall.
3. 33m 5+ Climb straight up behind the stance to the line of bulges that is

crossed on large holds to gain the fine sustained wall above. Go up this, trending gradually to the right to reach an exposed 'foothold stance' below a left-trending groove.

4. 40m 5 Swing round the right-bounding corner of the groove and traverse easily to the right for 8m before climbing straight up the sustained and sharp wall to reach the cliff top and the end of a great outing.

Descent: The stances on the route are equipped to allow an abseil descent back to the base of the wall (providing you brought double ropes). This is speedy but a bit of a gripper, especially locating the stance at the foot of the final pitch as it lurks below an overhang. A second alternative is to go the top of the mountain and descend as for GUBIA NORMAL, trainers recommended.

The next area to be described is the Sectors ESPOLON and POLLA BOBA. These are reached by following the horizontal path beyond SECTOR FINA Y SEGURA to where the gorge narrows.

Note: These routes are described from left to right, walking up the slope as this is the normal approach route.

SECTOR ESPOLON

On the right side of the narrowest point of the gorge at Gubia a striking ridge shoots skywards. This is in fact the protruding end of the extension of the sheet of rock that forms the PARET DES COLOMS on the other side of the ravine. Located here is a small collection of short routes on the grey and yellow wall just to the right of the toe of the buttress and the much longer (and much more worthwhile?) classics of GUBIA NORMAL and QUAN ES FA FOSC. The two classics are described first, then the shorter offerings.

Just beyond the foot of GUBIA NORMAL the gorge starts to open out again. High on the right is a huge and very impressive west-facing wall that will doubtless keep a couple of generations going with 'super-projects'. Immediately ahead at this point and just above and to the right of the path is a dark slab climbed by the rather tatty-looking:

56. FAKIR 6a 10m

On the other side of the stream bed is another dark slab tackled by the slightly better-looking:

57. VITAMINA 6a+ 10m

The next two classic routes share a common and undistinguished first pitch from the narrowest point of the ravine. Above this the first, GUBIA NORMAL,

Sector Espolon & Polla Boba

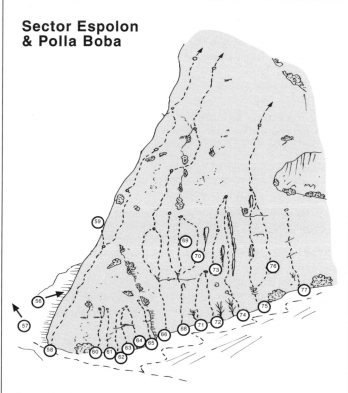

Sector Espolon

56. Fakir 6a 10m
57. Vitamina 6a+ 10m
58. Gubia Normal *** 4+ 240m
   (aka Albahida)
59. Quan Es Fa Fosc *** 5+ 133m
   (aka Super Nova)
60. Chitas Marchitas * 6b 12m
61. Charly Danone * 7a 14m
62. Jodete Y Baila 6c 14m
63. Fi De Ric ** 6a 14m
64. Puta Perro * 6b 14m
65. Tranky Compi ** 5+ 14m

Sector Polla Boba

66. La Ley Del Deseo *** 5 160m
67. Sourisa Vertical ** 5+ 46m
68. Master *** 6a 46m
69. Polla Boba *** 5+ 45m
70. Mejico Lindo ** 6a 45m
71. Iquizerda * 4 14m
72. Derecha 5 14m
73. Left-Hand Tufa System ** 6b 26m
74. Oasis *** 6a+ 40m
75. Unnamed *** 6b 34m
76. Los Bomberos *** 6a+ 147m
77. Hambre Eterna * 22m 6a+

follows the classical ridge towards its right edge whilst the other, QUAN ES FA FOSC, takes the left-bounding arête of the ridge.

58. GUBIA NORMAL (aka ALBAHIDA) *** 4+ 240m

The most striking feature at Gubia offers a magnificent outing at an amenable grade (about UK VS 4c). The island is worth visiting just to do this route! It follows the eye-catching ridge which is clearly visible from the island's airport if you know where to look. It then follows easier rock to the top of the mountain. A descent back to the base of the route is not an easy option as the climb is not equipped for an abseil descent; the simplest arrangement is to carry trainers in a light sack and then descend the back of the mountain (see below). The route contains quite a bit of fixed gear but much of it is old; carry a light rack and double ropes if you have any doubt about your ability. From the top of the climbing it is also possible to abseil down LA LEY DEL DESEO (see below), though this is exposed and a little gripping if you are not familiar with the route.

The detailed description here is from my ascent of the route. Many other variations are obviously possible at much the same grade, some of which may have more fixed gear. If in doubt keep heading upwards! Many of the stances are numbered in rather faded red paint and there are occasional red arrows, usually at the stances, to indicate the general direction of the subsequent pitch.

Start at the foot of the left-hand spur of the ridge at some red-painted writing and a red cross. There is also a start up the right-hand spur that is supposed to be rather harder and may contain rather more fixed gear. It may be worth 5, though I have not done it.

1. 40m 2 Follow the easy ridge up to the right and then back to the left to below a vegetated groove (no fixed gear). The arête on the left of the groove gives the safest option and leads to a recess with a bolt ladder (QUAN ES FA FOSC 5+, see below) rising out of its left side.

2. 28m 4+ Step out past bushes to reach the right rib of the recess and climb rough rock to an insubstantial *in situ* thread (a much bigger thread is available just above, not *in situ*). Continue up the steep sharp wall (first crux) until the climbing begins to ease and it is possible to trend up and left to a belay in another recess. There may be an easier variation to this pitch further to the right.

3. 28m 3+ Move out right onto the exposed rib and climb into a shallow corner passing a hidden peg that is well past its 'sell-by date'. Follow the ridge above on great rock until a comfy stance (and hiding place) in yet another recess is reached.

4. 34m 3+ Head up and right to reach the obvious flake crack (prominent orange

Dave Gregory on Hawai 5-0 (4+), a good introduction to Gubia

Willie Jeffrey following the crux pitch of Estricnina (5+), Gubia

peg) and climb it, taking care with one or two large blocks, to gain access to the face above. Continue up this to reach ledges on the right with two brand new bolts and then climb an easy open groove to a belay 8m higher in a recess containing a large tree.

5. 40m 4 Behind the tree is a steep wall which is best approached from the right. Climb up to an old peg then trend left across the wall (second crux) to better holds before climbing straight up again to regain the open crest of the buttress. Continue straight up this past a selection of *in situ* threads (and possible stances) to a foot-hold stance at two of the larger threads.

6. 35m 3 Continue straight up the rib on great rock (easier but inferior floral variations are available to either side) to a stance below the bulge that blocks the ridge.

7. 35m 3 Move awkwardly right into a crack behind a bush and climb round the arête to a deep corner. Climb this, taking care when passing the huge jammed block, then either climb the groove or the rib to its right to arrive at a projecting shoulder and, just a little higher, the sudden end to the climbing. Thread and tree belays. If you have timed things right you should have at least an hour's daylight left. If not, it is time to get a move on!

Descent: From the top of the climbing the easiest way off the cliff is to continue up the ridge. This is exposed in places and care is needed with occasional loose blocks, though a rope should not be needed by the competent. Most tricky sections can be passed on the right (especially as there is a huge drop to the left), and gradually the ridge opens out and slabby scrambling leads to the summit of the mountain; about 20 minutes from the top of the climbing. From the ruined buildings on the summit an indistinct path leads northwards through bushes to reach a well-made gravel road in 5 minutes. Turn right along it. This weaves its way down hill (45 minutes) to arrive at a farm complete with a big dog on a long chain (try barking back at it!). Just beyond here is the main road. Turn right and walk for 0.5km to arrive back at the taverna: how very convenient. About one and a half hours from the end of the climbing.

Running parallel to the left of the GUBIA NORMAL's pitches 2 to 5 is a clean rib of rock with a three-pitch bolt ladder up it. This only requires 10 quick-draws and double ropes, and is the excellent:

59. QUAN ES FA FOSC (aka SUPER NOVA) *** 5+ 133m
A great climb: steep, direct and exposed on marvellous rock and with the added bonus that it is well bolted.

1. 40m 2 As for GUBIA NORMAL to the bolt belay in the recess.

2. 30m 5 8 clips. Step left and climb the rounded rib on very sharp rock until the angle drops back and a small uncomfortable stance in a hollow is reached.

3. 30m 5+ 9 clips. Traverse out left from the recess then follow the bolt ladder, generally trending slightly rightwards until again things ease off and a stance in a yellow bay is reached.

4. 33m 5+ 8 clips. This pitch might be considered the crux – mainly because it is steeper and more exposed than those below, rather than its being any more technical. Step left out of the recess and enjoy the situations! Now follow the rib with sustained interest to eventually arrive at two large bolts equipped with maillions.

Either continue slight rightwards up the easy upper section of the NORMAL, approximately 70m to the top of the ridge (see above for the way off), or descend the line of the route by abseil.

The short routes on the grey and yellow wall are described next. The first of these starts just to the left of a prickly bush and close to the left edge of the wall.

60. CHITAS MARCHITAS * 6b 12m
Climb the easier lower rib then continue past two small white tufas and up the final grey pillar on tiny sharp holds to reach the lower-off.

The next four routes all start at a flat area in the bushes below the centre of the slab that runs up to steeper rock in the middle of the wall.

61. CHARLY DANONE * 7a 14m
Climb the easy slab then continue up the thin grey wall to gain the foot of an unusual crozzly tufa. Sharp climbing up this leads to the singular bolt lower-off.

62. JODETE Y BAILA 6c 14m
Hard climbing with rather antiquated protection. Climb the centre of the slab and from the patch of yellow rock below its right edge pull into the prominent 'blank' scoop. Up this to a lonesome bolt lower-off.

The next route is the easiest and arguably the best on this section of rock.

63. FI DE RIC ** 6a 14m
Climb up the centre of the slab then link a line of good but well-spaced pockets and flakes up the centre of the widest orange streak by a series of long reaches to gain easier rock. The lower-off is just above.

64. PUTA PERRO * 6b 14m
Climb the slab easily rightwards to the first bolt then use a couple of unusual 'stuck

on' holds to get established on the steep wall above. A difficult couple of moves (marginally easier on the right?) on sharp holds leads to better pockets, and a quick sprint over the final bulge reaches the belay on the previous climb.

The final route climbs the right arête of the wall.

65. TRANKY COMPI ** 5+ 14m
Start just left of the easy vegetated groove that separates this area from SECTOR POLLA BOBA, and climb this pleasant sustained pitch on sharp rock past half a dozen bolt runners.

SECTOR POLLA BOBA
Below and to the right of the soaring ridge of GUBIA NORMAL is an attractive face of rock, 50m high and split horizontally by a narrow ledge system. (This should not be confused with the much-small-bolt-spattered face near the toe of the buttress which is part of the SECTOR ESPOLON, described above). The SECTOR POLLA BOBA has a collection of worthwhile routes that are not too tough, are well protected, are on great rock and which face south: altogether not a bad combination. The lower wall contains two pitches either of which can be used to access the five pitches that continue from the midway ledge. There are no real stances above the top of the routes, so lowering back to the stance in the centre of the wall is the easiest option. With a bit of organisation it is possible to tick the whole sector in a couple of very pleasant (or hectic) hours' climbing.

The routes are described from left to right.

Note: The two initial pitches make worthwhile objectives in their own right, and at a lower grade than most of the stuff above, if you do not feel the need to extend yourself high off the ground by venturing onto the upper walls.

At the base of the face is a well-beaten area directly underneath the centre of the lower wall.

66. LA LEY DEL DESEO *** 5 160m
An excellent and long climb offering a perfect introduction to continental (or island!) ethics. This already great route has been extended upwards for two more pitches, making it the best route of its grade on the island.
1. 22m 5 From the flat area at the foot of the wall step left and follow the bolt line, with a tricky move over a bulge to reach a stance at the left edge of the ledge system.
2. 24m 5 Climb directly above the stance on excellent rock following the bolt line with sustained interest to reach large holds by the final bolt. From here

continue with a touch of faith; good holds continue to arrive and lead to the substantial belays not too far away!

3. 22m 4+ Continue up the line marked by the silver dots; pleasantly sustained climbing leads up the open rib to a stance where the cliff rears up again and things look a touch more serious.

4. 30m 4+ Climb the steeper rock via a tricky sequence, then more sustained climbing in ever more dramatic situations leads to paired bolts at a cleaned ledge. There is also another pair of bolts 5m higher.

5. 22m 4+ Move right and climb the slab before trending up and left to a stance behind trees.

6. 40m 4+ Step right and then climb the slab, passing a tree early on, then continue to ledges and a belay just below where GUBIA NORMAL comes around from the left. Top out or descend by abseil. At this point it may occur to you that double ropes might be a good idea.

67. SOURISA VERTICAL ** 5+ 46m

1. 22m 5 Follow either line of bolts up the lower wall, the right-hand one being marginally easier, then move right or left to a stance.

2. 24m 5+ Climb up, passing to the left of the prominent bush right of the arête. From here continue directly up the wall before bearing away left with plenty of protection and a goodly set of holds to eventually pass a peg runner and reach a stance on the arête of the cliff.

68. MASTER *** 6a 46m

The central line on the wall is one of the best hereabouts, with the upper pitch being steep, sustained, direct and interesting.

1. 22m 5 From the flat area follow the right-hand bolt line up scoopy rock immediately to the left of a low-profile yellow tufa. A bulging section is taken on good holds, then easier climbing leads to a move right to a cramped stance on a flake with a wire cable belay. The remains of the battered bush that just manages to survive behind the flake are guaranteed to snag your ropes and fray your nerves.

2. 24m 6a Climb directly up the wall to the bulging section and press on straight through it to easier terrain just beyond. Continue in the same line to another tricky and rather run-out section to arrive thankfully at a large pocket. Then cross the final bulges on a series of excellent holds to a solid lower-off point.

69. POLLA BOBA *** 5+ 45m

The original route of the wall remains well worth doing.

1. 23m 5 As for the first pitch of MASTER to the wire cable belay.

2. 22m 5+ Climb up the wall trending slightly rightwards (though not as rightwards as the next route) to a bulge which cuts across the wall and contains some odd calcareous growths sprouting from the rock. Cross the bulge with difficulty then continue on good, though spaced, holds to the lowering station of the previous climb.

70. MEJICO LINDO ** 6a 45m

A worthwhile if somewhat unbalanced route, with the top pitch quite a bit harder than the first.

1. 23m 5 As for the first pitch of MASTER to the wire cable belay.

2. 22m 6a Follow a line just to the right of the bolt ladder (fourth from the left) until it is possible to swing right under a bulge. Cross this by fingery moves and continue up the ensuing scoop until it blanks out. Lurch up and left with difficulty to reach the lowering point just a little higher.

Up to the right of the lower wall of POLLA BOBA SECTOR, with its two approach pitches, are two new low-grade climbs that lead to a steeper terrain. This 'steeper terrain' is the wall with the three prominent tufa systems. The two lower-grade climbs start where a solid tree sprouts from the rock, 1m from the ground.

71. IQUIZERDA * 4 14m

The left-hand bolt line is pleasantly sustained throughout. Six clips.

72. DERECHA 5 14m

The right-hand line is easy apart from the tricky bulge at half-height.

Above the lower-off used by the previous two climbs is an extension pitch:

73. LEFT-HAND TUFA SYSTEM ** 6b 26m

Steep climbing between the two left-hand tufa systems leads to a possible stance after five bolts, then more of the same, in a similar distance, until a lower-off on the right appears.

Ten metres up and right is a flatter area, where three great routes start.

74. OASIS *** 6a+ 40m

A magnificent outing between the two right-hand tufa systems. Trend left up easy rock to the first bolt (8m), the head between the tufa systems on sharp grey rock. Harder moves are required to reach the first big 'blob', then steadier climbing to a tricky exit from the groove. A final easier section leads to the belay. Lowering to the stance above the two easier routes mentioned above is the simplest way down.

75. UNNAMED *** 6b 34m

Climb straight up the easy scoop then on up the gradually steepening wall to a crucial pocketed section climbed trending rightwards just above half-height. Above this, easy-street eventually joins LOS BOMBEROS up the right-hand side of a squat tufa.

76. LOS BOMBEROS *** 6a+ 147m

A great outing, one of the Gubia triptych. Don't consider yourself an aficionado until you have done PRINCESA, SEXO DEBIL and this one. Take 15 quick-draws and double ropes for the descent. The grades are just a little stiff; add half a notch if you want. Pitch 1 (the easy one) is well worth doing in its own right, 5+ ** 34m.

1. **34m 5+** Climb up the easy scoop then trend right to climb the steep pocketed wall and the right-hand side of a tufa to a small stance.
2. **28m 6a** Step right and continue up the steep wall to an easing in the angle and another small stance.
3. **45m 6a+** A monster of a pitch, sustained and sharp.
4. **40m 6a+** And more of the same: simply superb.

77. HAMBRE ETERNA * 6a+ 22m

Start 10m further up the slope at the last bolt line in this area. Thin moves to pass the diagonal overlap at 12m form the crux, then easier, and gradually more floral, climbing leads to a lower-off by bushes.

Paret Des Coloms

The magnificent west wall of Gubia is home to over 30 routes, a good number of which are great classics. They vary in length from 20m to three pitches, and in grade from 5 to tough 7b+. The whole area is known as the PARET DES COLOMS and is rather arbitrarily divided into three sectors, from right to left, SEIS PELAS, ALGO SALVAJE and PAPA MORENO. Although the face generally varies in angle from steep to very steep, there are some more reasonable pitches scattered amongst the 'E big numbers', especially on the slabbier skirt of rock that runs along much of the base of the cliff. The whole cliff looks rather intimidating when seen from the opposite side of the gorge, but it turns out to be more friendly on close acquaintance, especially in the morning when it is full in the sun. Many of the harder climbs follow bizarre tufa pillars and chandeliers and some of these weep after prolonged rain. Other climbs, most notably those on the clean barrel-shaped buttress at the right side of the face, dry very rapidly after rain.

The foot of the cliff is most easily approached by walking up the dry stream bed to a point immediately below the last large solitary pine tree on the left side of the valley. A steep path, difficult to pick out at the start, weaves up the hillside to arrive right below the centre of the cliff, which is in the sun until a couple of hours after midday.

Note: It is best to avoid attempting to cut directly across the ravine because of its incised nature and some very exotic (i.e. prickly) scrub.

In keeping with the rest of the cliff, the routes are described from right to left.

SECTOR SEIS PELAS

This section of cliff stretches from the right-hand boundary of the face as far left as an area of slabby, scrappy rock about 10m to the left of the big black hole that disappears into the heart of the cliff.

The first routes described start from a small hollow at the very right toe of the buttress. This is reached by a short diagonal scramble up a brushy slab and is recognised by having a trio of old bolts set in its left side.

Note: There also appears to be a route which starts up the scruffy slab to the right of the first climb described (GUATON). The bolted second pitch up the convoluted red rock and to the right looks well worthwhile, but no grades are available.

To the right of the trio of old bolts is a line of large and brand new bolts heading straight up the face. These are the protection on the common first pitch of two excellent face climbs.

78. GUATON *** 5+ 50m
A fine climb with two good pitches, the lower one of which is worthwhile at 5 **.
1. 22m 5 Climb rough rock directly above the stance then continue up smoother rock, keeping to the left of a flake to pull over a bulge to reach the base of a projecting tufa pillar. Climb the left side of this by laybacking and fat pinch-gripping to a small, comfortable stance with substantial belays.
2. 28m 5+ Step out right and climb up to gain the line of golden-coloured bolts running up the wall. Follow these directly or slightly more easily by climbing the red hollows just to the right. At the level of a very large (unoccupied?) bird's nest head straight over the bulge, finishing with a long reach for the chains.

79. DANZOMANIA *** 6b 90m
An excellent sustained route, one of the longest on this side of the ravine.
1. 22m 5 As for the first pitch of GUATON, to the small stance (see above).
2. 30m 6b Climb straight up the wall past a couple of old bolts and a peg, then trend left following new dark speckled bolts by very sustained moves on sharp holds until a tricky sequence leads to a bulge. Once through this, easier climbing protected by rather spaced and more elderly bolts leads to a stance below an open grassy groove.
3. 28m 6a The left wall of the open groove is approached easily and then gives

Sector Seis Pelas & Algo Salvaje

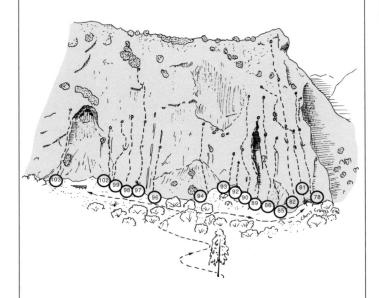

Sector Seis Pelas

78. Guaton *** 5+ 50m
79. Danzomania *** 6b 90m
80. Chungui Chunguez *** 6c 52m
81. Estricnina *** 5+ 66m
82. Tia Melis *** 5+ 90m
83. Vol De Nuit ** 6b 60m
84. Gay Power *** 7a 30m
85. Los Pasteles De Isabel
    *** 7a 35/60m
86. Leather Face *** 7b 45m
87. Tao *** 6b+ 42m
88. Centro * 5 20m
89. Comechochos ** 6b 42m
90. Decadencia Corperal *** 7b 60m
91. Pellojo De Tiburon ** 6c+ 30m
92. Mes Rapit Suc El Vent ** 5+ 15m
93. Humi ** 5+ 18m

Sector Algo Salvaje

94. La Peladora *** 6b+ 24m
95. Pesadilla Final * 6b 50m
96. Perque Triunfin Els Canalles
    *** 6b 20m
97. Si Lo Se No Vengo *** 6c 60m
98. Pinon Fijo *** 7b+ 26m
99. Algo Salvaje *** 6b 26m
100. Front 242 *** 7a+ 25m
101. Tres Menos Cuarto ** 7b 25m
102. Sal De Arenal *** 6c 22m
103. Esto No Es Quinto Superior
     *** 6c 22m
104. Peor Imposible ** 7a 36m

more sustained and sharp climbing until things ease and your tattered fingers can be given a rest. Abseil descent.

80. CHUNGUI CHUNGUEZ *** 6c 52m

The second pitch offers superb, sustained and fingery face dancing. The first is a worthwhile outing at ** 5. Start at the trio of old bolts on the left side of the hollow directly below a white tufa at 20m that has a vague resemblance to a pale pair of buttocks when seen from this position (honest).

1. 22m 5 From the trio of old bolts climb straight up the wall to reach the white pillar. Gain a standing position on this awkwardly, then continue more easily to a stance in a small hollow with a selection of belays.

2. 30m 6c Directly above the stance is a line of closely spaced, and occasionally paired, bolts. This is followed with escalating difficulty to a 'thread' handhold, from where harder moves lead up and left to steeper rock and better holds. From this point things ease, though the interest is maintained to an odd set of belays and a cramped stance. Lower back to the previous stance or belay here and then descend by abseil.

Using the same first pitch as the previous route is a fine excursion that follows a sneaky line up this impressive buttress. Good protection, perfect rock and exciting positions combine to make a classic outing:

81. ESTRICNINA *** 5+ 66m

A great climb with only a couple of tricky moves which are very well protected. Start as for CHUNGUI CHUNGUEZ.

1. 22m 5 From the trio of old bolts climb straight up the wall, following a line of discrete bolts, to reach the 'buttock-shaped' pillar. Gain a standing position on this with difficulty then continue more easily to an isolated stance in a small hollow with a selection of belays.

2. 20m 5+ Crossing the wall to the left of the stance is a vague line of weakness which is followed into the middle of nowhere. The belay chains above the first pitch of TIA MELIS (see below) offer a substantial running belay to protect the crux moves up and left to a hidden peg before it is possible to swing left into a shallow cave. After clipping the chain and bolt belays, regain your composure, then you can begin to enjoy the positions.

3. 24m 5 Swing left out of the cave then climb up the wall above until it is possible to trend left into an open shallow groove. Up this to reach a solid tree, in a hollow, equipped with chains. Abseil descent.

On the left side of the buttress tackled by ESTRICNINA is the long and magnificent 'drop of water' line followed by:

82. TIA MELIS *** 5+ 90m

1. 24m 5+ Start left of the shallow hollow at the foot of ESTRICNINA by a stunted tree and climb to a bolt (difficult to spot from below) by a patch of orange rock immediately beneath a small hole in the cliff. Once this is located continue directly up the face by sustained climbing, then make thinner moves up smoother rock to reach a prominent diagonal flake crack with orange staining below it and, just a little higher, the chunky chain belay (no stance).
2. 22m 5+ Make a couple of thin moves up and out right to a hole then climb directly up the cliff by more superb sustained climbing (no sneaking off left) to a stance.
3. 24m 5+ A new line of bolts runs up the steep slab above. Follow these almost to the cliff top.

To the left of the direct line of TIA MELIS a line of grassy hollows trends slightly leftward up the cliff face. The odd piece of ancient fixed gear points to this having been climbed in antiquity, though it is not marked on the present edition of the local topo. Re-equipped it would offer a great low-grade way up the cliff. Any philanthropic takers?

To the left of the easy break is an impressive smooth wall, the most eye-catching feature of which is the red 'drainpipe tufa', climbed by the classic LOS PASTELES DE ISABEL. Below this section of wall is a grey apron of rather shrubby rock, bounded on its left (directly below the 'drainpipe') by a cleaner slabby section with bolt runners. The next three routes start up this.

83. VOL DE NUIT ** 6b 60m

Fine steep wall-climbing spoilt only by the possibility of escape to the right part way up the first pitch.

1. Climb easily to the apex of the slab (10m) and clip the first bolt on the steeper section of GAY POWER. Step right and climb the wall, right then left, to reach a rather fragile fretted pocket. From here continue directly up the wall by steep climbing on good holds to eventually climb a short bulging section reach the cave stance above the second pitch of ESTRICNINA.
2. Bridge out of the roof of the cave (spooky) then continue straight up the wall above until it is possible to trend right into an open shallow groove. Pull onto the wall above this then traverse diagonally to the right, passing above one lower-off to reach another on the edge of the buttress. Abseil descent.

84. GAY POWER *** 7a 30m

Very thin face climbing that is especially difficulty if the largest of the many micro-holds are not chalked up. Climb to the top of the slabby grey apron (10m) then head up the wall on an increasingly sketchy series of holds. The crux arrives just before things ease, and a lower-off is reached a little higher.

The 'drainpipe' is climbed by the major classic of:

85. LOS PASTELES DE ISABEL *** 7a 35/60m

1. 30m 7a Start up the slabby grey apron as for the two previous climbs then step out left onto the wall and make thin moves on small holds to reach the base of the tufa. Shin up the left side of this by sustained climbing to gain a squatted rest on its top with difficulty, then loop out left and back right to reach and follow better holds over a bulge to a small stance and lower-off.
2. 25m 6c Head up the easier-angled wall above the lower-off until things begin to rear up and more fingery face-climbing is required to reach another set of chains and the end of a great route.

To the left is the great black cave that disappears into the cliff, and below and to the right of this is the left-hand edge of the slabby apron that runs across the base of this section of the cliff. The last route on the smooth wall to the right of the hole starts here and provides a gain pitch of brilliant pocket pulling:

86. LEATHER FACE *** 7b 45m

Either start as for the previous routes and then trend left to a spiky tree at the base of the steepest part of the wall, or perhaps better reach the same place from direct below by climbing the lower section of the next route. From the flattened area behind the spiky tree step out right (no climbing up left and stepping in!) onto the wall. This gives very sustained and gradually steepening pocket pulling, with thin moves up left to a juggy tufa. Above this the angle increases, and fortunately the holds get bigger and better; keep on cranking. Just above the bulges is a resting place (the old stance). The fine face above gives more superb and gradually steepening face-climbing to complete this superb outing.

The rock around the great black cave that disappears up into the bowels of the cliff has been developed to give a selection of pitches across a range of grades. There are three short pitches into the cave, and from the mutual stance in the base of the black hole there are two harder ways on. There is obvious scope here for mixing and matching.

A prominent scoop runs up into the base of the cave and to its right is a steep rib rising above a hollow and leading onto a slab.

87. TAO *** 6b+ 42m

A good climb best done in one pitch. The upper section is bizarre and provides an appropriate introduction to the tufa climbing at Gubia. Thankfully upgraded from 6a.

Climb the edge of the hollow, then steeper rock (jugs galore) to reach the slab. From here trend left passing below the tree on LEATHER FACE until it is possible to drift up and left to ledges in the base of the chimney. (A worthwhile pitch in its own right, * 5, with one short awkward section.) Cross to the right side of the chimney and climb the groove until it is possible to tackle the bizarre chandeliers by some monkey business (taking care not to pull the whole affair down) to a bulge which is crossed by a quick powerful sequence. A lowering point is located just above.

88. CENTRO * 5 20m
The central line just right of a prominent scoop is steep to start, quite sustained and is on very sharp rock. From the belay in the base of the chimney go exploring the beckoning hole above or lower-off rapidly back to sanity.

89. COMECHOCHOS ** 6b 42m
A bizarre climb following the prominent scoop and then the inside left wall of the chimney. The first pitch makes for a worthwhile climb at ** 5, and the grade of the second pitch depends on how soon you can (or are able to) make use of the opposite wall of the chimney.
1.   20m 5 Climb the scoop by pleasant bridging to a belay below the orifice – an excellent pitch.
2.   22m 6b Climb the left wall above (using holds on the right when required) until things steepen and the roof is crossed with difficulty until is possible to bridge across to the opposite wall. The belays are just above the lip of the overhang, and if required there is a resting ledge a little higher on the other side of the chimney.

The fine grey pillar to the left of the black hole is climbed by the first-rate though arduous:

90. DECADENCIA CORPERAL *** 7b 60m
1.   30m 6b Start just around to the left of the groove that runs up into the hole and climb rightwards before swinging back left at a well-hidden peg runner. From here sustained climbing using poor pockets and thin edges leads to a final steep sprint to a set of chains in a hollow. An excellent pitch.
2.   7b 30m The bolts continue up the steep wall and so do the holds, but only just! A very sustained piece of climbing on which it is difficult to identify a crux move, though it is probably the one that you fell off.

Immediately to the left of the first pitch of DECADENCIA CORPERAL is another recently bolted line running straight up the fine face:

91. PELLOJO DE TIBURON ** 6c+ 30m

More thin climbing, never too steep, but quite taxing enough due to its sharp and sustained nature. Two upper pitches trend left, no details known. The name means 'shark skin' – and yes, I did make it up!

To the left of the grey pillar climbed by the previous two routes is an easy-looking left-slanting break that was the line chosen by the original route on this section of face: SEIS PELAS. The first pitch trends left up this break and passes a steeper section to a set of shoddy belays in the base of the large orange hollow high on the face. The second and crucial pitch trends right following the top edge of the grey pillar to a belay at the top of DECADENCIA CORPERAL. It has not been re-equipped at the time of writing, though the local guide gives it 5+, 6c.

The last piece of rock to be described on this sector is the clean wall below and to the left of the initial pitch of SEIS PELAS. There are two short but excellent and amenable face climbs here. These are directly below the right edge of a prominent huge orange bowl high on the cliff. The right hand line is:

92. MES RAPIT SUC EL VENT ** 5+ 15m

A fine sustained pitch, well protected and generally on good but sharp holds. Keep clipping and keep pulling all the way to the chains.

93. HUMI ** 5+ 18m

The left-hand line is the slightly harder twin and has a steep sustained lower section and a tricky bulge thrown in for the crux.

To the left is another section of tree-ridden grey rock that is initially slabby and runs up into steeper orange terrain above. This is the right-hand end of the central part of the cliff known as:

SECTOR ALGO SALVAJE

The central section of the PARET DES COLOMS is perhaps the most impressive developed wall at Gubia. This section of cliff is bounded on the right by a slabby apron of grey rock directly below the huge orange bay high in the centre of the cliff, and on the left by the smoother slabby face left of the deepest caves directly above the old stone-built platform. Between these two features are a dozen or so routes offering some of the wildest pitches in the area. Many of the climbs follow most unusual tufa features, and the climbing is generally steep and powerful rather that overly technical. Chipped and drilled holds are quite a common feature on the harder climbs!

On the right edge of this area is a brown wall bounded by grey streaks to left and right. There is a recently bolted route up the centre of this which looks good and hard, though I have not been able to find a grade for it.

Starting up the grey slabby apron at the right side of this section of the wall is well worthwhile:

94. LA PELADORA *** 6b+ 24m
Climb the easy slabby rock to where the colour and angle change. Steeper sustained and quality climbing on pockets leads to lowering chains just as the angle falls back.

Climbing the left side of the same section of rock is the marginally less worthwhile outing:

95. PESADILLA FINAL * 6b 50m
Climb the grey slab then trend left up steeper orange rock using a fine selection of pockets until a final tricky move over the bulges leads to a belay just above the change of angle. There is a second easier pitch 5 up the walls above, but the skull and crossbones plus the description 'roca molta decomposta' on the Spanish topo suggests where the route name 'Final Nightmare' came from – and after all, you are on holiday.

Left again and just before the most imposing section of the wall is an indeterminate area of rock with several bushes and some large orange patches of rock 10m off the ground. The two-pitch route MORGUE 5,6b climbs this, though it does not look like an especially edifying exercise, being a bit too reminiscent of some of Cheedale's better offerings.

Left again the rock becomes ever more impressive. The lower section of the wall is marked by three grotesque phalluses sprouting from the rock. To the right of these is a large, pale grey active tufa and right again is a cleaner grey wall. The wall is climbed by the excellent:

96. PERQUE TRIUNFIN ELS CANALLES *** 6b 20m
A fine sustained pitch of face-climbing on sharp holds and with the crux sequence involving a short leftwards traverse at half-height. The lower-offs are situated at the point where the rock turns dirty – now there's a novel idea.

To the left is the long impressive tufa system described earlier. This is one of the last to dry out after seepage begins. To the left of this are the unmistakable large growths mentioned above. These have been described as 'elephant's legs' and by other less repeatable comparisons; the mind boggles. Two hard and excellent routes start here:

97. SI LO SE NO VENGO *** 6c 60m

Climb between the growths then press on up the sustained pocketed wall to technical and fingery moves past the fourth bolt to gain a slender ramp on the right. Easier climbing reaches a good rest on a 'sheep's head' at 25m, then a final tricky sequence reaches a belay just a little higher. A second pitch continues up and left before heading up the crest of the wall, 22m, 6a.

Also starting by the protrusions is a route regarded as one of the best routes on the wall by those in the know. It is certainly one of the hardest.

98. PINON FIJO *** 7b+ 26m

From the growths climb the wall trending slightly leftwards following the pale grey streak past a hollow and a difficult clip (reinforced extension sling in place) to an optional breather in the cave of ALGO SALVAJE. Step back right and continue to the chains by some large, and some not-so-large, holds.

To the left is the only white streak on this section of the cliff. This is tackled by the easiest route in the area, though it is no push-over. This is the great classic of:

99. ALGO SALVAJE *** 6b 26m

Climb up rightwards to the white streak via an overhanging scoop which leads to some large holes. Exit right from the scoop and battle up to and past a large hanging lump to reach an overhang. At this point the translation of the name (Something Wild) becomes ever more apt. Cross the overhang to reach an overdue resting ledge before stepping left and climbing the juggy wall to the lower-offs. Superb.

100. FRONT 242 *** 7a+ 25m

A tough climb which offers some brilliant moves despite (or because of) the drilled pockets. Start as for the previous route but trend left up the smooth wall before making moves right then left past a disappointing pocket to a mono-doigt from where the crux span up and rightwards can be made. A short sprint to the belays remains. Steep stuff.

To the left is a section of orange scoops. Climbing through these is:

101. TRES MENOS CUARTO ** 7b 25m

Bridge up through the scoops and tufas to a 'curly' overlap and thread where the rock turns grey. Continue up the grey streak using an undercut mono-doigt to reach better holds, from where an immense reach gains a distant edge. Thankfully easier climbing leads to a lower-off below a large clumpy bush.

102. SAL DE ARENAL *** 6c 22m

A short-lived but excellent piece of exercise climbing the right edge of the large area of red rock to the right of a tall white tufa with a bush on top. Trend left up slabby rock then climb the wall past a small tree via a ragged crack. From the last resting place storm the twin tufas by frantic upside down laybacking to reach a thread and two-bolt belay to right of a prominent bush. The route might be considered 6a by the criminally muscular.

To the left is an impressive, though undeveloped, area of face right above the old stone platform. The cliff here consists of a large inverted funnel with a variety of holes disappearing up into the rock. There is obviously scope here for some exciting trips into upside-down land, though the rather scrappy approach up slabs has delayed development.

103. ESTO NO ES QUINTO SUPERIOR *** 6c 22m

A good route with some wild positions and a fierce and spectacular crux. The name is very true. Start to the left of the old platform and climb a slab past bushes to reach a prominent pocket with an orange streak below it. Climb over bulges on prickly rock then continue to ledges below steeper country. Layback up the tufas until all appears lost, from where a massive reach leftwards off a poor layaway gains brief respite at jugs. Pull back right with difficulty from where better holds lead to a lower-off on the slab above.

To the left, roughly following the arête of the wall, is a route called ES POAL, which is given the odd grade (considering the chipped holds on other parts of the cliff) of 6b & A0. No other details are known, though the local guide suggests it is not equipped.

Around to the left is a much more open and slabby section of cliff that only contains one route at present. The slab is climbed by the thin:

104. PEOR IMPOSIBLE ** 7a 36m

1. 12m 4 Climb the lower slab trending right to a stance on ledges below the smoother rock.
2. 24m 7a Trend up and left to by-pass the first bulge before heading back right towards the centre of the face. This gives thin sustained climbing on razor edges until another bulge is passed and easier moves lead to the lower-off.

SECTOR PAPA MORENO

The final sector at Gubia is the band of rock that runs leftwards up the hillside to the left of the caves and tufas of SECTOR 242. At present there are only four climbs here, though there is obvious scope for more, especially further up the hillside.

The first route is the three-pitch:

105. PUENTE AEREO 5,5,5+ 60m
Climbs the lower walls to reach a groove high on the cliff, and is not equipped.

Further up the slope is a pedestal, and starting on top of this is:

106. PAPA MORENO ** 6b+ 20m

Still further up the hill past some impressive tufas are the final two climbs, both of which are two pitches long:

107. AMOR BRUJO * 6a,6a 40m
the right-hand line, and

108. PECHO LATA 6b,6b 40m
on the left, which is not equipped at present.

CALA MAGRANER

Character

When working on my original guide to Mallorca, back in 1994, Cala Magraner proved to be a bit elusive. Now it is a well-known venue providing 50 plus routes, generally towards the lower end of the grade spectrum. Those who like their sport well the wrong side of vertical should find the 25 or so offerings on Cave Crag and El Cuenco to their satisfaction. The main crag has been reported variously as 'the most idyllic crag on the island' to 'a disappointing venue'. Well, it has a pleasant setting, a good selection of lower- and middle-grade routes, the climbs are well bolted and they all face due south; what more people expect is bit of a mystery to me. Stories of invasions of smelly seaweed pushed on-shore by winter storms may occasionally make the far right-hand side of the cliff unappetising. If you are after sensibly graded and sunny sport climbs then look no further; and, of course, don't forget the picnic!

Access

The main cliff is situated on the south-east coast of the island between Porto Cristo and Calas de Mallorca. Eight kilometres south of Porto Cristo is the impressive castle/fortified house of Son Forteza Vey. Driving south from here the road descends some sweeping bends for 1km until a parking place at the entrance

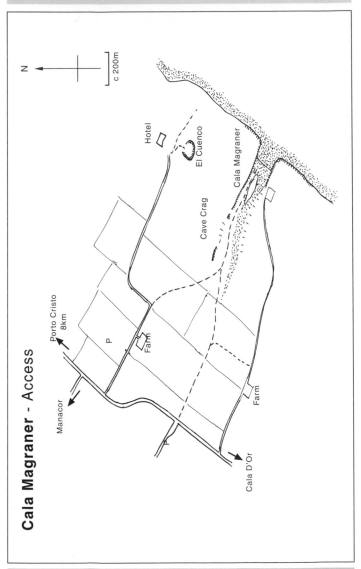

Cala Magraner - Access

N ← c 200m

Hotel

El Cuenco

Cala Magraner

Cave Crag

Porto Cristo
8km

P

Farm

Manacor

Farm

Cala D'Or

of an unsurfaced road on the right (with an assortment of post boxes on its right side) is reached. Cross the main road and fence, then follow the dried-up river bed gently downhill all the way to the sea. The first 10 minutes are easy going, then as the stream bed narrows a path on the left can be followed for another 10 minutes. A couple of gates on the right are traversed, and just beyond these the track leads into a mini-gorge with a lagoon separated from the sea by a pebble bar. To the right of the centre of the climbing area is a ruined building, the location of which aids finding specific routes. The approach takes a very gentle 25 minutes from the car. If the valley is fenced off, as occasionally happens, it is possible to head up and right, following the first of the fences, to a good track beyond the farm (with its mandatory mad dogs) which leads all the way to the lagoon.

An alternative that involves a bit less walking is to drive down the track just north of the parking place described above, signed 'Agritourismo', for 0.9km to parking by the gates. Continue down the arrow-straight track, passing the farm, until the road swings left at a right-angled bend. Follow a vague track down rightwards along the edge of the field and into the valley. The cliffs are another 5 to 10 minutes away. Whichever approach is used close (and open!) all gates properly.

For El Cuenco follow the latter approach above, but continue all the way down the track to a newly built hotel. The crag takes the form of a deep hole a short distance to the right and is reached by a track through the trees.

The Climbs

All the routes here are described from right to left as the sea is perhaps the most obvious reference point (at least nobody is going to move it!). Despite the fact that the Mediterranean is effectively non-tidal, the sea level does change because of weather conditions, and the accessibility of the routes on the far right-hand side of the cliff does vary. Research has finally revealed some of the correct names of the routes, though my source has to remain a secret.

RIGHT-HAND SECTION

The first five routes can be tricky to access if the sea is at all rough.

1. * 6b+ 15m
Trend diagonally rightwards above the sea passing one hole to reach a cave (solo?). Climb out of this steeply; 'glue-ins' protect.

A short distance to the left, and above the tide-line is a low-grade, shallow, bolted corner. Right of this is a steeper white wall with three lines of bolts.

2. * 5+ 17m
The rightmost line passing some small shrubs early on.

Cala Magraner - Right-Hand and Central Sections

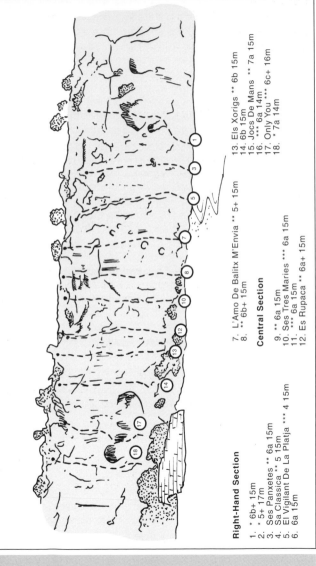

Right-Hand Section

1. * 6b+ 15m
2. * 5+ 17m
3. Ses Panxetes ** 6a 15m
4. Sa Classica ** 5 15m
5. El Vigilant De La Platja *** 4 15m
6. 6a 15m

7. L'Amo De Balitx M'Envia ** 5+ 15m
8. ** 6b+ 15m

Central Section

9. ** 6a 15m
10. Ses Tres Maries *** 6a 15m
11. *** 6a 15m
12. Es Rupaca ** 6a+ 15m

13. Els Xorigs ** 6b 15m
14. 6b 15m
15. Jocs De Mans ** 7a 15m
16. *** 6a 14m
17. Only You *** 6c+ 16m
18. * 7a 14m

3. SES PANXETES ** 6a 15m
The central line with a fingery start into a bay then easier above; 'glue-ins' protect.

4. SA CLASSICA ** 5 15m
The white rib immediately right of the groove on a continuous series of good holds; 'glue-ins' protect.

5. EL VIGILANT DE LA PLATJA *** 4 15m
The open shallow groove mentioned above gives a great introduction to sport climbing. Quite steep but juggy and well protected throughout.

6. 6a 15m
A blunt rib protected by a couple of old bolts (hard direct, easier with a lateral approach) leads to easier climbing, a poor thread, a bolt with maillon and finally twin rings on a ledge just below the cliff top.

7. L'AMO DE BALITX M'ENVIA ** 5+ 15m
Two metres to the left and past some good unclimbed rock is a route passing just to the right of two conspicuous orange holds. Passing the second of these is the crux; 'glue-ins' protect.

8. ** 6b+ 15m
Eight metres to left, start below the prominent stacked bulges high on the cliff. Climb slabby rock, bolts close together, to below the bulges. Lowering off from the ring here gives a pleasant * 5 10m. Attack the bulges centrally; passing the second one is the crux.

CENTRAL SECTION

9. ** 6a 15m
Tackle the slabby wall to the left of the fall-line from the roof, pull leftwards over a narrow slanting bulge (crux), then climb a deep crack past the right side of another bulge and reach left to a lower-off shared with the next climb.

10. SES TRES MARIES *** 6a 15m
Climb the wall passing the large stuck-on 'blob' awkwardly and finishing over a juggy bulge.

11. *** 6a 15m
The delicate pale slab is climbed directly with thin moves just short of the belays.

12. ES RUPACA ** 6a+ 15m
The innocuous shallow groove in the slab is climbed with continuous 'interest' passing many large new bolts.

Cala Magraner - Left Hand and Far Left Hand Sections

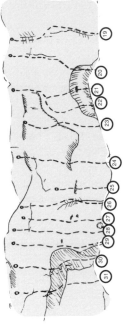

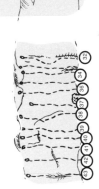

Left Hand Section

19. ** 5+ 14
20. Pipiricot ** 6a 14m
21. Sa Sesta *** 6b 15m
22. Galiano M'engana 6b+ 15m
23. Penta ** 6c+ 14m
24. Pixotades Per Ses Galtes ** 6c 16m
25. Perello * 4+ 10m
26. Jardiners Sense Fronteres * 3 14m
27. Herbofilia ** 3 14m

28. Paramuero * 5 12m
29. Sa Nyosclo * 5+ 12m
30. ** 6c+ 14m
31. ** 7a+ 14m

Far Left Hand Section

32. ** 6a 10m
33. Miguelin El Travieso * 6c 10m
34. Mou Els Peus * 6b+ 10m
35. Tootsie * 6b 10m
36. * 6c 10m

37. 6a+ 8m
38. ** 6a+ 10m
39. Sense Voler ** 6a 10m
40. * 6a+ 10m
41. Lladre De Somnis * 6c 10m
42. Metal Fatigue * 7a 10m
43. Al Loro Manolo * 6c 10m

13. ELS XORIGS ** 6b 15m

To the left and behind the biggest bush in the area, climb straight up the steep slab and then cross the bulges with difficulty. It is possible to avoid this final section (the crux) by a loop out to the right, * 6a.

To the left is large cave behind the ruined building. Just to the right of this is a thin seam:

14. 6b 15m

A thin crack is followed to tricky bulges. The crux is at half-height. Some of the bolts and the lower-off are in poorish condition at present (Jan 2000).

15. JOCS DE MANS ** 7a 15m

Start at the right edge of the cave and follow the handrail out left and get established on the warty wall above with difficulty. Climb this to a tricky finish.

16. *** 6a 14m

The central line starts by climbing the pillar, then swing right and jug-haul to enter and climb a groove. The lower-offs are in the bulges above.

17. ONLY YOU *** 6c+ 16m

The left-hand line up the steep white rock in the cave systems. Climb thin cracks to tufas and continue through the bulges. One of the best hereabouts.

18. * 7a 14m

The rough brown rib to the left has a crucial couple of moves around the bulge. A loop out to the left misses the crux and the point (6b).

LEFT-HAND SECTION

To the left is another area of undeveloped slabby rock (left of and behind the ruined building) and then another set of routes based around an area with two caves, separated by some easier terrain, and all tucked in behind some wiry bushes. Just to the right of the cave is a new route climbing into a shallow groove:

19. ** 5+ 14m

The steep pocketed wall, tufa rib and groove above are excellent.

20. PIPIRICOT ** 6a 14m

The right-hand line out of the right-hand cave has a tough fingery start, then step right and climb the easier scoop.

21. SA SESTA *** 6b 15m

The central line out of the cave has a strenuous start and a couple of delicate moves to reach the hanging flake. Swing left then back right.

22. GALIANO M'ENGANA ** 6b+ 15m
The left-hand line starting from the cave is fingery, sustained and markedly under-graded! Start up bubbly rock, climb left then back right to join and finish as for the previous climb.

23. PENTA ** 6c+ 14m
To the left of the cave is this tough route that starts at some rippled tufas, then crosses a thin diagonal overlap by sustained climbing.

24. PIXOTADES PER SES GALTES ** 6c 16m
A route starting at a ground-level cave and following the white streak up the gently leaning wall to the left with rusty-red bolts and occasional 'surprising' holds.

To the left and between the two caves are five pleasant lower-grade lines up grey slabby rock. Starting behind a tree is:

25. PERELLO * 4+ 10m
The short right-hand line, finishing at a steepening.

26. JARDINERS SENSE FRONTERES ** 3 14m
The central shallow groove is equipped with nine 'glue-ins' runners and great rock. A beginner's dream.

27. HERBOFILIA ** 4 12m
The broad rib just left of the shallow groove and right of an evergreen bush.

28. PARAMUERO * 5 12m
The steepening slab just left again is tricky towards the top, especially if you are puritanical.

29. SA NYOSCLO * 5+ 12m
The right edge of the blob-encrusted cave has tricky layaway moves at the change of angle.

30. ** 6c+ 14m
Tackle the hanging 'chandelier' and climb out of the cave on the left, then continue up the tough wall above.

31. ** 7a+ 14m
Follow the line of lumps and bumps out of the centre of the cave, then the wall and bulges above.

Fifty metres to the left of the blob-encrusted cave is the next area of development, a series of short, red-streaked walls.

FAR LEFT-HAND SECTION

32. ** 6a 10m
The short jamming crack on the far right is trickiest where the crack isn't.

33. MIGUELIN EL TRAVIESO * 6c 10m
The steep sharp wall just right of a spindly thorn tree.

34. MOU ELS PEUS * 6b+ 10m
The orange wall just left of the spindly tree has three bolt runners.

35. TOOTSIE * 6b 10m
The yellow rock is climbed up a series of small tufas.

36. * 6c 10m
Just to the left again; tough and with some sloping holds.

37. 6a+ 8m
The short wall left of the bushes.

38. ** 6a+ 10m
The left-slanting crack is followed to and through bulges.

39. SENSE VOLER ** 6a 10m
To the left is a pleasantly sustained wall with four bolt runners.

40. * 6a+ 10m
Just left, and below a block at the top of the cliff is this pocketed wall.

41. LLADRE DE SOMNIS * 6c 10m
An orange streak leads to a hanging flake.

42. METAL FATIGUE * 7a 10m
The white wall is climbed with difficulty, passing a small overlap.

43. AL LORO MANOLO * 6c 10m
An open shallow groove left of thin twinned trees leads to a tricky wall and is the last offering here.

Fifteen metres further left is a short wall with three routes, and on the right is a cave:

44. ? 12m
From the cave a thin crack leads past old bolts to a substantial lower-off.

45. 6a+ 12m
A bit of an eliminate; try to avoid the crack if you can.

46. * 6a 10m
The crack is better.

47. 5 10m
The wall just left is also unremarkable.

Forty metres left is a cave with three short hard climbs:

48. 7a 10m
The chipped right edge of the cave and tough bulge above.

49. 7c+ 8m
The taxing centre of the roof.

50. 7a+ 8m
The left edge of the cave.

CAVE CRAG

Five minutes' walk back towards the road is a south-facing tufa-encrusted cave, the first rock passed on the way to the cliff. Here are ten impressive lines breaching its roofs for those who thought the main cliff 'a path'. The routes all look well worthwhile and are all 18m to 20m long (see diagram). From left to right these are:

MC1. 7c+
MC2. 7c
MC3. 8a
MC4. 8a
MC5. 8a+
MC6. 7a+
MC7. 7b+
MC8. 7a+
MC9. 7a+
MC10. 7a

EL CUENCO

The last developed area is the amazing underground cliff, or open- topped cave of El Cuenco (the Eye Socket). See 'Access' section for how to get there. On the northern side of the hole a path descends into the gloom. As a winter venue the setting is far from ideal, being damp and gloomy, but in the summer it makes a great escape from the heat. All the routes are in the upper grades and the whole place has a very intimidating atmosphere. There have been some access problems linked to the proximity of the newly built hotel, so keeping a low profile is a good idea. The quality of the routes is not known, though they all look superb; any

Cala Magraner - Cave Crag

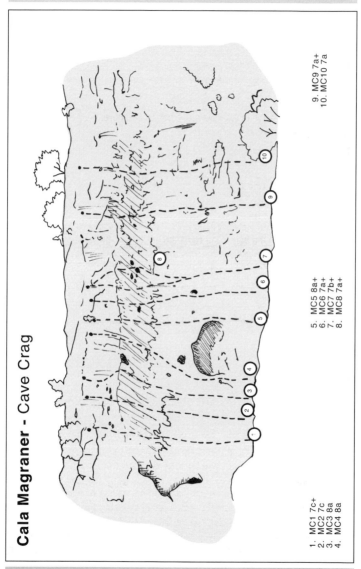

1. MC1 7c+
2. MC2 7c
3. MC3 8a
4. MC4 8a

5. MC5 8a+
6. MC6 7a+
7. MC7 7b+
8. MC8 7a+

9. MC9 7a+
10. MC10 7a

Cala Magraner - El Cuenco

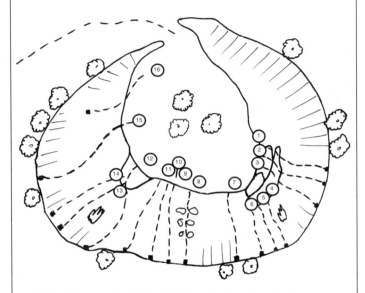

Note: Between routes 3-4 and 12-13 are two large bees' nests active in summer - AVOID

1. La Pandilla Basura 7a
2. Ximbomba Electrica 7a+
3. Sa Variant 7a
4. James Brown 6c+
5. Sense Nom 8a+
6. Project 8?
7. American Psico 8a
8. Espanis Sico 8?
9. MC-5 8b
10. Lime Spiders 8?
11. Tuthan Kamon 8b
12. La Mouche Au Plat 8a
13. S'Inacabada 7b
14. Mackintosch 7b+
15. Show Porno 7c
16. La Trena 7c+

feedback gratefully received. See diagram for route locations.
From left to right (clockwise looking in) the routes are:

1. **LA PANDILLA BASURA** 7a
2. **XIMBOMBA ELECTRICA** 7a+
3. **SA VARIANT** 7a
4. **JAMES BROWN** 6c+
5. **SENSE NOM** 8a+
6. **PROJECT** 8?
7. **AMERICAN PSICO** 8a
8. **ESPANIS SICO** 8?
9. **MC-5** 8b
10. **LIME SPIDERS** 8?
11. **TUTHAN KAMON** 8b
12. **LA MOUCHE AU PLAT** 8a
13. **S'INACABADA** 7b
14. **MACKINTOSCH** 7b+
15. **SHOW PORNO** 7c
16. **LA TRENA** 7c+

EL PARADON –
PUIG MAJOR ANTICIMA

On the southern slopes of the island's highest mountain is a superb tower of clean white limestone, over 200m high and approached by what looks like about a 45 minute walk. Unfortunately there is a NATO listening station on the very top of the Puig Major, keeping a watchful eye (or should that be ear) over the whole of the western basin of the Mediterranean, and there is a considerable military presence at the foot of the road that leads to the peak. I have not climbed here, but the crag looks worth a visit if you fancy getting away from them scruffy little sport routes that pepper the whole island! The information here is from an old topo from the local climbing shop, and is several years old. Please treat the information with care! Any feedback would be gratefully received.

Access: (See section 'Can Nyic', Access map.) Just to the east of the army base and the road to the summit of the mountain (and conveniently hidden by a bend!) there is parking on the right and stiles on the left that offer a way through the fencing. Follow tracks rightwards around the prominent hill and into the valley

Puig Major Anticima - El Paradon

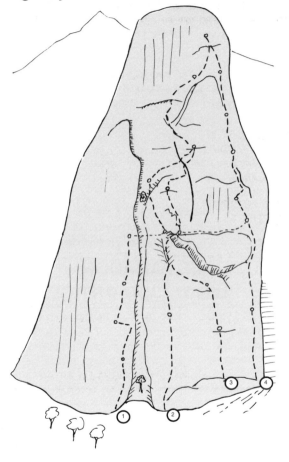

1. Socu 5,5,5
2. Ye Ye 6a+,6a

3. Puig 5+,4,6a,6a,3,4
4. Cosi 5+,5+,5+,5,5,4,4

that runs towards the cliff. There are four routes here of amenable grade, the local topo suggests two 50m ropes as well and nuts and friends are required. Descent is either on foot to the right of the face or by abseiling down COSI.

The routes are listed from left to right, and all are situated to the right of the huge orange walls at the left-hand side of the face.

1. SOCU 5,5,5
A 3- to 4-pitch outing up the left bounding rib of the central 'canal'. After the fourth stance a traverse right across the couloir offers an extension up the upper section of the tower. This trends left to re-enter the couloir then back right to join the upper section of PUIG.

2. YE YE 6a+,6a
A harder route with quite a bit of fixed gear, with two long pitches up the walls to the right of the canal to reach the large ledge at one-third height. Continue up one of the other routes, escape to the right or abseil off.

3. PUIG 5+,4,6a,6a,3,4,
The central line on the face to the right of the couloir heads towards the large overhangs before trending leftwards under these to where a groove leads to the ledges. The upper section climbs straight up the wall before trending right to cross a diagonal crack to a ledge. From here a long pitch goes left then right to reach easy ground.

4. COSI 5+,5+,5+,5,5,4,4
The right-hand side of the face is climbed in two long pitches to reach the ledges. The route then climbs a crack on the right and the gradually easing arête above.

LAS PERCHAS

Character
Two contrasting cliffs make the area worth a visit. Perhaps the main attraction is spectacular cave with a small number of exceedingly steep climbs. This crag faces due north, but this hardly matters; it is so steep that even if the cliff faced due south it wouldn't see much sun, such is the angle of the rock! Not surprisingly the climbing is very powerful, relying on pockets and sporadic tufas to climb walls that vary in angle from very steep to indecently steep. This is definitely a suitable destination for the criminally muscular.

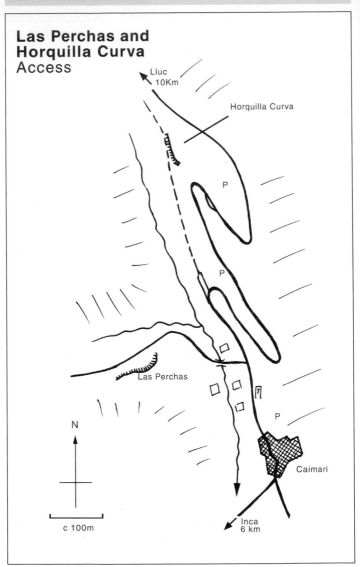

**Las Perchas and
Horquilla Curva**
Access

Lluc
10Km

Horquilla Curva

P

P

Las Perchas

N

P

Caimari

c 100m

Inca
6 km

Colin Binks on the retiring gem of Placa Aspera (6a+), Gubia

Only You (6c+), Cala Magraner

Slab climbers (or at least those who prefer their sport angled a little either side of vertical) are catered for by the sunny little crag close to the parking area.

Access

From Inca follow the road north to Selva and on to the small village of Caimari, tucked in close under the hills. Drive north out of Caimari for a short distance to the 'Luch 10km' sign. Just past this are several narrow entrances on the left; take note of the one with the small red arrow on the gate post. Drive past this to reach the first sharp bend as the road begins to climb into the hills and park here at a recently created 'mirador/parking', where the two-hour footpath to the monastery at Lluc begins. For the cave walk back down the main road and follow the track mentioned above to the cliff, 15 minutes from the car. For the Horquilla Curva Crag walk up the track to the cliff, 5 minutes away. It is also possible to drive on round the next two bends and park on the edge of the road, 50m up the hill from the cliff, if you really can't face the extended approach described above.

The climbs in the cave are described first, from left to right.

The first three routes are to be found around the left arête of the cave.

1. UNNAMED * 6b 12m
On the far left, a short line.

2. PETIT POI * 6b+ 12m
The easy-looking groove in the left arête of the cliff is the usual warm-up for the rest of the cliff. Steep climbing up the juggy groove leads to a more technical exit. Four clips.

3. BALL DE BOT * 7a 16m
A slight rib to the right of the hole is climbed steeply to easier angled rock to the lower-offs. Six clips.

4. EMPIRE STATE *** 8a+ 20m
Another steep number. The overhanging wall right of the arête is followed rightwards to a belay in the right wall of the large groove around the lip. Seven clips.

5. PEU DERET *** 8b+ 20m
Start in the back left corner of main cave and follow the left-trending bolt line to a lower-off just around the lip.

6. COMANDO MADRID *** 8b+ 25m
Start as for the previous route but climb across the overhang to a hole in the centre

Las Perchas

1. * 6b 12m
2. Petit Poi * 6b+ 12m
3. Ball De Bot * 7a 16m
4. Empire State *** 8a+ 20m
5. Peu Deret *** 8b+ 20m
6. Comando Madrid *** 8b+ 25m
7. American Express
   *** 8c/project 25m

8. Master Hit *** 8b+ 22m
9. Colgado *** 7b 16m
10. Es Penjat ** 7a 16m
11. A Vista De Pajaro ** 8a+ 14m
12. Motor Head *** 7c+ 16m
13. Terrorvision *** 8a 16m
14. Toten Hosen *** 7c 15m
15. Bon Apetit *** 8a 15m

16. Penhouse *** 7c 15m
17. Hoodoo Gurus *** 7b 15m
18. Picados ** 7c+ 12m

of the roof, and then continue in the same vein to the twin-bolt lower-offs around the lip.

7. AMERICAN EXPRESS *** 8c/project 25m
Start in the back right-hand corner of the cave and follow the bolt line. The route is 7b to the first lower-off and another world beyond this!

To the right and under the right edge of the major cave is a tall thin cave entrance. The next route starts directly above this and is reached most easily by scrambling round to the left, though the belayer may want to stay on the ground rather then risk being pulled off the ledge by an airborne leader.

8. MASTER HIT *** 8b+ 22m
Swing out right then trend left across the never-ending roof to belays around the lip. As far as the fixed karabiner on the fifth bolt is a pocketed 7c+.

To the right is a prominent small tree 10m up the cliff, under a large overhang.

9. COLGADO *** 7b 16m
Just left of the fall-line from the tree. A tricky leaning lower wall to a good rest (you will need it) on ledges on the right. Step back left then tackle the tufa-encrusted roof to reach a leaning wall above. The crux moves lurk here and involve getting up and right to the lower-offs. Seven clips.

10. ES PENJAT ** 7a 16m
Start as for the last route but trend right and climb a leaning rib above until forced out right into a groove. A memorable route that is sparingly bolted.

11. A VISTA DE PAJARO ** 8a+ 14m
The next line to the right heads straight through the bulges before trending right to the lower-off.

12. MOTOR HEAD *** 7c+ 16m
Right again climb up to black holes at 5m using a series of 'chips', then continue into and up the steeply leaning ramp/groove above. Six clips.

13. TERRORVISION *** 8a 16m
Start at low-relief tufa with a pocket in its top left corner, and climb the line past an old wooden wedge at 5m. Above this climb through a hollow then trend gradually leftwards up the face passing a hole. Seven clips.

14. TOTEN HOSEN *** 7c 15m
To the right the overhanging orange wall is climbed on well-chalked pockets, passing a 'black hole' to eventually reach a tufa and then the lower-offs. Five clips.

15. BON APETIT *** 8a 15m
Start from a pair of 'elephant's legs' in the back of the cave (paired bolts at start). More butch climbing up overhanging tufas blobs and flanges.

16. PENHOUSE *** 7c 15m
Start as for the last route but swing right early on and climb the bigger tufa.

17. HOODOO GURUS *** 7b 15m
Start just to the right of a prominent blackened cave. Climb the leaning lower wall on pockets to prominent tufas. Battle powerfully up these to the lower-off. Five clips.

At the right edge of the cliff the crag runs out into ivy-coated hillside. The last route starts 7m left of the ivy:

18. PICADOS ** 7c+ 12m
Climb the white scoop to reach grey rock above and the solitary lower-off bolt. A short route offering hard, well-chipped face-climbing. Three clips.

HORQUILLA CURVA

A pleasantly situated crag with a small selection of routes on typically sharp rock. The crag is easy of access, gets the afternoon sun and is worth an hour or two if you climb in the 6s. I resisted the temptation to call it Higher Perchas. The routes are listed from right to left.

The first three routes climb the steep slab at the right-hand side of the cliff:

19. * 6c 16m
Up the slope to the right of the bushes is a steep pitch with a tricky first clip.

20. * 6a 20m
A shoddy start (from the toilet!) trending right up scrappy ground leads to much better climbing up the centre of the steep slab. 8 bolts.

21. *** 6b 24m
The route of the cliff, starts as for the last climb and then gives excellent sustained climbing up the left-hand side of the slab, with the crux low down and a jig out to the left at the top. 10 bolts.

To the left of more bushes are two short blunt ribs, both sprouting bolts.

22. 6b 14m
An easy start leads to a short, steep and tricky wall. Given the very mean grade of 5 elsewhere.

Horquilla Curva

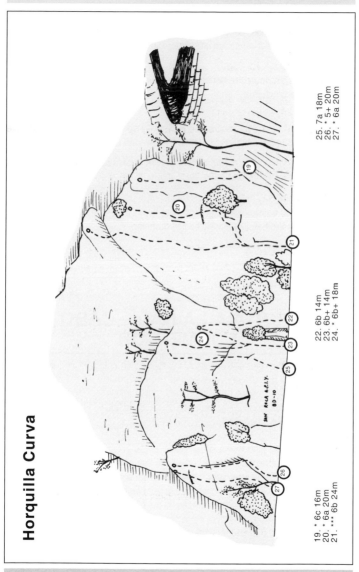

19. * 6c 16m
20. * 6a 20m
21. *** 6b 24m

22. 6b 14m
23. 6b+ 14m
24. * 6b+ 18m

25. 7a 18m
26. * 5+ 20m
27. * 6a 20m

23. 6b+ 14m
The left-hand start, then keep left and climb the short sharp wall to the left-hand end of the same lower-off as the last climb.

24. * 6b+ 18m
The left-hand start described above, then trend left up the leaning wall to a lower-off just left of a small tree.

25. 7a 18m
Climb easy and floral rock for 8m to the first bolt steeper rock, which is followed strenuously until pockets lead out right to the lower-off used by the previous climb.

The final two, very well-bolted, routes are 14m further left, where there is a right-slanting groove behind a thin tree:

26. * 5+ 20m
Climb the slanting groove and grotty corner before thin left-trending cracks give better climbing. Well endowed with 11 bolt runners.

27. * 6a 20m
The centre of the buttress on pocketed rock gives a pleasant pitch. 10 bolt runners.

PUNTA A LA NAO – CABO FORMENTOR

Dave Lyon and Terry Taylor have added two new routes (March 1998) to the prominent headland beyond the first mirador (the parking for Creveta), the Punta a la Nao. These descriptions have not be checked, though it is has to be assumed that the routes are fully bolted.

Access

From the first mirador the Punta a la Nao can be seen as a long headland jutting out into the sea. There is a west-facing 80m high sea cliff at the far end of this, below the prow of the headland which forms its highest point. Park either at the mirador or, if you want to save 5 minutes, at the first lay-by on the right about 1km further along the road. From this small lay-by (small white road-marker with the black 7 on it) cross the road, pass through a gap in the short wall, cross the water pipe and follow the path down through the trees towards the headland. The path continues out to the headland and the prominent prow is reached in about 12 to 15 minutes. (See section 'Creveta', Situation & Access map.)

CYBERSEX ** 6a+ 55m
Abseil down past the thread belay at the top of pitch one and continue to the bolt belay on a ledge a short distance above the sea (double 60m ropes required?).
1. 6a+ 20m A pleasant pitch with short-lived difficulties on the initial pillar.
2. 5 35m An easier pitch up the large grey slab above.

ROBOT WARS *** 7a 65m
Also reached by abseil from the cliff top, although there is the bolt on the slab just below the top which acts as the final belay. Abseil to the double-bolt belay 40m down. Arrange a second abseil a further 25m down to the stance about 8m above sea.
1. 7a 25m Superb climbing on perfect rock and following the left curving fault line from the belay. The difficulties increase throughout the pitch as the angle gradually increases.
2. 6b+ 40m A long pitch on the upper slab with a thin central section. The final roof is the crux, leading back to the bolt belay just below the cliff edge.

PUERTO PI

Character
A slightly scruffy bouldering area whose main asset is its great accessibility, being situated on the southern side of the bay only a short drive from Palma in one direction and from the resorts of Palma Nova and Magaluf in the other. I have no doubt that there are many other areas of greater worth scattered around the island, but if you are looking for somewhere for a quick work-out, only minutes from the road, Peurto Pi fits the bill admirably. The rock consists of a long 5m high outcrop that overhangs considerably for much of its length. The rock is pocketed and is generally exceptionally rough, though the broken glass and other detritus don't really do the place any favours.

Access
Follow the road around the harbour at Palma in a southerly direction to the first turn-off, located at a major junction, with traffic lights, just a short way past the

Santa Ponca-
Access & Routes

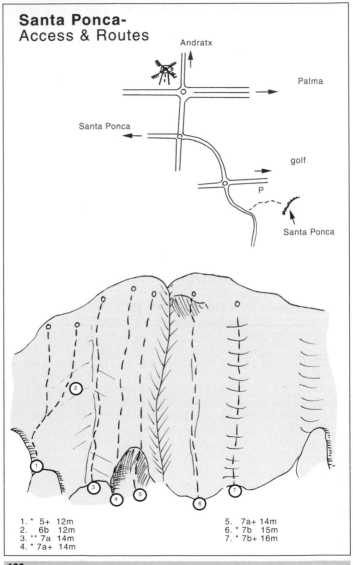

1. * 5+   12m
2.   6b   12m
3. ** 7a   14m
4. * 7a+ 14m
5.   7a+ 14m
6. * 7b   15m
7. * 7b+ 16m

military harbour. Take a left turn here. If coming from the resorts to the south, a right turn is made at the foot of the long hill that runs down towards the harbour. Follow the road up the hill, then, as it bends round to the left roadside, parking is available where there is a break in the chain on the right. Leave no valuables in the car.

The rocks are reached by a short scramble down the bank. Enjoy the setting and get pumping.

SANTA PONCA

Character

A small cliff of good rock which is worth a visit if you are in the area, and can climb to a suitable standard. The cliff faces north-east and so can be a shady retreat on hot days. Generally the routes are short, hard and under-graded. Be warned.

Access

The cliff is the conspicuous smooth white lump that overlooks the golf course at Santa Ponca. Take the coastal road past Palma Nova and Magaluf and on towards Andraxt. At a roundabout with a newly restored windmill turn left towards Santa Ponca and follow signs for 'Golf'. At the entrance to the golf course turn right and take the road that winds up the hill towards the cliff sticking out of the trees. Park on the roadside at a long right-hand bend, then follow any one of a series of tracks that wend up through the trees to reach the base of the cliff less than 5 minutes away.

The routes are listed from left to right.

1. * 5+ 12m
Climb a short easy crack then step onto the wall and follow a continuously surprising set of pockets. Steep and quite satisfying.

2. 6b 12m
Start as for the previous climb but swing awkwardly right onto the face and make a couple of moves on razors to reach better holds, leaving a short steep sprint to the belays.

Just to the right the cliff swings round to face north. The arête that divides the two faces is:

3. ** 7a 14m
The leaning arête is steep, sharp and technical. Climb diagonally leftwards on poor pockets then head straight up the sustained pocketed rib above.

4. * 7a+ 14m
Start to the right of the arête. Pull through the roofs with difficulty then continue up the smooth white wall above.

5. 7a+ 14m
The steep line just to the left of the scruffy gully that divides this section of the cliff is strenuous and fingery.

6. * 7b 15m
To the right of the central gully is a discontinuous crack-line that runs out into steeper rock just below the cliff top. The crack is much harder than it looks, being largely holdless and precarious. Eventually good holds arrive and more thuggish climbing leads to the lower-offs.

7. * 7b+ 16m
The last route on the cliff is an open white scoop that gives a technical, precarious and sustained pitch. Most definitely not one for strong arms.

SES TRET

Character
The cliff is also known as Roca Blanca on some topos. A most unusual crag for Spain in that part of it has been quarried in the past. Before you turn the page in search of something better, be assured: this is no Horseshoe Quarry; indeed the rock is generally very solid. Unfortunately the angle of the cliff means that all the climbs are of a high standard of difficulty, with nothing to interest climbers operating in the 'fives' and 'sixes'. The crag faces due north and so is sheltered from the sun, and much of it is steep enough to stay dry even in heavy rain. Rather conveniently, due to the quarrymen's activity, the base of the crag has a continuous 'dotted line' painted along it, with the dots being a standard 1m apart. This does away with the need to find names for the climbs, though it does make for rather boring climbing talk, adding ever more numbers to the melting pot. Most of the routes are chipped to a greater or lesser degree.

Ses Tret

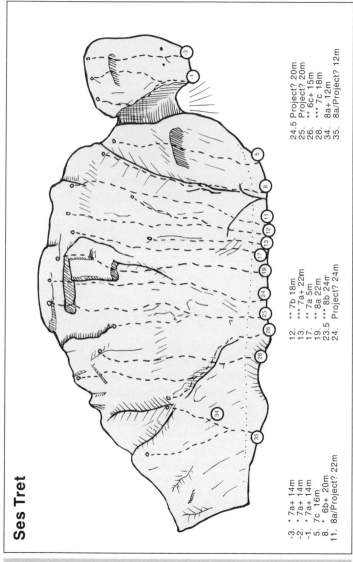

-3. * 7a+ 14m
-2. * 7a+ 14m
-1. * 7a+ 14m
5.   * 7c 16m
8.   * 6b+ 20m
11. 8a/Project? 22m

12. ** 7b 18m
13. *** 7a+ 22m
17. ** 7a 5m
19. ** 8a 22m
23.5 *** 8b 24m
24. Project? 24m

24.5 Project? 20m
25. Project? 20m
26. ** 6c+ 15m
28. *** 7c 18m
34. 8a+ 12m
35. 8a/Project? 12m

Access

The crag is hidden just off the main road from Palma to Valdemossa. Some 15km to the north of Palma the road cuts through a short rocky ravine with a prominent slabby cliff above the road on the right. Immediately upon exiting from this there is an extensive (and scruffy) parking area on the left. This is easily overshot on the first visit; a couple of kilometres further up the road is a right turn that allows you to turn around and have a second go! Leave nothing in the car, then follow the left-hand track past a locked gate as it rises gradually until the cliff appears on the left 400m down the track. A short steep scramble leads up to it. Several other buttresses are passed on the way to the main cliff, and although they feature the odd bit of gear they are largely undeveloped at present and are all fairly uninspiring.

The routes are describe briefly from left to right, and the painted numbers are used to locate them.

Number 35. 8a/Project? 12m

Head straight up the wall on the far left. It leans at an angle close to 45 degrees and not all of the holds are entirely natural!

Number 34. 8a+ 12m

Up the wall following gold then red bolts trending slightly leftwards to a lower-off in the groove above.

To the right is an even steeper prow of rock with no routes at present and at the right-hand side of this is:

Number 28. *** 7c 18m

A fearsomely steep line tackling the leaning lower wall to a rest on the ramp of the next climb, and then attacking the severely tilted rock above with gusto. Excellent and well-chipped.

Number 26. ** 6c+ 15m

A diagonal pocketed ramp-line is followed steeply leftwards to ledges and a lower-off at the world's largest karabiner. A good warming 'pump up' for this section of the cliff, though stripping the gear can be problematical. A more direct finish above the end of the ramp is apparently an open project.

Number 25. Project? 20m

Start at the foot of the ramp and initially climb straight up the crag. At the third bolt trend left up the steep sustained ragged crack-line.

Number 24.5. Project? 20m

As for Number 25 to the third bolt then straight on up the overhanging orange rock above and over a prow to the lower-offs. Undeniably steep.

Number 24. Project? 24m
Start at a right-trending seam. At the fifth bolt (with fixed karabiner) move left into an orange scoop and then press on over the roof above. The lower-off is located just below the top of the cliff.

Number 23.5. *** 8b 24m
Start up the right-trending seam and press on to reach a rest in an orange niche. From here do battle with the square roof and the black prow that hangs over it.

Number 19. ** 8a 22m
Straight up the 'easier-angled' wall to the right to enter an orange rounded scoop. Climb out of this to reach a ragged crack-line and then a tufa, which is followed to the lower-offs.

Number 17. ** 7a 15m
Head up right to reach ledges below a ragged crack-line then press on up this, before trending leftwards to reach a lower-off where the wall becomes smooth.

Number 13. *** 7a+ 22m
Despite its allotted number this is one of the best routes on the crag, with a technical lower section and exciting finale up the centre of the head wall. Climb the smooth lower wall then press on up a tufa, passing an overlap with difficulty. Climb into a bay for a breather, then push on up the leaning wall using a discontinuous crack system until it is possible to step left and then lean back right to reach the lower-offs. Simply stunning.

Number 12. ** 7b 18m
Climb the ragged crack to an optional lower-off in bay, or if you feel up to it step right to join the next route and continue up the tilted prow via a thin crack.

Number 11. 8a/Project 22m
A very fingery-looking pitch up the centre of the wall just left of the prominent groove line, protected by white bolts and finishing over the big prow.

Number 8. * 6b+ 20m
The steep twisting bridging-groove that defines the right side of the central section of the cliff is protected by bright red bolts. The warm-up for the cliff. Despite being the only climb on the cliff suitable for normal mortals it is considerably steeper than it looks, and thus requires some powerful climbing.

Number 5. 7c 16m
The short leaning buttress is no push-over.

Around to the right are three more steep lines on a huge boulder. Unlike the main cliff this section of rock does not bear any numbers, but to continue the theme of the main sector of cliff they are listed as:

Number -1. * 7a+ 14m
The leftmost line up an overhanging rib has a tricky start and is climbed mostly, and surprisingly, on its steeper left side.

Number -2. * 7a+ 14m
The central line follows the previous route to the third bolt and then swings right to climb a steep orange scoop and formidable roof on pocketed rock.

Number -3. * 7a+ 14m
From boulders reach a chiselled hold which is used to pull into a series of scoops. Step left and climb the overhanging groove precariously on sloping holds and then the final easier leaning wall direct.

PORT DE SOLLER (S'ATALAIA)

Character

A cliff of contrasts in a pleasant, if slightly scruffy, setting and easy of access from the town of Port de Soller, which is quite awkward to get to from almost anywhere on the island! The cliff is divided into a short set of rather scruffy walls with a selection of lower-grade routes and an impressive tufa cave with some more memorable offerings. Development of the left side of the cliff is continuing at the present and, judging by the extent of the rock, will go on for some time. It is worth mentioning that the cliffs are in the sun from about mid-afternoon until it sets. Once the sun bathes the rocks in golden light any imperfections in the setting are soon forgotten.

Note: in recent months there has been a massive building programme on the very edge of the cliff, where the original hotels have been extended leftwards. The whole area is fenced off, and signs in English and Spanish warn against climbing. Judging by the size of some of the blocks of rock that are lying on the path at the foot of the cliff this is probably a good idea, at least until the fencing and signs are removed.

Access

Soller is reached most easily via the C711 that runs north from Palma passing the cliff of Gubia and the town of Bunyola. A new toll tunnel (520 pesetas, Jan 2000) has finally opened, cutting out the horrendously twisty road over the pass and making climbing here a more viable option. An alternative to the drive is to take the train to Soller, then the tram to the terminus at Port de Soller, a steep 5 minute walk from the cliffs. (See appendix for train times.)

From the tunnel exit drive past the town of Soller and along the sea front at Port de Soller. Follow the railway track to its end and take the last available right turn (by a leather boutique), which winds steeply uphill and over a brow until there is an opening on the left that heads towards the sea. Turn down here and park as soon as possible. The routes are described from right to left, as this is the usual approach. I have been unable to come up with names for the small scruffy routes at the start of the cliff and so have simply numbered. The first selection of 14 climbs is pretty poor and may have been adversely affected by the building operations. Their original descriptions are included here for completeness.

SECTOR INICIACION

The initial two routes (the best here) lie below the projecting hotel wall that juts out high above, and the first of these is up the tall grey tower directly below the corner of the wall:

1. * 5 20m

Climb the rib up the right side of the face and continue up the upper arête. A lower-off is available, removing the need to enter the palatial grounds above.

2. * 5+ 20m

Start up the tricky bulging face to the left of the arête and pass these obstacles to gain the easier and well-positioned upper section.

3. 5 14m

To left are flat ledges at 3m. From these climb to more ledges then scale the wall directly above via a slippery bulge (with chips) to reach chains in the base of the easy groove above.

4. 4+ 10m

Two metres to the left is a short bulging wall with diagonal right to left cracks crossing it. Climb directly up the centre of this to a lower-off on the ledges above.

The white wall to left is prominently spattered with bolts. On the right side of this is a groove:

5. 3+ 10m

Climb the open groove to the right of the white wall. The start is steep and the rest is easier.

6. 5 10m

The centre of the well-bolted white wall has tricky moves past the third bolt and a quick sprint to a lower-off above.

The next two routes start from a couple of flat rocks on ground:

7. 4+ 10m

Take a line up ruddy rock via a prominent excavated niche.

8. 4 10m

To the left is a left-trending bolt line passing red rock scars. Some of the rock still feels rather temporary, so climb it with care.

Five metres left is a bizarre line of seven huge home-made brackets. These provide the very encouraging protection on:

9. 6a 10m

A very sharp lower wall is climbed, starting off a small ramp, and with the climbing easing rapidly as height is gained.

10. * 5+ 13m

Just left of the 'mega-brackets' is a bulging wall and shallow corner leading to a small robust tree. A short distance above is a solitary bolt and crab lower-off. 'The best of the rest'.

Several hundred metres further along the track a small scrambly path leads to a prominent pale rock-scar/buttress with four short routes that share a lower-off. They are not especially worthwhile, but for completeness they are:

11. PIC NIC * 7a 12m

12. ? 6c 12m

13. ? 6b 12m

14. ? 6b+ 12m

SECTOR SA COVA

A short distance left again the cliff becomes more worthwhile, starting with an impressive tufa cave which is home to seven routes. All of the routes here climb some amazing tufa features, and all are strenuous. The cave is a superbly sheltered sun-trap late in the day when the sun hammers straight into it. Just the

Port De Soller (S'Atalaia)
Sector Sa Cova

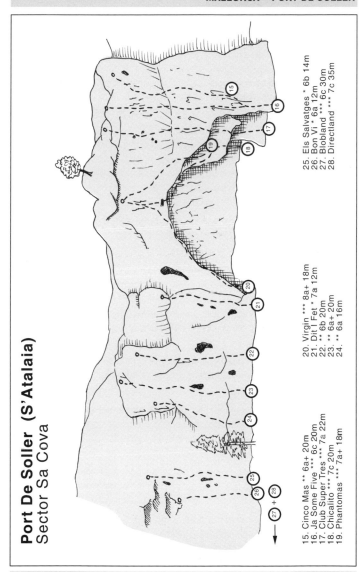

15. Cinco Mas ** 6a+ 20m
16. Ja Some Five *** 6c 20m
17. Club Super Tres *** 7e 22m
18. Chicalito *** 7c 20m
19. Phantomas *** 7a+ 18m

20. Virgin *** 8a+ 18m
21. Dit I Fet * 7a 12m
22. ** 6b 20m
23. ** 6a+ 20m
24. ** 6a 16m

25. Els Salvatges * 6b 14m
26. Bon Vi * 6a 12m
27. Blobland *** 6c 30m
28. Directland *** 7c 35m

spot for boosting up the tan. The first two climbs here share a common start up the right rib of the cave.

15. CINCO MAS ** 6a+ 20m

A good climb with a tough finale. Swing onto the initial rib then trend right past a hole towards a hanging 'dong'. Just short of this move left, then make steep pulls (lowering off from the fixed karabiner here is worth 5 *) to where a swing right along a diagonal crack gives access to a final difficult sequence to the chains.

16. JA SOME FIVE *** 6c 20m

Start as for the previous climb then climb the edge of the cave until the wall starts to lean. A demanding sequence past a series of 'stuck-on' tufas reaches sloping ledges and a hidden jug, then a baffling final set of moves allows a rightward exit onto a slab to reach the belay. It is also possible (and cheating?) to step left to join the finish of the next route.

Inside the right edge of cave are the next three contributions. The first one parallels the previous pair of routes, with the other two crossing the impressive roofs just to the left.

17. CLUB SUPER TRES *** 7a 22m

Great climbing, powerful and sustained, a 7a that thinks it is a 7b. Pull onto the wall over a tricky overhang and continue up 'tufatastic' rock to where it starts to lean severely. A hard move on disappointing pockets gains a hanging proboscis, then easier but still steep moves up the wall conclude a great pitch.

The next two climbs share a common start and find separate ways around the lip of the cave, with one finishing direct through the roofs and the other trending left below the lip to pull round onto the leaning head wall.

18. CHICALITO *** 7c 20m

Step right out of the back of the cave then pull over a roof to tufas and a good deep hole. From this power straight through the overhangs above with difficulty to eventually reach better holds that lead left to the lower-off.

19. PHANTOMAS *** 7a+ 18m

A test of stamina. Follow the previous climb to the deep hole then trend left below the lip to a bigger hole and a semi-rest. Tackle the bulge direct above using a series of good, but spaced, pockets to reach black tufas and then the lower-off.

The compelling line out from the back of the cave is unclimbed at the time of writing, though it looks an obvious challenge. At the left side of the cave is a route that traverses the whole of the underside of the lip from left to right:

20. VIRGIN *** 8a+ 18m

An obviously over-strenuous outing despite the size of many of the holds, and a suitable challenge for those who thought the last route 'duff'. Follow the underside of the left edge of the cave to eventually (after two more years in the gym?) join the previous route.

21. DIT I FET * 7a 12m

Starting at the left edge of the cave is a ragged seam running straight up the wall and into a brown bay. A short but action-packed pitch which is rather 'sequential'.

To the left of the cave is an area of more amenable rock consisting of an open scoop and then a rounded buttress. Beyond the rounded buttress is a tree growing just to the left of an alcove. There are three easier offerings here. Climbing out of the alcove is:

22. ? ** 6b 20m

Exit from the scoop via the prominent undercut and tootle up the white tufa-streaked wall to a steeper section of grey/brown sharp rock. Finish up this with gusto!

23. ? ** 6a+ 20m

To the left of the tree stood close to the rock are some spiky bushes on the wall and then a bright white buttress climbed on its right side by a line protected by silver bolts. The route heads left of a grey streak past large holes, then up the tilted brown wall to chains on its rim.

24. ? ** 6a 16m

Left again is a line marked by dark red/brown brackets running straight up a steep white wall to a short leaning section and on to a lower-off in a cave.

To the left are two shorter offerings, close together.

25. ELS SALVATGES * 6b 14m

The steepening wall to a finish right of the roofs.

26. BON VI ⁴ 6a 12m

The pleasant wall to a lower-off below the big overhang.

Left again the cliff gets considerably higher and more impressive. It is slabby in its lower section. The names are made up but in common use:

27. BLOBLAND *** 6c 30m

A line of large gold ring bolts runs left across the lower slab to a hollow below much steeper rock. Then it trends back right across a weakness in the steep head wall to a large silver solitary lower-off bolt in a cave. Excellent.

28. DIRECTLAND *** 7c 35m
To the left again and behind a big tree is an easy groove most easily reached from the right and leading to a short wall running into the hollow of the previous climb. Continue straight up the steep, sustained and hard wall above.

A short distance left in the back right-hand corner of a flat-floored bay (which doubles as a sun-trap and toilet) is:

29. DORIS * 7b 12m
Climb the steep wall and large formidable-looking roof to chains on its left arête.

Some 120m to the left is another smaller cave, with three routes:

30. ? 8a 16m
The right arête of the cave.

31. ? 7a 16m
The left arête, starting in the cave.

32. ? 6c 14b
Just left again.

A recent development at Port de Soller is the COVA DES CINGLES, an impressive sea cave below the main cliff and accessed by traversing a narrow ledge. There are currently only five routes here:

33. MIGUELIN EL POLITOXICOMANO ? ? 7a
The wall to the left of the cave.

34. CRISTO EL TRANSEXUAL ? ? 7a
The left arête of the cave and the wall above.

35. BLAU FERRARI ? ? 8a
The right arête of the cave then the butch bulging roof is tackled leftwards.

36. ALLIENS ? ? 6b
Follow the previous route but nip up the wall when things start to get really steep.

37. EL FOLLA-GUIRIS ? ? 6a
Start as for the previous two routes, but keep to the wall on the right.

CALA SANTANYI – PLAYA DE TIJUANA

Character

A fine set of mostly tough climbs in a superb setting, definitely **the** crag for the non-climbing members of the team. The climbing is generally fingery and is on very sharp rock that is not as soft as first appearances might suggest. The cliffs have the atmosphere of Pembroke's Trevallen, with the added attraction of continental-style protection and the blue Mediterranean as a backdrop instead of the Bristol Channel. Mention should also be made of the superb beaches, bars and cafes nearby. Why fly halfway round the world to the Seychelles? Paradise is a lot nearer than that! All the routes here have fixed protection, though some of the bolts had suffered serious corrosion due to the proximity of the sea. From 1994 onwards a replacement programme has been going on, with almost all the old bolts being replaced by substantial glued stainless steel affairs.

Access

The cliffs are located below the headland to the east of the superb beach and inlet of Cala Santanyi. On first acquaintance the easiest way to get to the cliffs is thus: take the main road across the island to the town of Santanyi (Santany on some maps), where signs lead in 3km to a right turn to Cala Santanyi. The road winds down into a narrow valley where there is parking for the beach. Drive past this (if you can) and up a winding road past several hotels. Take a right turn at a triangular roundabout (a trianglabout?) containing a tree, then take another right turn signed 'Hostal Villa Sireno & Apartments' at a tear-drop shaped roundabout with plants. Continue for 300m to yet another right turn (signed 'Inmobiliaria Brossa, Palmeria' and opposite a plaque in the wall: 'Carrer de S'Atalaia Vella'). A short distance further on, parking is available at an open area by a derelict lighthouse. Leave nothing valuable in the car.

Facing the sea, walk right through scrub for 200m, past a collapsed stone wall, and descend easy slopes to the extensive wave-cut platform that runs below all the cliffs. On hot days the sea is very inviting, though the undercut nature of the rock makes getting in and out of the water tricky, especially if there is a swell running. Perhaps a visit to the beach at Cala Santanyi is a better idea.

Walking back towards the car along the wave-cut platform, you pass a rather

Cala Santanyi - Playa De Tijuana

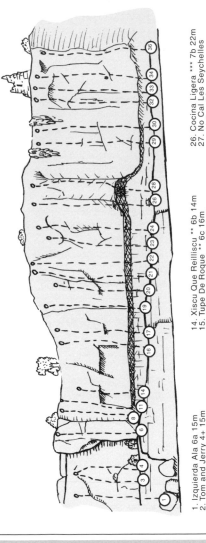

1. Izquierda Ala 6a 15m
2. Tom and Jerry 4+ 15m
3. Ebam 4+ 15m
4. Ebamsa 5 15m
5. Arista * 6b 15m
6. Finger Killer * 6c 15m
7. Angula * 5 15m
8. Vino Tinto * 6a 15m
9. Tapas * 6a 16m
10. Tatas * 5+ 15m
11. Blame It On the Rain 6c+ 14m
12. Honeymoon 7a 15m
13. Never Mind The Bolsillos 7a 12m

14. Xiscu Que Reilliscu ** 6b 14m
15. Tupe De Roque ** 6c 16m
16. Escuela De Calor *** 6b 20m
17. Un Dimanche A La Campagne
    ** 7a 20m
18. Tocino For Pepino * 6c+ 20m
19. Flesh For Dani *** 7b 20m
20. Compiedras ** 7a+ 16m
21. Cancamos ** 7b 20m
22. Miguels *** 7a+ 22m
23. La Calle Del Ritmo *** 7b+ 22m
24. Psicomambo *** 6c 22m
25. Peli ** 7a 12m

26. Cocina Ligera *** 7b 22m
27. No Cal Les Seychelles
    ** 7a+ 22m
28. Colesterol Party*** 6a 22m
29. Batchcamft ** 7a 18m
30. Tenacidad *** 8a 22m
31. Poseidon *** 7a+ 22m
32. Chuter Fou *** 7b 20m
33. Go Jonhy *** 8a 18m
34. Rompepiernas ** 6c+ 22m
35. Naranja ** 7a 20m
36. Espolon ** 6b+ 20m

indeterminate horizontally striated wall just before some huge boulders perched on the edge. A large cactus hangs over the top of the wall and its right side is bound by a deep red corner. There are several routes on this wall, and although they are not especially spectacular their setting makes them just about worth the effort if you climb in the lower grades. The routes start from a long narrow conglomerate ledge reached by a short unsavoury scramble.

1. IZQUIERDA ALA 6a 15m
The most left-hand line has a tricky start that eases immediately.

2. TOM AND JERRY 4+ 15m
Start from the left end of the ledge, 3m right of a tree, and climb directly up the lower wall and bubbly black slab above. It is worth noting that the final bolt runner can be removed by hand! A lower-off is available just to the left of the cactus below the crest of the wall.

3. EBAM 4+ 15m
The central line. Climb an orange bulging wall leftwards to slabbier rock and then follow a crack-line rightwards up easier rock to a lowering point to the right of the cactus bush.

4. EBAMSA 5 15m
Start 2m left of the main corner and climb straight up the gradually easing black slab. Passing the first bolt is the crux of the climb, and a belay is available just to the left of the overhang near the top of the cliff.

The large red corner offers an obvious challenge to any traditionalists who have brought a rucksack full of big nuts on holiday and who are suffering withdrawal symptoms from 'real climbing'. The pale striated wall and massive roof to the right offer a more modern challenge – out with that bolt gun.

Around to the right is a scruffy open corner, and starting from the ledge at its foot, and reached by a short scramble, are several short but interesting climbs.

5. ARISTA * 6b 15m
The left arête of the bay is climbed on its right side with one short taxing section which can be climbed by 'barn-door laybacking' or a quick jump. Easier rock remains.

6. FINGER KILLER * 6c 15m
The centre of the left wall of the corner has a short 'blank' central section that is passed by precarious use of a couple of razor edges.

7. ANGULO * 5 15m
The open corner to a finish on the right wall.

8. VINO TINTO * 6a 15m
The wall immediately right of the corner requires a rather blinkered approach.

9. TAPAS * 6a 16m
Just to the right of the corner the steepening wall is rather harder than it looks, offering steep fingery moves past thin diagonal cracks.

10. TATAS * 5+ 15m
The centre of the right wall of the corner is a bit longer and a bit harder. It sports a mixture of old and new bolts. The route starts off with a slabby section and then steepens to a long reach through bulges using an unhelpful set of 'stuck-on' flowstone holds. Twin lowering bolts are found 1m below the cliff top.

11. BLAME IT ON THE RAIN 6c+ 14m
From the right-hand edge of the ledge climb directly up the right side of the wall.

12. HONEYMOON 7a 15m
From the right-hand edge of the ledge traverse out towards the arête and climb it on its left side.

Around to the right the buttress is severely undercut with a sharp arête in its centre. The left side of this is climbed by:

13. NEVER MIND THE BOLSILLOS 7a 12m
The left-hand side of the bulges are short and powerful.

14. XISCU QUE REILLISCU ** 6b 14m
A short but action-packed pitch. Power over the initial overhang from the right then glorious jug-pulling leads up the leaning grey wall above to lower-offs, where the angle eases.

15. TUPE DE ROQUE ** 6c 16m
Start just to the right under the centre of the wide white roof at 7m, and climb up to it. Step right and pull back leftwards across the edge of the roof with difficulty before heading straight up to the chains.

Running to the right from the previous climbs the cliff is undercut by a series of flat white overhangs 3m off the ledge. Despite some obvious lines this section is undeveloped at present. Twenty-five metres along the ledge and just right of a hanging corner is a red arête. On its right side is the recently rebolted:

16. ESCUELA DE CALOR *** 6b 20m

A great pitch of contrasting styles. After a tricky start over a roof, juggy climbing leads leftwards up the lower wall. This is best completed quickly to gain easier-angled rock above. A couple of technical moves up the wall give access to easier rock and the belays.

A short distance to the right is a hanging left-facing corner rising above the flat roof. The wall to the left of the corner is climbed by:

17. UN DIMANCHE A LA CAMPAGNE ** 7a 20m

Gain the bolt ladder from the corner then step left and sprint up the leaning wall to reach (marginally) easier-angled rock above by a tricky move. This is still tricky and climbed trending rightwards to an artificial-feeling last couple of moves to reach the belays.

The hanging corner still contains old bolts at the time of writing. It is climbed in part by:

18. TOCINO FOR PEPINO * 6c+ 20m

Climb directly into the base of the corner using a long reach to pass the roof then follow it until forced out onto the left wall. Step left again and join the final tricky section of the previous route.

To the right the roof gets ever larger, and the rock below it leaves something to be desired. There are several routes in this section, though quite how they get across this formidable obstacle is somewhat open to question. Either the local climbers are very tall or some form of combined tactics has been used to reach the initial holds on many of the routes. Bringing a short step-ladder might not be bad idea.

Eight metres to the right of the corner of TOCINO FOR PEPINO and just past an open scoop is a steep crack-line with new bolts (and old rust marks) running alongside it.

19. FLESH FOR DANI *** 7b 20m

The roof is 3m across and 3m off the ground! Improvise a way around this using drilled holds, then follow the steep sustained and technical crack-line up the gently leaning wall to the lower-offs.

20. COMPIEDRAS ** 7a+ 16m

Eight metres right again is shallow crack in a groove above the lip of the overhang. The roof proves formidable! Once through it, step left and follow small holds up the brown-streaked arête which eventually eases. Hard for the grade.

Just to the right is a route with odd-looking rather rusty bolts set in much fresher looking glue.

21. CANCAMOS ** 7b 20m
Climb the initial overhang then trend left into the shallow open groove. Up this then continue (if you can) up the more open wall above. The route offers good climbing rather spoilt by a final hideous move.

22. MIGUELS *** 7a+ 22m
Start as for previous route to get through the initial overhang, then follow the line directly up the leaning wall at the junction of the yellow and brown rock. Magnificent technical climbing throughout with a baffling sequence up the final blind groove.

23. LA CALLE DEL RITMO *** 7b+ 22m
Starting above a huge white block on a vegetated section of the ledge is an open groove in the left side of a bay. Start right of the groove and climb the centre of the smooth white face before trending slightly left to enter and climb the red groove by fierce sustained moves.

24. PSICOMAMBO *** 6c 22m
At the right side of the open bay is a line of bolts above the lip of the overhang. Pass the roof by using a prominent red pocket. Once over the roof swing awkwardly out right then step back left to follow the pleasantly technical open groove. The sting in the tail is a final tricky (and fingery) sequence to the lower-offs.

To the right the ledge that has run below the whole face fizzles out and the base of the cliff steps down 3m. Around the arête to the right is an impressive red corner severely undercut at its base and rising above a cave that tunnels up into the cliff. This corner is the classical COLESTEROL PARTY. To the left of the corner there are three much steeper routes.

25. PELI ** 7a 12m
Climbing the impressively steep left arête of the cliff is this short and sharp offering.

Climbing the centre of the severely overhanging face and marked by new bolts is:

26. COCINA LIGERA *** 7b 22m
Climb through the initial overhanging wall by zig-zagging left then right before pulling out left onto the impressive left arête of the corner. Up this in a dramatic position to the lower-offs.

27. NO CAL LES SEYCHELLES ** 7a+ 22m
Start just left of the big corner and head up the short awkward wall into the base of the cave. Step left and climb steeply through the bulges, trending leftwards until it is possible to pull over onto the wall. Up this to a crucial blind reach (try up and right) to easier climbing that leads to lower-offs in the centre of the wall above.

28. COLESTEROL PARTY *** 6a 22m
A superb pitch; the best lower-grade route on the cliff by far. Climb a short soft wall to ledges below the cave that disappears up into the cliff. Pull through the roof left then swing right on a collection of massive holds. Follow the main corner by sustained bridging past plenty of bolts to a lower-off in the left wall just below the cliff top.

To the right of the big red corner a huge prickly pear cactus hangs threateningly over the cliff top. Sunbathing directly below it is probably not a brilliant idea, as it drops spiky fruit at irregular intervals!

29. BATCHCAMFT ** 7a 18m
The blunt arête to the left of the fall-line from the cactus is well bolted and well 'ard, offering thin sustained climbing with a difficult clip thrown in for good measure.

30. TENACIDAD ** 8a 22m
Five metres right of the fall line from the cactus is a bolt line up the centre of a leaning red wall. It is climbed direct, apart from a slight jig to the right at about half-height. A tough pitch on tiny holds; obviously for the tenacious only.

Two metres further right and just to the right of a thin wriggling crack-line a set of new bolts runs straight up the wall and protects one of the best pitches on the cliff:

31. POSEIDON *** 7a+ 22m
An easy slab leads to gradually steepening rock and more technical moves to reach a baffling sequence through bulges using pockets. Above this, more steep moves (just keep going!) lead to the lower-offs. A great pitch on which a three-pronged fork up the backside might just give you the impetus to succeed.

32. CHUTER FOU *** 7b 20m
Just to right is a bulging arête with a shallow white leaning groove up its right-hand side. Climb easily into the base of the groove and then follow this, with useful tufas, as it leans to the right. Difficulties are considerable and sustained.

33. GO JONHY *** 8a 18m
Start to the right of the leaning white groove and climb into the centre of a bay 7m

up. From here take a deep breath and then head straight up the sustained leaning wall, always bearing the route's name in mind.

34. ROMPEPIERNAS ** 6c+ 22m

To the right again and 10m before the arête of the cliff is a prominent brown stripe with bolts up it. Streak (not literally) up this to good holds amongst tufas high up and then finish more easily. The name means 'break a leg', but you don't have to.

35. NARANJA ** 7a 20m

Just before the arête of the cliff is a bright orange wall. This gives fine climbing on good, though often hidden, holds and with two hard moves thrown in just to keep you on your toes.

36. ESPOLON ** 6b+ 20m

The right arête of the main section of the cliff gives a good introduction to the harder climbs the place has to offer. Start on the left and make difficult moves up and right on improving holds until a rest in a hollow can be had. Step back left and pull over the bulges to the (toilet) chain belay.

Around to the right the cliff is undeveloped apart from one route up the blankest section of wall, no grade known. There are obviously some strong natural lines available across a spread of grades on this section of the cliff, and as it faces the morning sun it is only a matter of time. Across the next inlet the cliffs continue to Cala Figuera and beyond. There has been a little development here on some of the larger boulders and there is scope for lots more.

VALLDEMOSSA

Character

A pleasant set of very accessible climbs in a magnificent setting. The cliffs are in the sun from shortly after midday until it slips majestically into the Mediterranean. As might be expected with such an accessible piece of rock there has been quite a bit of development here since my last guide. Despite this there is still an awful lot of undeveloped rock in this valley.

Access

From Palma follow the road that runs due north for 15km (not the almost parallel 711 to Soller) to the small pleasant town of Valldemossa (various spellings of the name appear to exist). Drive through here following the coastal road westwards towards Andratx for a short distance until a signed right turn points to Port de Valldemossa. This twists round a small valley and then begins to descend past a quarried wall rising directly from the tarmac. Just past an impressive overhang that juts out over the road there is limited parking on the right in a lay-by (about 3–5 cars depending how well parked they are). If this is full there is further parking either before the road starts to descend or further on down the hill.

Note: Despite its constricted width, the road sees quite a lot of traffic, including occasional large lorries. Please park with common sense and keep an ear alerted for traffic.

The routes are described from right to left. The first routes are located 50m back up the road, where a clean grey pillar of rock rising straight from the road is liberally spattered with bolts. The five routes here offer pleasant enough sport on quality rock. Be prepared to skedaddle if you hear approaching traffic.

1. DERECHO COSTILLA * 6b 16m
The rightmost line is a clean grey rib which is gained via a tricky lower wall and is followed by sustained and fingery climbing on small sharp holds.

The next four routes to the left share a common belay. That being the case, it won't have escaped your notice that if you get up the easiest line the other routes can be top-roped for a bit of safe exercise or as a stress-free way of upping the route tally for the holiday.

2. RECTO CRESTA * 6a 16m
Start just left of a recess and use big holds to attain easier-angled rock, which is followed leftwards onto the face. Up this by pleasant climbing until a final couple of tricky moves gain the lower-off.

The next three climbs are very crowded. The creator of these would have done a better job just putting up two lines here and giving them a bit more independence.

3. TRIPLET DERECHO 6a 16m
Gain a ledge at 3m and then swing right to the foot of the bolt ladder. This leads steeply at first to a couple of taxing moves past a 'long gone' flake hold and then on more easily to the lower-off.

4. PERFIDO ENCANTO * 6b 16m
The nicest of the trio. From the ledge of the previous climb head straight up the rib by sustained moves on good rock. An action-packed little pitch.

Valldemossa - Roadside Cliffs

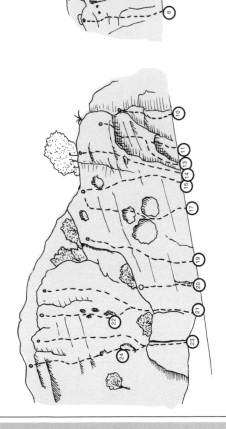

1. Derecho Costilla * 6b 16m
2. Recto Cresta * 6a 16m
3. Triplet Derecho 6a 16m
4. Perfido Encanto * 6b 16m
5. Rompe Dedos 6b+ 16m
6. Zurdo 5+ 12m
7. Izquierdo 4 8m
8. Centro 4 8m

9. Derecho 4+ 8m
10. Dali 6a 10m
11. Sostre Den Burot *** 6c 12m
12. Pepino ** 6b+ 14m
13. Pepa ** 6a 14m
14. Deidro * 6a 14m
15. Fito ** 6b 16m
16. Variante 6a 16m

17. Sophi *** 5+ 16m
18. El Jubilado * 5 18m
19. Via De Clau ** 6a+ 15m
20. Something * 6c 10m
21. Intrepido ** 6c 20m
22. Palm Olive ** 7b+ 20m
23. The Steep Route * 6b 20m
24. Kiko ** 6a+ 20m

5. ROMPE DEDOS 6b+ 16m

The left-hand line is sustained and tough, with the exit onto the upper slab offering a brief heart-flutterer. Move delicately up and right to the lower-offs. Upgraded from a stingy 6a.

A short distance down the road is an unspectacular route up a short rib:

6. ZURDO 5+ 12m

A route that is rather better than it appears, and that's not difficult – it looks very uninspiring. Start up an awkward groove, then a steep couple of moves over a bulge lead to a short 'slap' to gain the upper wall.

Further down the road and 50m from the roof that forms the right-hand end of the main cliff is a very small buttress, El Tonel, with three short offerings.

7. IZQUIERDO 4 8m

8. CENTRO 4 8m

9. DERECHO 4+ 8m

Further down the road is a large roof that hangs right over the road. To the right of this feature is a nondescript route up a short tilted wall:

10. DALI 6a 10m

Climb the steep rib and ensuing bulge to twin bolts hidden on the ledge above.

11. SOSTRE DEN BUROT *** 6c 12m

Climb the right-slanting groove with difficulty (or do the first bulge direct with even more difficulty, 7a+), then yard leftwards across the roof on buckets to a couple of powerful moves to the chains. When lowering off keep an eye out for traffic, especially big lorries and double-decker buses!

The wide slabby wall that backs the parking place now has a pleasing collection of worthwhile climbs across a range of grades. The first two of these both start up the steep arête immediately left of the cave of SOSTRE DEN BUROT. Both routes climb the initial rib and then go their separate ways.

12. PEPINO ** 6b+ 14m

Up the rib then move out right onto the steep and generally holdless wall. Climb this and the overlap to a lower-off just below the tree-covered ledges.

13. PEPA ** 6a 14m

Start as for the previous route, then trend slightly left up the steep and sustained slab and cross the overlap to reach easy ground.

14. DIEDRO * 6a 14m

Use any of the starts hereabouts to gain access to the easy groove above. Unbalanced whichever way you approach it.

Also starting from the edge of the tarmac is the original route of this section of rock.

15. FITO ** 6b 16m

Climb the easy-looking (it isn't) slab leftwards then continue up the centre of the steep wall connecting good holds by tricky moves until a final precarious and strenuous stretch gains the chains.

16. VARIANTE 6a 16m

Just to the left is another bolted line that can be used as a more direct start to the above route with no change in grade. It can also be used as an illogically difficult direct start to the much easier upper groove of EL JUBILADO.

Climbing through the strange collection of cavities in the centre of the wall is the elegant line of:

17. SOPHI *** 5+ 16m

Start just right of a deep drain and climb a thin break leftwards then head up into the first hollow, where a sit-down rest can be had. Pull awkwardly over the bulges then continue straight up the wall by sustained and interesting climbing on great rock until level with the belays on the right. Traverse right and lower-off.

An interesting route can be had by following the diagonal crack that runs rightwards across the lower part of the slab. Done originally as a traditional climb by a homesick OAP, this has now been bolted up.

18. EL JUBILADO * 5 18m

Start below the left edge of the large hollow at 10m and follow the rising crack-line rightwards until the obvious upper groove can be reached. This leads to the trees; abseil off. The name means 'the retired one' after its first ascensionist.

To the left is another line climbing through a diagonal bulge just to the right of the point where the bank starts to rise:

19. VIA DE CLAU ** 6a+ 15m

Start below the bulge and climb the sustained wall on continually surprising holds. Slant right to the left edge of the hollow in the centre of the wall then swing back left and scale the next bulge. The right edge of a shallow groove is followed until almost at the level of a ledge, then swing right to reach the belays via a classical high step.

Pete O'Donovan hanging around on Colgado (7b), Las Perchas

Just left is a short innocuous-looking thin crack.

20. SOMETHING * 6c 10m

A tough nut to crack (and it would be a tough crack to nut) being both very short and very sharp. If you wondered what Gary Gibson does on his holidays, now you know.

To the left is a short steep crack that leads to a grassy diagonal break at 12m, above the left edge of which rises an impressively steep wall with two bolt lines.

21. INTREPIDO ** 6c 20m

Climb the stubborn crack to the vegetated break then step left and storm the well-pocketed wall until a thin leftwards traverse (crux) gains a hidden flake. Swing right and make a final tough pull up to reach the chains, making sure that you clip them before pump out. Almost too exciting to be a holiday route! Originally a hairy (airy?) 6a+.

22. PALM OLIVE ** 7b+ 20m

Start as for the last climb to the break then step left and follow the left-hand line by steep sustained and technical climbing with a particularly thin cross-hands move on razor edges forming the technical crux. Another offering from GG.

Left again the path rises up the bank, and a short distance up here a tall fallen flake stands close to the rock. There are three bolt lines here, two of which share a common start before going on to find their different ways up the head wall. The far right-hand line is apparently a project. Using the same start is:

23. THE STEEP ROUTE * 6b 20m

Climb the flake then step out onto the wall (easier higher up) before tackling the holes and bulges above in a generally leftwards direction. Pull over the final bulge to reach easier rock and the chains some distance above.

24. KIKO ** 6a+ 20m

A fine strenuous pitch starting at the bottom left corner of the flake. Step right onto to the flake and climb easily to its top. Cross ledges, then follow the steepening groove to another ledge and then storm the pocketed wall above. Keep slightly left to a bulge then trend strenuously right under this to a resting ledge. Swing steeply back left to reach the lower-offs.

To the left is another route on poorer rock that is 6b.

The rest of the routes at Valldemossa are situated a steep 5 minute scramble up the bank from the parking place. Here the cliff consists of two open corners: the

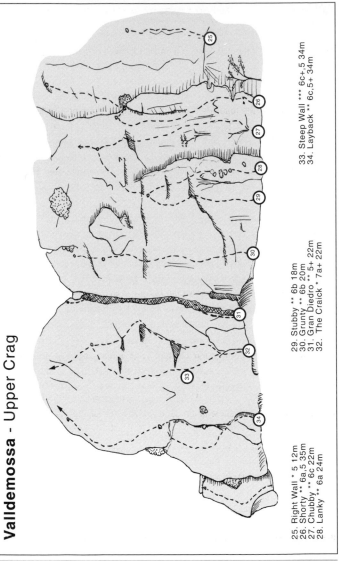

Valldemossa - Upper Crag

25. Right Wall * 5 12m
26. Shorty ** 6a,5 35m
27. Chubby ** 6c 22m
28. Lanky * 6a 24m

29. Stubby ** 6b 18m
30. Grunty ** 6b 20m
31. Gran Diedro ** 5+ 22m
32. The Craick * 7a+ 22m

33. Steep Wall *** 6c+,5 34m
34. Layback ** 6c,5+ 34m

right-hand one is steep and gloomy, the left-hand more open and popular. The routes are described from right to left, starting in the right-hand bay. The second corner is well worth a visit, especially after mid-afternoon, when the sun shines onto this section of the cliff. From the parking follow tracks steeply up left below the rock, with a short loop out right and then cross some easy-angled slabs to reach the face.

Note: this whole area was originally reached by parking before the road starts to descend below the roadside cliff, then following any one of a series of vague paths along the cliff top to a pleasant picnic-type area above the climbs, and making an abseil approach down the left wall of the corner.

Note 2: I originally made up several of the names on this cliff and these appear to have stuck, having appeared in several guides. Some of the newer routes have been named to preserve the theme. Can you guess which?

25. RIGHT WALL * 5 12m
A pleasant if slippery outing up the discontinuous crack in the right wall of the corner.

To the left is a short route to a small tree lower-off then a deep tree-filled corner. The left wall of the bay has six more routes. All are apparently in the 6c to 7a+ range, with steeper offerings on the right and easier-angled (relatively) fare to the left. Any feedback on these would be gratefully received. Just around the arête is a fine north-facing fluted wall, home to six excellent routes.

26. SHORTY ** 6a,5 35m
A worthwhile route, though the bolts in the first pitch are about ready for a face-lift. Start under the right arête of the wall and make steep pulls to gain the flutings. Climb straight up the wall on sharp holds until jugs on the left allow steeper moves into a groove. Traverse right passing one stance to a second on a ledge on the right (20m). Follow the juggy rib behind the stance to lower-offs in the lip of a bulge (15m). Note it is also possible to top out if you want to visit the cliff top. A descent can then be made (by 15m and 25m abseils) down the left wall of the large corner.

27. CHUBBY ** 6c 22m
The next (newer) bolt line left gives good climbing up the flutings, a juggy bulge and tough sequence to get back into balance.

28. LANKY ** 6a 24m
Another climb that could do with rebolting to return it to its former glory. Climb the pocketed rib and slabby wall to a lower-off just below an overlap. Without weighting the belay make a tricky pull to reach the overlap, then the slabs are climbed

trending to the right to the lower-off of the previous route. **Note:** The route used to have an easier upper pitch, though this appears to have fallen into disrepair.

29. STUBBY ** 6b 18m
Effectively a direct start to LANKY. Start just to the left and climb the flutings until increasingly technical moves gain jugs at the overlap. Easier moves lead to the lower-off, or continue up the delicate upper section of LANKY for a longer 'tick'.

30. GRUNTY ** 6b 20m
Start just right of the chimney and pull onto the fluted wall. Climb this with escalating difficulty until a sustained thin sequence of moves gains jugs over the bulge. Continue by a 'delicate layback' up the left-hand side of the immense detached flake!

31. GRAN DIEDRO ** 5+ 22m
A unique and intimidating pitch up the soaring corner line which is well worth the effort. Bridge the left-hand side of lower chimney then pull across right into the upper section. Back and foot, jam and squirm this to the corking chockstone and improvise past this to the lower-offs in the left-hand rib.

The left wall of the great corner has three worthwhile, if arduous, climbs.

32. THE CRAICK * 7a+ 22m
Start just left of the big corner/chimney and follow a crack up and right and the steep pocketed seam through the bulges. No resting out to the right!

33. STEEP WALL *** 6c+,5 34m
Start as for the previous climb, but trend left and follow the wall on better than expected holds to a taxing section just before the angle drops back, 22m. A peasant pitch up the slab above leads to the cliff top, 12m.

34. LAYBACK ** 6c,5+ 34m
The central crack-line is entered steeply and followed with conviction, especially where it ends. There is a stance a short distance above, 16m. A pitch up the rib on the left is available, leading to the cliff top, 18m.

To the left are three more bolt lines, the first one starting as for the last route, and the others climbing the steep bulges further left. They are all thought to be 7c. Any takers for checking them?

SON XANQUETE – CABO FORMENTOR

A recent small collection of mostly short, steep and hard routes in an isolated setting out on the Formentor peninsula. The place is most useful for climbers stopping on the northern side of the island who think Creveta too much of a slab. There are several projects for those into that kind of thing and quite a bit of undeveloped rock. The cliff is rather insignificant (up to 15m high) when you take a look at the amount of rock on the rest of headland, but at least it is a start! The routes have been developed by the Club Pollença de Montanysme – many thanks for that!

Note: If you have trouble pronouncing the names, it is worth knowing that 'x' in Catalan is pronounced as 'ch'. So no xeating, xipping or xuffing about.

Access

Drive from Port de Pollença towards Cabo Formentor. Pass the mirador parking for Creveta and continue out towards the Formentor lighthouse for approximately another 10km. The cliff is situated just below the exit of the only tunnel on this section of road. There is one parking place on the left as you exit the tunnel (3 cars) and some more small lay-bys further on near the next mirador. From the parking place by the tunnel walk up the road and cross the crash barrier just past the kilometre post and the tunnel sign. Continue down the hillside past a large fallen block and around the right-hand side of the cliff to reach its base. There is another cairned path leading from the middle of the crash barrier to the top of the cliff if you can't wait to get a top rope on (see map and diagram).

Some of the first bolts are quite high so a clip stick might be found useful if you don't want to end up in the bushes!

The routes are listed from right to left (see diagram). All lengths are approximate, though you definitely will not need a 60m rope here!

On the right-hand side of the cliff are three short and steep offerings, and they set the scene for the rest of the place:

1. UNNAMED 5+ 8m
The first line on the cliff.

2. MAO SE LA TU 6a 8m

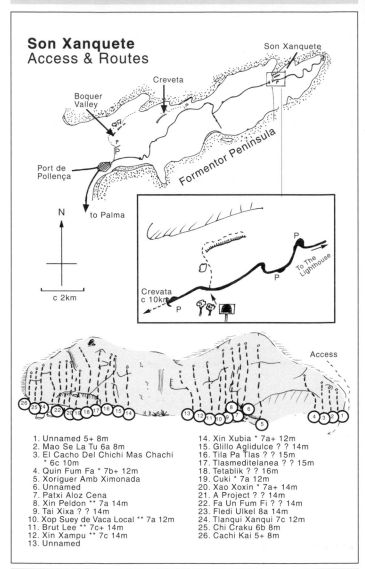

Son Xanquete
Access & Routes

Son Xanquete

Creveta

Boquer
Valley

Formentor Peninsula

Port de
Pollença

N

to Palma

c 2km

Crevata
c 10km

P

To The Lighthouse

Access

1. Unnamed 5+ 8m
2. Mao Se La Tu 6a 8m
3. El Cacho Del Chichi Mas Chachi * 6c 10m
4. Quin Fum Fa * 7b+ 12m
5. Xoriguer Amb Ximonada
6. Unnamed
7. Patxi Aloz Cena
8. Xin Peldon ** 7a 14m
9. Tai Xixa ? ? 14m
10. Xop Suey de Vaca Local ** 7a 12m
11. Brut Lee ** 7c+ 14m
12. Xin Xampu ** 7c 14m
13. Unnamed

14. Xin Xubia * 7a+ 12m
15. Glillo Aglidulce ? ? 14m
16. Tila Pa Tlas ? ? 15m
17. Tlasmeditelanea ? ? 15m
18. Tetablik ? ? 16m
19. Cuki * 7a 12m
20. Xao Xoxin * 7a+ 14m
21. A Project ? ? 14m
22. Fa Un Fum Fi ? ? 14m
23. Fledi Ulkel 8a 14m
24. Tlanqui Xanqui 7c 12m
25. Chi Craku 6b 8m
26. Cachi Kai 5+ 8m

Next left is this three-bolt offering.

3. EL CACHO DEL CHICHI MAS CHACHI * 6c 10m
Just to the left with a steady start and hard finish.

4. QUIN FUM FA * 7b 12m
Left again – another climb of escalating difficulty.

To the left are three projects:

5. XORIGUER AMB XIMONADA, 6. UNNAMED and 7. PATXI ALOZ CENA.

Starting from a ledge is:

8. XIN PELDON ** 7a 14m
A steep pitch with a bolt-on hold to finish.

9. TAI CHICHA ? ? 14m
Currently contains old rusty studs, possibly a project cum aid route!

10. XOP SUEY DE VACA LOCAL ** 7a 12m
A sharp outing that has also been given 7c.

11. BRUT LEE ** 7c+ 14m
A blobby outing with the crux where the blobs aren't.

12. XIN XAMPU ** 7c 14m
Currently the last (climbed) line on the right-hand side of the face.

Just left is a project, **13. UNNAMED**.

Pass round behind the scratchy bushes and below more leaning rock (and a snake pit) to reach the left-hand side of the cliff.

14. XIN XUBI * 7a+ 12m
The left-trending line 10m left of the bushes eases with height.

To the left are four projects that will be the best routes on the cliff when they are completed:

15. GLILLO AGLIDULCE ? ? 14m

16. TILA PA TLAS ? ? 15m

17. TLASMEDITELANEA ? ? 15m

18. TETABLIK ? ? 16m

19. CUKI * 7a 12m
An awkward start, steep centre and tough blobby finish.

20. XAO XOXIN * 7a+ 14m
More uphill blobby work just to the left.

21. A PROJECT ? ? 14m

22. FA UN FUM FI ? ? 14m
Another project.

23. FLEDI ULKEL 8a 14m
This one has been climbed, but is tough at Mallorcan 8a!

24. TLANQUI XANQUI 7c 12m
The last offering of the hard offerings is short, steep and sharp.

25. CHI CRAKU 6b 8m
The penultimate route.

26. CACHI KAI 5+ 8m
The crag finishes pretty much as it started!!

OTHER AREAS

Here are brief notes on a few localities that have at least some development and might be of interest if you are in the area or just want to get away from the crowds.

CALA SAN VINCENTE

This small but popular resort is situated at the end of the valley that runs parallel and to the north-west of the Boquer Valley. It is worth a visit to gaze across at the huge cliffs of the Caval Bernatt across the bay and wonder just how good the rock really is. Between the resort's two beaches is a rocky headland sticking out into the bay. There are quite a number of old and very rusty bolts splattered around the wall that runs out over the sea, and the occasional name and grade painted below some of the easier lines towards the right side of the face. Unfortunately much of the rock is not as good as you might have come to expect on the island. The cliff also has some obvious potential for girdling and bouldering. As the Mediterranean is effectively non-tidal, all you need is a calm day, chalk bag, swimming trunks and rock boots.

SA COMA (not checked)

Above the village of the same name (between Cala Millor and Porto Cristo) is a small crag with about a dozen routes, mostly in the 6s. Any feedback would be welcome.

CALA LLOMBARTS AND CALA FIGUERA

Two small areas to the south and north of CALA SANTANYI might be worth a look, though current information suggests that the original bolts have rusted away.

TORRENTE DE PAREIS

There are two areas of limited climbing development around the spectacular gorge of the Torrente de Pareis. The descent of the gorge itself is a classic half-day through-trip, passing some magnificent rock scenery. It is best attempted after a dry spell and requires a pick-up team to collect you at the exit from the gorge. See June Parker's *Walking in Mallorca* (Cicerone) for full details.

The **bottom end** of the gorge, Sa Calobra, is reached by a tortuous road usually occupied by many huge coaches shunting the tourists in and out. There is a wealth of rock hereabouts, but the inaccessibility of the place has led to very limited development. There are also some impressive pieces of rock half-way down the road at the point, most notably where it passes between a huge tower and the mountainside. From the car parks, bars and restaurants, a series of short tunnels leads through the cliffs to reach the beach at the lower end of the Torrente de Pareis. Above the first of these is an old bolt ladder that runs a long way up the face and looks like an old aid route. Around to the left of the second tunnel a concrete walkway runs under the cliff and above the sea. There are two routes that start from this – both look worthwhile and not too hard. On exiting from the final tunnel there is a bay on the right with a black slab that runs up into steeper rock. There are two more climbs here that share a common start up the slab and then follow different ways up the steep upper section. While you are there check out the number of cats! In the centre of the gravel beach at Sa Calobra there is a rock tower about 20m high, and there are three steep and worthwhile-looking pitches on the western side of this obelisk. On the far side of the gorge is a tall wall that rises above a seasonal pool and contains at least one route. I have also heard rumours of routes on a steep fluted wall about 30 minutes' walk up the ravine, and on a large sea cliff around the next headland from the beach. Also the bouldering hereabouts is great.

The other area of development at Sa Calobra is at the **top end** of the gorge and this is most easily reached from Escorca, which is the parking place for the start of the aforementioned through-trip. A footpath is followed through olive groves and then starts a long descent on a well-made path to the top end of the narrow section of the gorge. On the descent the impressive tower visible on the far side of the gorge is where the routes are located. Opposite the point where the narrow side branch of Sa Fosca joins the main gorge from the left is the towering cliff of THE ENTREFOC. There are (at least) two multi-pitch climbs on this magnificent

The Entrefoc

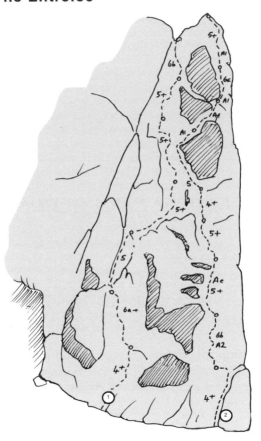

1. Via Rectal 4+, 6a/b, 5, 5+, 5+, 5+, 6b

2. Via Antonio G. Picazo 4+, 6b/A2, 5+/Ae, 5+, 4+, 5/A1, 5/A1, 6a/A1, 5+/A1

300m pillar, and it goes without saying that they are not sport climbs. A full rack and double ropes would appear eminently sensible for an attempt on either of these routes. According to the topo I have seen to the cliff, starting at the crack to the left of the foot of the main arête of the buttress is the VIA ANTONIO G. PICAZO, which is eight pitches long. The pitch grades are 4+, 6b/A2, 5+/Ae, 5+, 4+, 5/A1, 5/A1, 6a/A1 and 5+/A1. It may well be free climbable at a not too lofty grade.

Up the bank to the left is the more amenable sounding VIA RECTAL (up the backside of the cliff??), which starts at a right-slanting ramp and has six long pitches graded 4+, 6a/b, 5, 5+, 5+, 5+ and 6b. For both climbs a descent is available by scrambling off the back of the cliff and descending back to the point where the path from Escorca arrives at the river. Although these routes are long and something of an unknown quantity, they are probably nothing when compared to the walk back up to the car!

PRACTICAL INFORMATION

THE MAJORCA BULLETIN

This is a useful daily newspaper written for expatriate Brits. It is available in newsagents for 100 pesetas and is free in most bars. It always makes a big deal about the weather back home and is worth buying for that alone. It also carries a lot of useful phone numbers – police, ambulance, consulates, etc – and has a list of all the 24-hour chemists open each day.

TOURIST INFORMATION

Every resort has a Tourist Information Office that will help you with accommodation, car hire and the like. The staff invariably speak English and are very accommodating, though remember that office hours are the norm, and that in Spain that includes a siesta. If you cannot locate the local Tourist Information phone the main Palma office on 712216 and they will point you in the right direction.

SHOPPING

There are several truly huge hypermarkets that are worth stocking up at, in the interest of economics, as savings are in the order of 25% to 30% over the smaller supermarkets. They sell absolutely everything and accept Visa as well as sterling!

The 'Continente' on the right side of the motorway when travelling towards Palma is convenient, though there are others on a similar scale scattered around the island. Also look for 'Mercadona' and 'Pryca' – you can not miss them! Alcoholic drinks are especially cheap from the hypermarkets (e.g. 70 pesetas for a litre of beer, 450 pesetas for a 750cl bottle of whiskey, and wine upwards from 70 pesetas a litre). Have a good holiday and don't forget the climbing!

EATING OUT

The island has literally tens of thousands of good eating places. For cheapness (around 400 pesetas for chicken and chips) look for the places with photographs of the meals outside. For something more up-market, and not necessarily a lot more expensive, go for the restaurants with Spanish names. As you might expect, the seafood is often exceptional.

CLIMBING SHOPS

The only climbing shop in Mallorca is in the centre of Palma at Via Sindicat 21, Pati (Tel. 716731), which is just to the east of the larger Plaza Major. The shop is called Es Refugi and moved a couple of years ago around the corner from its original location (which is now a sex shop). It carries stock at prices rather cheaper than back home. Boots are the best bargain, but they do not carry a very large range of sizes, especially if you have got big British feet. Visa is accepted. The easiest way to get to the shop is to park in one of the pay and display car parks on the sea front and then to walk past the cathedral in a north-easterly direction. It takes about 15 minutes if you don't get lost. Try using a map!

THE BRITISH CONSULATE

If you need the consulate (and fingers crossed that you don't) it is situated outside the western edge of the Plaza Major (Tel. 712445 or 712085), conveniently 2 minutes' walk from the climbing shop.

24-HOUR PETROL STATIONS

Many of the island's petrol stations are not open on Sundays, or over Bank Holiday (and those appear to be almost weekly). There are 24-hour petrol stations at the airport, Campos, Callade la Calma, Santanyi, Manacor, Inca, Andratx, Puerto Alcudia and of course in Palma. Not all of them stock unleaded. If in doubt keep at least half a tank full.

TRAINS

Trains leave from the Plaza Espana in Palma for Soller and Inca.

Palma to Soller
8:00, 10:40, 13:00, 15:15, 19:45

Soller to Palma
6:45, 9:15, 11:50, 14:10, 18:30

Trains run to and from Inca, in the middle of the island, roughly every hour from 6:00 in the morning to 22:00 at night.

FERRIES

Ferries run from Palma to the other Balearics and to the Spanish mainland. An island-hopping holiday is a possibility.

Ferries from Palma (winter timetable) to:
Barcelona: 23:30 every day and 13:00 Tuesdays and Saturdays
Valencia: 12:00 every day except Sunday; 24:00 Sunday
Ibiza: 10:00 Wednesday and Friday
Mahon: 9:00 Sunday

OTHER ACTIVITIES

What is there to do if you fancy giving your fingers a rest day? Well apart from the hill walking, bars and restaurants, the beaches, the discos and the nicknack shops, there are a few other things to pass the time away. For starters try one of the show caves. They are warm, dry and on a scale unimagined in the UK. Entry prices initially appear rather high, though you will get your money's worth. If you fancy something different go wind-surfing, snorkelling or for a ride in a glass-bottomed boat. For more excitement give the water park 'Agualandia' a try. It is located between Benisalem and Inca on the C713. Also at Inca are leather factory shops that are renowned throughout Spain – just the place for that last minute present. For something more relaxing try bird watching. Take a trip to the vast reed beds at La Albufera between Alcudia and Ca'n Picaort, on the north coast. There is a network of footpaths and hides, and rarities are commonplace!

If all that fails to entertain you, get up in 'them thar hills', locate your own crag X and get it developed.

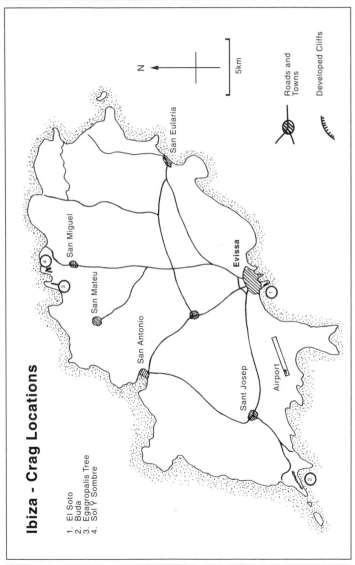

Ibiza - Crag Locations

1. El Soto
2. Buda
3. Egagropalis Tree
4. Sol Y Sombre

N

5km

Roads and Towns

Developed Cliffs

San Eularia

San Miguel

San Mateu

Evissa

San Antonio

Sant Josep

Airport

IBIZA

Introduction

The rock climbing on the large island of Mallorca has become better known to a gradually increasing audience, as has the general pleasantness of the island as a winter destination, especially its superb wild mountains. In fact, British hill walkers have been escaping the cold rain of our own hills for this Mediterranean paradise for a number of years and rock climbers are just beginning to catch on. It turns out that all of the Balearic islands are composed of limestone, and although Minorca is generally low lying, the smaller island of Ibiza is quite rugged, with hills rising to almost 500m and extensive sea cliffs ringing large parts of the coastline. Of course Ibiza does have a famous place in the 'Brits abroad, summer on the Costa' syndrome and an August week spent in San Antonio would put most climbers off all forms of mortal life for ever. On the other hand the winters here are exceptionally quiet, the place has some of the finest beaches in the Mediterranean and Ibiza is reported to have the most equable climate of all the Mediterranean islands. At the moment there is enough climbing here to fill a week for most folk, though the island is perhaps best used as somewhere to get a winter break in the sun and to mix climbing with other less energetic activities. The proximity of Mallorca and the existence of frequent ferry crossings points to the possibility of a two-centre holiday, if you fancy a change of scene or doing a bit of 'island hopping'.

Flights to Ibiza are cheap and frequent throughout the summer; in the winter they are rather less frequent and even less expensive. There is ample accommodation, though a base on the south coast is probably the best bet as this is the most central, with the roads radiating from Evissa (as the locals call Ibiza town) offering easy access to the whole island. A car is pretty much essential. See the Mallorca section for the details of Premier Car Hire, who have a depot on the island. Camping is generally discouraged, a throwback to the rosy days of hippydom when the island was a venue for the 'flower power brigade', though with a bit of discretion it would probably be possible to bivouac near the chief cliff of Buda. Sleeping on one of the beaches is liable to get you moved on by the local police, unless you can find somewhere well out of the way. At present there are only 15 or so climbers on the island and they are kept busy developing new cliffs. A call into the climbing shop in Evissa, which is at no.12 (the northern end) Calle de Ramon Muntaner (named after a local historical hero and not a climber), should elicit the whereabouts of the latest place to be and be seen. Buying any topos that are available will help with the cost of bolting new areas.

All of the routes described here are on limestone, much of which is very sharp. Good bolt protection is the norm, and as on Mallorca the grades tend to be a touch on the tough side. There is one extensively developed cliff on the island and three other less important venues. These are described here in clockwise manner, starting actually in Evissa city. Enjoy your visit.

EL SOTO

Character

A fairly uninspiring set of climbs unless you especially enjoy short brutal overhangs. The cliff is close to Evissa town and the setting is pleasant, especially late in the day when the low sun shines across the bay onto the cliff. There is also the potential for some good traversing as long as you don't mind falling into the sea when you finally pump out.

Access

The cliffs are located in a west-facing position below the rocky heathland that is situated on the promontory to the west of the fortified walls of the old city of Evissa. Tacking through the complex built-up area to this general vicinity should locate either one of a pair of rough roads that run out onto the heath. The higher one arrives on top of a small hill and the lower one ends close to the sea by a high wire fence. The cliffs are located under the highest part of the coast here, directly downhill from the higher parking point and a 2 minute uphill walk from the lower one (see access map). A loose open gully located in the centre of the cliff is descended, keeping to the right until it is possible to turn left (looking out), at which point a short easy traverse should locate the first bolts in a prominent block overhang. The climbs are described from left to right as they are approached.

Geography

The left and right extremities of the cliff both plunge straight into deep water and the developed section is located in the centre. This is split by an open corner that is wave-washed at its base and can be tricky to cross if any real size of sea is running. The present collections of climbs are centred around the two prominent overhangs that are the main features of the cliff.

After descending the gully and turning left (facing the sea) the first feature of note is a block overhang with two bolt lines through it. These are:

1. YASTA 5+ 8m
Gain the left-hand line from the left, pull powerfully over the roof and finish easily.

2. PATO 6a+ 8m
The right line tackles the roof at its widest point and gives a short, sharp struggle.

El Soto - Access & Routes

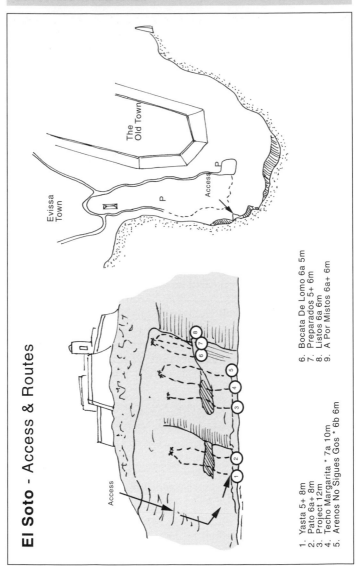

1. Yasta 5+ 8m
2. Pato 6a+ 8m
3. Project 12m
4. Techo Margarita * 7a 10m
5. Arenos No Sigues Gos * 6b 6m
6. Bocata De Lomo 6a 5m
7. Preparados 5+ 6m
8. Listos 6a 6m
9. A Por Mistos 6a+ 6m

Around the arête to the right is a leaning wall starting from the water's edge or, alternatively, from an undercut ledge 5m up. This face is supposed to have been climbed by MAS PIMIENTA MARIA (grade unknown), though it did not appear to have been bolted on our visit.

*To the right is a deep corner which can be tricky to cross if the sea is at all rough; traverse awkwardly round this or paddle across. On the other side of the inlet is a large block overhang above a slab, with **3. PROJECT** on the left and the most worthwhile (though it's not that good!) route on the cliff crossing it:*

4. TECHO MARGARITA * 7a 10m
Follow the bolt-protected crack-line across the roof using good holds, then at the lip swing right and make difficult moves to easier ground.

5. ARENOS NO SIGUES GOS * 6b 6m
The right edge of the roof is followed past a thin green thread and bolts until it is possible to gain the slab above.

6. BOCATA DE LOMO 6a 5m
Around to the right is a right-slanting white rib on the side wall, which is climbed to the lower-off used by the previous climb.

Around to the right is an easy ramp which slopes up to the right ending above a big drop into deep water. Above this ramp are three short climbs, only one of which is fully bolted at present.

Note: It is possible to escape back to the cliff top by climbing the short wall above the lower end on the ramp (Diff/grade 2) to gain easy ground and thus avoid the paddling. The rock is a little suspect so don't fall off. Unfortunately this isn't a suitable way down, chiefly because of the difficulty of identifying the correct place from above.

The final three climbs end at a mutual lower-off, and considering the poorly protected nature of two of these climbs they appear to make good candidates for top-roping.

7. PREPARADOS 5+ 6m
The left-hand line is climbed trending rightward to a lower-off just below the grass.

8. LISTOS 6a 6m
The central line is unbolted at present.

9. A POR MISTOS 6a+ 6m
The right-hand line has well-spaced bolts: don't fall off until you have the first one clipped.

BUDA

Character

On the eastern side of the Cap d'Oliva close to the south-western tip of the island are the extensive and relatively well-developed cliffs that go under the title of Buda. The rocks here look south-east over an idyllic bay and are in the sun until about 3pm. The routes vary in height from a tiny 5m to a grand 120m, and they are almost without exception very well bolted. Much of the rock here is astoundingly sharp, and a fall from most of the routes that are less than vertical is unthinkable, with severe lacerations to the ego being the least worrying consequence of such a tumble. On the harder routes the local climbers have taken to removing the sharpest edges from the holds; if you think this sounds like chipping, it is, but don't criticise it until you have tried a few of the routes and see what they are up against. It is perhaps worth noting that there is a large amount of undeveloped rock here, including an especially spectacular wall on the far left side of the cliff; a walk down the track towards the sea will reveal all.

Access

From Evissa take the road that runs west across the island towards Sant Josep de sa Talaia. Three kilometres before the town is a left turn to Es Cubells which cuts the corner and removes the need to go through Sant Josep. Rejoin the road to Es Cubells and then 1km before the village take a right turn and follow the recently upgraded road up the hill towards the tiny harbour of Cala d'Hort. Once over the crest of the hill the impressive towers of the island of Es Vedra come into view, and a couple of hundred metres down the hill on the left is a rough track with a plum-coloured sign to 'Torre des Savinar', almost directly opposite a concrete blockhouse with partially bricked-up windows. Turn down the rough track, initially passing a wider area then bearing left until a left turn leads steeply to a flat parking area on a col, close to the cliff. A rather unstable gully runs right under the base of the cliff, and a zig-zag well out to the left offers a rather easier way down.

Note: It is worth taking the short drive down to the beach at Cala d'Hort for the impressive views of the rocky island of Es Vedra and perhaps a quick brew and a bite at one of the restaurants here (and maybe even a couple of hours on the beach!).

Mention should also be made here of the cliff's population of bright green and very tame lizards. When you get your 'buttie box' out prepare to be mobbed!

Buda - Sector Overview

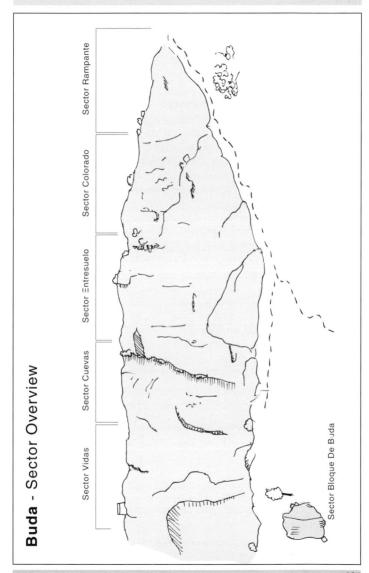

Sector Rampante

Sector Colorado

Sector Entresuelo

Sector Cuevas

Sector Vidas

Sector Bloque De Buda

Geography

The cliff is loosely divided into five sectors, though this division appears rather arbitrary due to the fairly continuous nature of the face. On the far right and just below the col by the parking is the SECTOR RAMPANTE, running along the side of the steep descent gully, which is home to many of the easier offerings on the cliff. Below this, towards the bottom of the slope and running leftwards almost to a prominent flat sandy area, is the SECTOR COLORADO. Beyond here is the rather nondescript SECTOR ENTRESUELO, and left again the massive caves that mark the SECTOR CUEVAS. To the left the cliff reaches its highest extent in the SECTOR VIDAS, and here lurk a small number of longer offerings amongst a lot of virgin rock. The impressive tilted wall even further to the left will doubtless offer some desperate sport in the fullness of time.

Each of the sectors and all of the routes are described from right to left, as this is the usual direction of approach.

SECTOR RAMPANTE

The first section of cliff comprises the easier-angled and rather shrubby walls that run along the side of the steep slope directly below the car park. Some of the Spanish grades are a touch on the mean side here and all the routes have their names painted on the rock, though some are rather faded.

At the top of the slope is:

CUERDAS Y CUCHILLOS 4+ 6m
A short, steep and sharp wall starts behind a tree and leads to a ledge and cave. Continue up the wall above.

CAP DE FABA 5 12m
Start from a small flat area and climb past a hanging block in the rim of a cave to where easier climbing leads to a lower-off close to the top of the wall.

Further down the slope is a 3m high flake.

E.G.B. 4+ 15m
Start by the flake and trend leftwards up the lower wall then continue up a rib and the steeper rock above.

SI NO LO VES NO TE LO DES * 6a 8m
Start below a conspicuous bright blue initial bolt just left of a bush. Climb the fine slabby rock to a possible belay on ledges. Lower off from here or better continue up:

TARARI QUE TE VI 5 12m
Follow the bolts up the wall above the lower-off of the previous route, trending slightly leftwards. Rather confusingly the name of this route is painted at the bottom of the cliff, next to the bolt line used by the next climb.

UNO MAS UNO * 5 16m
Start behind a bush, and climb past an odd rusty ring bolt into a hollow and on up the steeper rib above before trending right to the lower-off used by the previous climb.

FACSIMIL 4+ 15m
Left again, climb up past a yellow patch of rock onto rib and press on direct to ledges. Lower off.

PARAGIRDLING * 5 15m
A spelling mistake or a whole new sport? A couple of metres left start up a rib of quality rock and press on over some yellow blocks to the lower-off of the previous climb.

VARIANTE DE LEVANTE 5 15m
A rather trivial rhyming variation start to the previous route, climbing a rib past bushes then moving right to join the parent route.

ESKUARTAKO 4+ 4m
The short leaning wall leading to a tree with *in situ* slings is unremarkable in the extreme.

SECTOR COLORADO
This sector starts at a rounded arête some distance up the slope from the lowest point of the cliff and behind some trees growing close to the rock. This is just to the left of and down the slope from the easy break/ramp that bounds the left side of the SECTOR RAMPANTE.

The first routes are on the smooth yellow wall immediately to the left of the rounded arête.

1. PLOU POC 6a+ 7m
The short rounded arête is climbed on its left side and has a tough start and then eases rapidly. Wire cable lower-off.

2. STIRI 6b 8m
Start just left up the right rib of a hollow then make fingery moves up the right-trending shelving ramp to join and finish as for the previous climb.

Buda - Sector Colorado

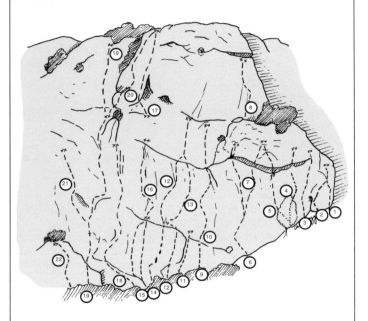

1. Plou Poc 6a+ 7m
2. Stiri 6b 8m
3. Nui For Rent * 12m
4. Incrudulo *** 7a 15m
5. Kolpez Kolpe *** 6b+ 20m
6. Espasmos De Terror ** 6c+ 22m
7. Eduardo Aqui Tienes Algo ** 7b 16m
8. Handmade 15m
9. Pikapiedra 6b 5m
10. Tocame Todo *** 7a 20m
11. Kantant Karamelles * 5+ 12m

12. Kemafsio ** 5,6c+ 33m
13. Inocentes Indecentes 7a+ 12m
14. Podenci Ibicenco * 5+ 12m
15. La Abeja No Me Deja ** 6a 14m
16. En Palma La Abeja ** 6c+ 12m
17. Red Hot Chilly Peppers ** 6c 18m
18. Chorrera De Dios *** 6b 25m
19. Percu Jones *** 5+,5+ 50m
20. Cave Man * 6a+ 12m
21. Gecco Blaster *** 6c+ 15m
22. Madonna Igual 6b 10m

3. NUI FOR RENT * 12m

The smooth-looking wall to the left is climbed starting from the left side of the hollow of STIRI. Up this on sharp holds (black bolts), gradually easing as height is gained. By the way, what is a nui anyway?

The next series of routes all climb up to and then cross the prominent narrow overhang that runs across the face 10m to 12m from the ground. The first two routes start in the same place, just to the left of wiry bush growing close to the rock.

4. INCRUDULO *** 7a 15m

A fierce pitch. Start at a 1m wide hole at head height and climb the fingery and technical wall to a lower-off on the lip of the roof above.

5. KOLPEZ KOLPE *** 6b+ 20m

Climb out left then up a small black tufa by technical moves. Cross the roof at a hanging 'dong', then trend left to a lower-off on the wall above.

6. ESPASMOS DE TERROR ** 6c+ 22m

At present a large *in situ* thread marks the start of this climb. Start out left along a ramp then head back to the right to pass a potential (you wouldn't, would you?) hanging belay, with difficulty, until it is possible to pull through the roof just left of the dong of the previous climb and to share its lower-off. Using the optional stance is a highly unethical way of reducing the grade of the pitch.

7. EDUARDO AQUI TIENES ALGO ** 7b 16m

Follow the previous climb until just short of its 'possible belay', then climb the tough wall trending left to reach and cross the roof at its widest point by the prominent wide crack.

Above the lower-off for the previous four climbs is a ledge, and rising from this is the unknown quantity of:

8. HANDMADE ? ? 15m

To the left of the previous climbs and rising from the foot of the slope is a flat section of wall, 10m high and with shrubby ledges above.

9. PIKAPIEDRA 6b 5m

The shortest route on the island climbs the wall on a series of chipped holds, protected by two white bolts. The crux move is reaching the good holds by the second bolt and can be problematical until you work out the correct approach. Single-bolt lower-off.

10. TOCAME TODO *** 7a 20m

Above the previous climb is a newly installed lower-off, and forging up the leaning orange wall just to the right of this is a tough cookie, easing gradually as height is gained.

11. KANTANT KARAMELLES * 5+ 12m

A prominent right-facing flake crack is reached by a tricky (6a?) rock-over and followed to a well-bolted exit to easier ground. Lower-offs to left and right.

12. KEMAFSIO ** 5, 6c+ 33m

A good tough climb, the first pitch offering pleasant sport at a sensible grade, while the upper one is more challenging.

1. 13m 5+   Climb the lower wall on sharp holds, passing a large thin flake and a mild run-out to the third bolt, then move left to a cramped belay on a lower-off .
2. 20m 6c+ From the belay, two bolt lines continue upwards. Move left to the left-hand line then climb steeply rightwards on sharp holds to gain a scoop. Trend right out of this to join the easier-angled upper section of INOCENTES INDECENTES.

13. INOCENTES INDECENTES 7a+ 12m

Start at the cramped stance of the previous climb then move right and make hard moves on well-spaced holds gradually easing in difficulty and angle.

14. PODENCI IBICENCO * 5+ 12m

Two bolt lines to the left of the conspicuous right-facing flake is a line up a right-trending scoop starting at the lowest point of the cliff. This is followed on good pockets with the occasional long reach. Lower-off from below the steeper rock above.

15. LA ABEJA NO ME DEJA ** 6a 14m

Just left again is a white scar and this route climbing yellow rock past some conspicuous holes. The crux is reaching the largest of the pockets; from here sprint for the chains.

Directly above the previous climb is a line of bolts that heads leftwards up the wall. This is:

16. EN PALMA LA ABEJA ** 6c+ 12m

Swing right then follow closely spaced bolts to the left across the tilted wall until a couple of blind moves gain easier-angled rock. From the lower-off at the top of the slab either head down or bring up the second man and have a go at the spectacular:

17. RED HOT CHILLY PEPPERS ** 6c 18m
Powerful climbing through the bevy of pocketed bulges above the lower-off of the previous climb.

Just to the left of the last route described at the base of the cliff (LA ABEJA NO ME DEJA) is a new route not listed on the present topo, offering steep thin face-climbing. It starts from the foot of a ramp and trends slightly right to reach the lower-off above LA ABEJA NO ME DEJA. If looks are anything to go by the route appears to be at least 6c.

18. CHORRERA DE DIOS *** 6b 25m
A tough pitch of high quality up the conspicuous flowstone pillar at the left end of this section of the wall. Follow the ramp up to the left then climb the undercut flake out to the right and make a vicious move on razors out right again to reach easier ground. Continue up the tufa system above on good but spaced holds, then make more taxing moves to lower-offs in the steeper rock above.

Around to the left of the ramp and tufa of CHORRERA DE DIOS is a ledge at 3m with several short routes starting from it (technically this is really the right side of the SECTOR ENTRESUELO). Starting up the right-hand line of white bolts by two white paint spots is:

19. PERCU JONES *** 5+, 5+ 50m
An entertaining route offering sustained and interesting climbing up a devious weakness.
1. 28m 5+ Follow the bolts up the short wall to easier ground then continue until it is possible to move out to the right along a large flake and climb a tricky wall (crux) to less taxing terrain and then a stance below a slab.
2. 12m 5+ Climb the very rough slab to a bulge and cross it into a groove. Follow this to a lower-off, or top out and scramble round to the right.

20. CAVE MAN * 6a+ 12m
Really a right-hand finish to the previous climb. Start from the final stance of PERCU JONES then climb the slab rightwards to below the overhangs. Cross the bulges right then left on generous holds to finish close to (or on) the arête.

21. GECCO BLASTER *** 6c+ 15m
Start as for the first pitch of PERCU JONES then move left to follow the bolts diagonally across the leaning wall to a lower-off where the situation eases. A strenuous and technical pitch.

2. MADONNA IGUAL 6b 10m
See Sectot Entresuelo (below).

SECTOR ENTRESUELO

A rather nondescript section of rock that nevertheless has some worthwhile climbs, the majority of which are rather on the short side. Perhaps the highlight of the area is the superb sandy 'beach' below the wall, just the spot to grab some rays! The first four routes start on the narrow ledge, 3m off the ground, that is also used as the launching pad for

1. PERCU JONES (see Sector Colorado above).

The first three climbs are short offerings that all end at the same lower-off.

2. MADONNA IGUAL 6b 10m
The right-hand route (the second bolt line left of the twinned paint spots) follows a thin ragged pocket line; short and not too sweet.

3. GROG'N ROLL * 6c 10m
Smooth-looking wall just to the left; short and savage.

4. FLUJO ROSA 6a 15m
Start at the left end of the ledge and climb steeply on good pockets before trending rightwards past a tree with *in situ* thread to the lower-off.

The next route is of rather more substance than those to the right.

5. EXPLOITED KLIMBERS ** 6a+ 30m
1. 15m 5+   Start as for FLUJO ROSA, but when it bears right pull onto the slab on sharp holds then continue more easily to a belay in a bay below overhanging rock.
2. 15m 6a+   Trend left up awkward rounded ledges to below an overhanging rib then battle up this on a generally unhelpful set of holds.

6. JOSELITO *** 7a+ 18m
The tough-looking line trending slightly to the right up the wall directly above the first stance of the previous climb.

A short distance to the left is another pair of short hard climbs (the place is full of them) that share the same lower-off.

7. MI OSITO DE PELUCHE * 7a+ 12m
Running straight up the smooth brown wall is this vicious little number.

8. DELICANTESSEN GROCK * 6b+ 12m
An awkward start leads to a swing out right, and a quick spring on spaced holds linked by high rock-overs gains the chains (you hope).

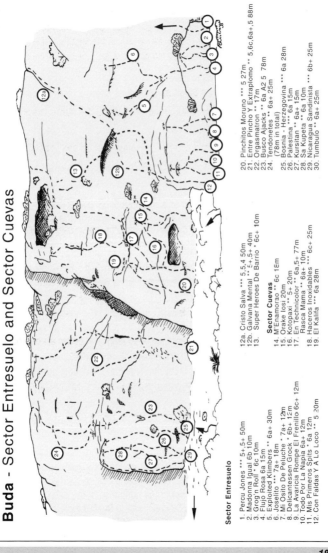

Buda - Sector Entresuelo and Sector Cuevas

Sector Entresuelo

1. Percu Jones *** 5,5+ 50m
2. Madonna Igual 6b 10m
3. Grog'n Roll * 6c 10m
4. Flujo Rosa 6a 15m
5. Exploited Klimbers *** 6a+ 30m
6. Joselito * 7a+ 18m
7. Mi Osito De Peluche * 7a+ 12m
8. Delicantes En Grock * 6b+ 12m
9. La Avaricia Nampe El Frenillo 6c+ 12m
10. Todo Por La Nampe 6a+ 12m
11. Mis Primeros Spits * 6a 12m
12. Con Faldas Y A Lo Loco ** 5 20m

12a. Cristo Salva *** 5,5,4 50m
12b. Galvana Mental ** 5+,5+ 40m
13. Super Heroes De Barrio * 6c+ 10m

Sector Cuevas

14. M'Enamorao ** 6c 15m
15. Orake Iosi.20m
16. Kotopaxi * 5+ 20m
17. En Technicolor * 6a,5+ 77m
     Rasca Manna ** 6a+ 10m
18. Haceros Inoxidables *** 6c+ 25m
19. El Kalifa ** 6a 28m

20. Pinchitos Moruno *** 5 27m
21. Entre Pincho Y Extraplomo ** 5,6c,6a+,5 88m
22. Orgasmatron ** 17m
23. Busco Ajacks ** 6a A2 5 78m
24. Tendonetes ** 6a+ 25m
     (78m in total)
25. Bosnia - Herzegovina *** 6a 28m
26. Palestina * 6a 15m
27. Kursitan * 6a+ 15m
28. Sa Kupeta 10m
29. Nicaragua Sandinista *** 6b+ 25m
30. Tumbulo * 6a+ 25m

Left again are three more short climbs, all of which finish at a lower-off on top of a short tilted section of rock above the left side of the wall.

9. LA AVARICIA ROMPE EL FRENILLO 6c+ 12m
Follow the line of white bolts past a prominent hole 7m up, then head up left along a ramp line to a finish up the right side of the tilted wall.

10. TODO POR LA NAPIA 6a+ 12m
The central line on the wall is a tough cookie for the grade on a nasty collection of pockets. Finish up the leaning wall on a much better set of holds.

11. MIS PRIMEROS SPITS * 6a 12m
The easiest route of the three is still quite hard work. Start below the left side of the wall and climb past a diamond-shaped hole. Move out right then continue on up the tilted wall above on biffos, or cop out by climbing up and left and leaning across to reach the lower-off.

The next climb is a pleasant pitch at a more sensible grade than the routes to the right, and it also offers a lead in for some extensions up the shrubby-looking rock overhead.

12. CON FALDAS Y A LO LOCO ** 5 20m
Follow the bolts up blocky rock and short steep walls to a lower-off on a good ledge system above. Either head down from here or, better, follow one of the next two routes onwards.

12A. CRISTO SALVA *** 5, 5, 4 50m
1. 20m 5+ From the belay on the ledge system traverse easily rightwards for 8m then climb the steep wall to a stance in a large cave.
2. 20m 5 Traverse horizontally right out of the cave for a short distance then climb the wall above the tree, firstly straight up then trending right to a stance.
3. 10m 4 Easy rock with the odd moment of interest leads to scrambling and the cliff top.

Starting in the same place (at the top of CON FALDAS Y A LO LOCO) but taking a rather more direct line is:

12B. GALVANA MENTAL ** 5+, 5+ 40m
1. 15m 5+ From the belay climb straight up the steep wall above to easier-angled terrain, then trend right to a belay in the cave as for the previous climb.
2. 25m 5+ Climb strenuously around the right edge of the cave roof to rapidly join and follow the rest of the previous route to the cliff top.

The final route in this sector starts from the cave stance of the previous two climbs and offers strenuous and exposed climbing in a rather out of the way setting.

13. SUPER HEROES DE BARRIO * 6c+ 10m

Start under the right edge of the cave and climb across the roof leftwards until it is possible to claw a way round onto the head wall. Continue horizontally to the lower-off then, once back in the cave, try to talk your second into stripping the pitch.

SECTOR CUEVAS

To the left the cliff becomes gradually more impressive as it runs out towards the sea. The first feature of note is a large cave rising above the 30m high shrubby slabs at the foot of the cliff, and high above, barely visible from the ground, is a much larger cave. Despite the difficulty in getting at the upper cave the effort is well worth it to examine this amazing hole in the cliff face. To the left of the lower cave is an impressive slab bounded on the left by a shrubby gully, and beyond this some impressively steep walls. Further to the left again is a fine pillar of grey rock, which forms the left side of the SECTOR CUEVAS and is home to some of the finest pitches on the cliff.

The first four climbs described are based around the lower cave, which is reached by a diagonal scramble from the right. Starting under the right edge of the cave is:

14. M'ENAMORAO ** 6c 18m

Climb up then leftwards towards a cramped rest in a hollow on the rim of the cave, before heading straight up the bulging wall past a deep undercut pocket to gain easier terrain. Continue more easily up rugged rock to the lower-off.

15. ORAKE IOSI ? ? 20m

Starts as for the previous climb as far as the hollow on the rim of the cave then continues leftwards to a lower-off shared with the next climb. The grade is unknown, though the section above the lip of the cave looks pretty tough.

The next four climbs all start at a point below the left rim of the cave and follow lines up the fine but abrasive slab above. Scramble up and left from the foot of the cliff to a point directly under the left edge of the cave. Prospective jug-jockeys should note that there are no routes out of the cave as yet. Go to it.

16. KOTOPAXI ** 5+ 20m

A good climb, though with some rather oddly placed bolts. Climb over the initial bulge by a white paint spot and head up the slab to the edge of the cave. Climb up left then traverse horizontally to the right (leaning down to clip the bolts and avoiding falling off) until it is possible to trend diagonally rightwards. One short thin section leads to easier climbing and the belays. Stripping the route is problematical so a (brave) second is required.

17. EN TECHNICOLOR ** 6a, 5+ 77m
A long and interesting trip up the full height of the cliff. The first pitch is the crux and it is possible to lower-off from the top of this, though the extension is worth doing just to get a look at the amazing cave at the final stance. Start as for the previous climb.

1. 25m 6a Pull over the initial bulges then head straight up the slab on rough rock until the bolt line splits. Trend right following spaced bolts then continue straight up to a stance on good ledges below the impressive impending wall tackled by HACEROS INOXIDABLES (see below).
2. 30m 5+ Walk rightwards along the ledge then climb straight up the wall, gradually easing as height is gained, until a ledge and belay just below 'the black hole' are reached. Bring up your second then go exploring.
3. 22m 4 Traverse horizontally to the right and then continue to the cliff top without too much difficulty.

18. HACEROS INOXIDABLES *** 6c+ 25m
A brilliant climb up the wall and bulging crack-line above the first stance of the previous wall.

Climb the sustained and technical (and chipped) wall to the roof below the crack. Pull over into the crack and then sprint up this in dramatic position before finishing up the still entertaining wall above. Mega.

19. EL KALIFA *** 6a 28m
Although really only a direct finish to the first pitch of EN TECHNICOLOR the route is well worth doing. Follow the first pitch of that route until it trends right, then continue past a recent scar (crux) to reach the prominent undercut flake that runs across the cliff. Follow this rightwards then pull over its right edge and follow easier rock to the chains.

20. PINCHITOS MORUNO *** 5 27m
To the left of and below the large lower cave is another smaller cave. Start out of this and climb through the bulges onto the slab. Follow the bolt line directly up this on very sharp rock, and with the occasional touch of interest, to a lower-off below scruffier rock. Excellent sport.

To the left is an open and shrubby corner that would doubtless be a well-polished and oft-travelled classic in Britain, whereas here it has been ignored. Where did I put that rack of hexes?

Colin Binks near the top of the superb Colesterol Party (6a), Cala Santanyi

John Addy on the Caval Bernat Ridge, Boquer Valley, Mallorca

A snow-capped El Tiede (12,200 feet) from Las Canadas, Tenerife

21. ENTRE PINCHO Y EXTRAPLOMO ** 5, 6c, 6a+, 5 88m

On the other side of the gully is a long and varied route that starts up an open rib. Unfortunately the start of the second pitch is much harder than the rest of the climb.

1. 22m 5+ Follow the bolt line up the rib over grey and then orange rock to a belay on top of the pillar below much more impressive terrain. This pitch is worth doing in its own right.
2. 22m 6c+ Climb the tough leaning wall on a series of 'excrescences' to gain entry to the wide leaning crack. Battle up this to a stance on ledges where the angle of the wall starts to fall back.
3. 22m 6a+ Climb the wall above the stance trending slightly to the right until it is possible to head left to reach more ledges and a small exposed stance.
4. 22m 5+ Again head left until it becomes logical to climb directly up the wall to a belay on the rim of the cliff. Scramble off.

To the left of the second pitch of the previous climb is a bolted line up a leaning wall. This is the impressive-looking

22. ORGASMATRON ** ? 17m

Across the previously mentioned gully is a fine high pillar of quality grey rock that is home to seven worthwhile routes. The ledges at the foot of the pillar are reached by an easy scramble from directly below.

23. BUSCO AJACKS ** 6a, A2, 5 78m

This route follows the most right-hand line on the buttress and starts just to the right of the fall line from a small but conspicuous bush about 12m from the ground. An interesting and varied route, with the rather illogical aid pitch being avoidable by climbing TENDONETES (see below).

1. 40m 6a Climb the wall on generally good holds, passing to the right of the bush and over the tip of a hanging flake, and passing bolts and threads galore to a good stance below the impending buttress above.
2. 20m A2 Aid up the buttress front until a stance in the groove on the left can be reached. Alternatively do TENDONETES (see below) to turn the outing into a *** affair.
3. 18m 5 Trend right up the groove, passing a couple of bulges to its termination, then continue more easily to the cliff top.

24. TENDONETES ** 6a+ 25m (78m in total)

The groove to the left of the middle pitch of the previous route is gained via a left-slanting ramp and followed with sustained interest to a stance where the angle drops back. Finish as for BUSCO AJACKS, 18m 5.

The next five climbs are centred around the front of the grey pillar. All offer fine strenuous climbing on good, if occasionally sharp, rock. There is a single-bolt belay on the ledges under the centre of the pillar.

Note: The groove line of TENDONETES, 20m ** 6a+, is directly above these routes and makes a logical way onto the cliff top for those who crave a summit experience.

25. BOSNIA - HERZEGOVINA *** 6a 28m
Traverse right from the belay and climb the steep juggy bulges, passing the occasional fragile holds, until the prominent bush can be reached. Climb straight past this obstruction then continue slightly leftwards to a good horizontal break before a finish up the superb rough wall to chains on the rim. Brill.

*The next two routes climb the centre of the pillar to a common lower-off. Either of them can be extended and made into a *** outing by continuing up the short and sharp SA KUPETA, which starts from these chains.*

26. PALESTINA *** 6a 15m
From the bolt belay on the ledges climb straight up the wall and through a sizeable bulge. Above this a sustained and intricate groove requires a forceful approach until a final tricky sequence reaches the chains. If you intend to continue up SA KUPETA, clip in and press on, as a rest on them is most definitely taboo!

27. KURSITAN ** 6a+ 15m
From the bolt belay on the ledges climb up and left to an *in situ* thread, then swing back to the right before climbing straight up the wall, then away finally rightwards, until a taxing sequence of moves is required to clip the chains. Once again the best trip involves pressing on up the head wall.

28. SA KUPETA ** 6a 10m
Is there a sharper route than this on the planet? From the 'hanging belay' above the two previous climbs head up the sustained slab on razor blades and broken glass. Ouch!

29. NICARAGUA SANDINISTA *** 6b+ 25m
The left arête of the buttress gives a fine sustained and airy piece of climbing. From the bolt belay trend left then climb steeply through bulges to gain a position on the arête. Blast up this direct (though a resting ledge on the left is very tempting) before powering through bulges and making a technical move on some odd holds to easier terrain. Continue up the crest of the arête in a spectacular position.

The final route in this section is something of an unknown quantity. The wall 6m left of the bolt belay is climbed by **30.TUMBULO, 6a+**, *a route which heads up* *into the corner that bounds the left side of the upper section of the pillar. From the ground it is difficult to see any bolts in the upper part of the groove; perhaps it had not been completed when we were there, or perhaps (horror of horrors) wires are needed.*

SECTOR VIDAS

The final section of cliff is this huge rambling wall to the left of the centre of the cliff. At present there are only three routes on this extensive face, and over to the left it gets ever more impressive. Of the three, one is a low-grade classic; one is a high-grade near classic; and one is an unknown quantity. Choose your poison.

1. LLAMALA LLAMAMADINGDONG ** 6b, 5, 5 95m

A fine direct line marred only by a patch of soft rock a short way up the crux pitch. The route is a significant pointer to what this cliff has in store for the future.

Scramble up to below the pillar of rock that forms the left edge of the Sector Cuevas then follow the ledge leftwards to its end. No fixed belays.

1. 28m 4 Step right and climb the short wall to easier rock, then trend left through the bushes then up a rough slab and large flake to reach a belay in a hollow.
2. 30m 6b+ Move left round the rib to the foot of the bolt line then follow the groove to the top of a small pillar. Climb the crux wall on disposable holds then trend right into a groove. Up this strenuously until it is possible to move out onto the exposed wall on the left, then climb this on surprising holds to a small stance in the base of a groove.
3. 15m 5 Move right into another groove and climb this to a more comfortable stance.
4. 18m 5+ Continue up the sustained and interesting groove above to a stance below the overhangs that cap this section of the wall.
5. 12m 4 Exit left to gain easy ground and the cliff top. Walk off to the right.

2. VIDAS EJEMPLARES *** 4, 5, 5, 5, 4- 120m

A long and committing expedition that cuts leftwards across the face following a natural weakness. The route has a rather British feel about it, as there is the odd patch of loose rock, and although most of the gear is in place much of it is rather antiquated. Despite these shortcomings the route is highly recommended to those who want a break from short, hard, well-protected climbs – as it is none of these! Carry a rack of medium wires and ten quick-draws.

1. 28m 4 As for the first pitch of LLAMALA LLAMAMADINGDONG.
2. 12m 5 Step down and move left into a crack (bolt) then traverse left to the second crack-line. This leads easily at first then more steeply (peg and old

bolt) to a cramped stance and new bolt belays on the edge of the world.

3. 25m 5+ Traverse left then cross the tricky slab (two old bolt runners protect this, the crux) and climb up to reach ledges. Move left around the corner to a flaky crack-line and follow this past several peg runners to a small but good stance. From here the trap is sprung as descent is no longer an option!

4. 30m 5 A serious pitch with little fixed gear. Climb the slab directly above the stance then trend left to below a corner. Pull past a tree into this then trend left again up the continuation slab (rather devious), passing a perched flake with care. At the level of the overhangs traverse 8m left to peg belays behind a tree.

5. 25m 4 Step left and then climb rugged ribs and short walls until the angle drops back and scrambling remains. Descend over the top of the hill to the right.

ATLANTIS is the major groove system around to the left of the two previous climbs. Its base is reached by continuing along the bottom of the cliff below the pillar of rock that forms the left edge of the Sector Cuevas. The route is four pitches long – 5+, 6a, 6c+A0, 5 – and at the time of writing it has not be re-equipped. The final stance is shared with VIDAS EJEMPLARES, and from here the route climbs directly to the cliff top. Perhaps this is that adventure route you have been looking for all holiday!

The final small collection of climbs at Buda is on the enormous boulder that lies some distance to the left of and below the climbs already described. The routes here are generally quite short (up to 18m) and hard, and perhaps the best reason for visiting this spot is the great overview that you get of the rest of the cliffs from here. On the other hand, if you want a small collection of tough cookies to throw yourself at, and in an idyllic setting, then look no further.

From right to left the four climbs here are:

MANZANO ** 6b 17m
The wall on the far right is the hors d'oeuvre.

LA REFINITIVA ** 7c 18m
The centre of the right-hand face is the main course.

ARISTA CON VISTAS * 7b 17m
The right side of the arête is the dessert.

FESTE HIPPIE *** 7a 17m
The left side of the arête is the cheese and biscuits.

OTHER AREAS

Situated on the north coast of the island are three small areas that can effectively be grouped together. Although they are not particularly high or extensive, their pleasant setting makes two of them (Egagropalis Tree and Sol y Sombre) worth a visit. The third area, Penyal de s'Aguila, has seen so little development at the moment that it cannot be recommended except for an exploration session. There is plenty of scope for new routes, both trad and sport, in all three areas and along extensive sections of the north coast.

EGAGROPALIS TREE

Character

A set of small walls that face south-east, offering superb views over part of the north coast of the island. There are about 20 varied routes here at present, with scope for more, and the place is worth at least one visit. Some of the rock is a little loose and much of it is very sharp. Development here is far from over, and there were several sets of chains suspended above unclimbed rock when we made our visit, so expect new climbs to appear between those described here.

Access

Follow the road from Evissa town northwards towards Sant Miguel de Balansat (15km). On entering the outskirts of the town take the first (or second) left turn and follow this for 1.3km to a right fork signed Es Portixol. This is followed for a further 2km until a left turn on a bend signed 'Cafe Ca n Sulavetas & Supermarket' can be taken. From this point the road is unsurfaced. Drive past the cafe and follow the main track for 0.8km to a Y-junction, and here take the right fork. Stay with this track for 0.9km, keeping left at a recently built low wall to arrive at low gate posts and a chain. Once through the chain take the left-hand track past a couple of white houses, up round some S-bends to a flat open area on a col, 0.6km from the chain. Parking here is recommended, though it is possible to turn left and drive up the steep, narrow and stony track for a couple of hundred metres to another parking area on top of the hill. (At this point it is probably worth checking the small print on your car hire paperwork. I think you will find that the hirer is liable for any damage to the underbody of the car, so watch that sump!)

Egagropalis Tree - Approach

From the top of the hill the cliff is visible to the north and is reached by a pleasant 30 minute walk. The direct approach is blocked by an incised valley, so locate a cairned path which initially heads off north-west (half-left when facing the cliff) from the parking area. Follow this down across scrubby slabs and into the trees. The path is quite well marked but it is narrow and the start is difficult to locate. The rough nature of the terrain in the area makes the effort in finding and following the track well worthwhile. It undulates through the trees and soon passes a small stone construction and barely discernible charcoal ring. Eventually the trees thin out and the cairns (and occasional arrows) are followed down and across scree and slabs into a gully. At the foot of this turn left past an impressive buttress (with two routes) to reach another gully. Descend this then turn left to pass under more undeveloped rock and arrive at the base of the central section of the best developed middle tier.

Geography

The cliff is divided into three tiers and the majority of the development has taken place on the central and most continuous one of these. The upper tier has some good roof potential, though the lower tier looks less promising. On the left side of the middle tier is a wide gully with routes on both arêtes, and to the right is a steep bulging wall rising from a ramp and running rightwards to a steep corner rising above a cave entrance. To the right a square buttress projects with a conspicuous tree on its top, and right again is an open slope. Beyond this is a bulging wall with a fine north-east-facing slab forming its right side.

The Climbs

On the descent to the main central tier a steeply overhanging buttress is passed; this contains two bolted climbs. The left-hand one is the most amenable, the very steep V-groove of BURRIDA DE RATJADA * 5+ 12m on the left, while to the right is the much more difficult KAKOJONO 6c 10m, crossing a flat roof.

On the left-hand side of the middle tier is:

SECTOR KARASKURA

NADA SINTI * 5+ 15m

ERES IDOTA ? ? 12m

1. MEJILLONES Y QUESO 5+ 12m
The sharp arête on the left side of the bay has a steep pull out of a cave to start and then uses massive sharp holds to climb the arête above.

In the very back of the bay is a set of chains above a short steep wall which still awaits the drill.

2. COMPANANIA SENTIMENTAL ** 6c 10m

The white wall on the right side of the bay has a fierce fingery start to reach the prominent large hole and then is slightly easier up the final wall. Very photogenic.

Around to the right is a steep wall rising above a slabby ramp and easily reached by a short scramble. The first climb tackles the steep left side of the wall.

The central section of the middle tier is:

SECTOR CAN SULAIETAS

3. ZORRATUTA NAGO ** 7c 18m

The bulging wall has a few well-spaced pockets. It looks both good and tough!

To the right and up the ramp a short distance are two bolt ladders up a less steep section of the wall, just to the left of some large overhangs. The two routes start separately but share a common lower-off. The left one starts from an overhung bay.

4. MALKOK *** 6b+ 18m

A fine varied pitch with some l-o-n-g reaches. Climb out of the hollow and trend left to gain a standing position on the easier-angled wall with difficulty. Continue up the wall linking large holds via extending moves until a final tricky sequence leads rightwards up a leaning rib to the chain.

5. PAIS DOGON ** 6c 18m

A tougher climb than appearances might initially suggest, with bolts that are rather unsportingly placed! Traverse left along a ledge to the first bolt then climb up and left (via a jig to the right) to enter the groove with great difficulty. Continue up and left with a long reach for a deep hole (beware of *in situ* birds), then press on up the easier groove and reach out left to the lower-off of the previous climb.

6. CORAZON DE TRAPO *** 7a 15m

The impressive roof to the right is approached via the pleasant wall and crossed leftwards on (mostly) good holds and a short jump to jugs in a bay. Grapple up the right arête of this to the lower-offs. A spectacular gorilla-thriller.

To the right is a step down in the ledge leading to a cave entrance, and above this is a smooth-looking groove protected by a bevy of bulges. Two climbs start up this, either from the cave or by stepping in from the ledge on the left.

Egagropalis Tree

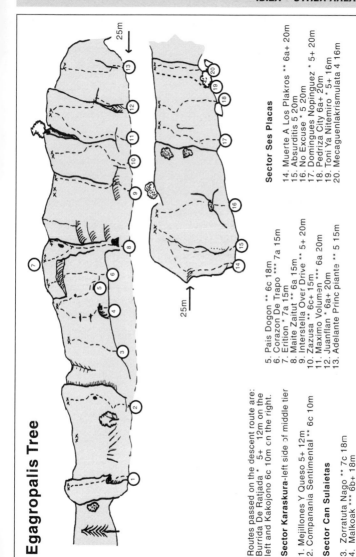

Routes passed on the descent route are:
Burrida De Ratjada * 5+ 12m on the
left and Kakojono 6c 10m on the right.

Sector **Karaskura**-left side of middle tier

1. Mejillones Y Queso 5+ 12m
2. Companania Sentimental ** 6c 10m

Sector **Can Sulaietas**

3. Zorratuta Nago ** 7c 18m
4. Malkoak *** 6b+ 18m

5. Pais Dogon ** 6c 18m
6. Corazon De Trapo *** 7a 15m
7. Erition* 7a 15m
8. Maite Zaitut ** 6a 15m
9. Interstella Over Drive ** 5+ 20m
10. Zazusa ** 6c+ 15m
11. Maximo Volumen *** 6a 20m
12. Juanflan * 6a+ 20m
13. Adelante Princ piante ** 5 15m

Sector **Ses Placas**

14. Muerte A Los Plakros ** 6a+ 20m
15. Absurdits 5 20m
16. No Excuse * 5 20m
17. Domingues Nopinguez * 5+ 20m
18. Pedriza City 6a+ 20m
19. Toni Ya Nitemiro * 5+ 16m
20. Mecaguenlakrismulata 4 16m

7. ERITION * 7a 15m

Enter the groove and climb it steeply to a deep hole with a rather fragile-feeling thread in it. From here take a big breath then head out leftwards following the lip of the roofs until a final difficult sequence up the head wall reaches the chains.

8. MAITE ZAITUT ** 6a 15m

The smooth-looking groove is less of a battle than appearances might suggest. Pull over the initial roofs to enter the groove, then follow it by jamming to a final well-positioned bit of bridging.

To the right again is a steep open book corner with a good flake crack in its back. The smooth-looking wall to the left of the corner has a belay installed at its top, but an ascent looks fairly unlikely without a considerable degree of sculpting. Access to the corner itself is guarded by a sizeable roof.

9. INTERSTELLA OVER DRIVE ** 5+ 20m

Battle round the roof (the expected hidden jug never materialises) then follow the fine sustained corner to the chains by bridging, jamming and laybacking. Pulling on the initial bolt would lower the grade to 5.

10. ZAZUSA ** 6c+ 15m

The right wall of the main corner has a tough start using some micro-tufas, then moves out to the arête via a prominent flat hold, before swinging back into the centre of the wall to finish.

To the right a square buttress protrudes from the general line of the face. It is topped by a conspicuous tree and bounded by two deep cracks. This is home to two climbs that attempt to climb the front face of the buttress.

11. MAXIMO VOLUMEN *** 6a 20m

Climb steeply up the right side of the left arête of the tower, using holds round the corner as and when needed, until forced to step right onto the face and slant rightwards towards the chains.

12. JUANFLAN * 6a+ 20m

Bridge up the steep right-hand crack system and make a baffling mantelshelf onto the good ledge above. Step out left and climb the sustained face on sharp holds to the lower-off.

Around to the right is an arête and a steep face of good rock bounded on its right side by a deep crack.

13. ADELANTE PRINCIPIANTE ** 5 15m

Climb the crack until it is possible to step onto the face (or do the direct start past the bolt at UK 6b), then climb the steep face on generous holds, apart from the last couple of moves.

Across the gully and 25m to the right is a rather scruffy-looking buttress that has a clean slab on its right side. There are some worthwhile routes here, though a bit of selectivity is required. This is the SECTOR SES PLACAS.

14. MUERTE A LOS PLAKROS ** 6a+ 20m

Start under the prow of the buttress and pull over a roof using temporary-feeling holds to enter a scoop. Continue up and over the beak above by a short jig to the right, and then back left to gain a jug on the lip and thus the slab above. Unless the logical finish has been bolted trend right to join and finish as for the next route.

15. ABSURDITIS 5 20m

A grotty start leads to greater things. Begin under the right edge of the front of the buttress and grovel leftwards into a constricted groove. Pull out of the top of this into a crack and continue up the fine slab above.

16. NO EXCUSE * 5 20m

To the right is a flake with a bush growing on its top. Climb past this up cleaned cracks (no bolts in the lower section so wires are required) then on up better rock to the lower-off of the previous climb.

To the right is a clean and well-scarred grey slab. On the extreme left edge of this is:

17. DOMINGUES NOPINGUEZ * 5+ 20m

Start just to the right of the bolt line and follow it by sustained moves on sharp holds to flaky jugs at 10m. Easier climbing remains, with a final long reach to the chains.

18. PEDREZA CITY 6a+ 20m

A technical gem up the centre of the slab offering sustained and thin climbing. Passing the third bolt is particularly perplexing. Try a sneaky left to right traverse.

19. TONI YA NITEMIRO * 5+ 16m

The slab immediately to the left of the corner gives another sustained pitch.

20. MECAGUENLAKRISMULATA 4 16m

The smooth corner on the right is approached over blocks and bushes. The climbing is OK, but the effort in reaching it is not really repaid in full.

SECTOR SOL Y SOMBRE

Character

An area with only limited development at the moment, though in a pleasant setting and worth an afternoon if you enjoy technical face-climbing. There are only ten or so routes here at present, two on an east-facing wall (Sector Sol) and the rest on a west-facing wall (Sector Sombre). The names suggest the local climbers get up early because on our visit Sector Sol was in the shade and Sector Sombre was being illuminated by the afternoon sun. Across the bay from the Sector Sol there are some impressive walls beneath a hardly less impressive hotel complex; possibly worth a visit if you are looking for an area to develop.

Access

Follow the road from Evissa town northwards towards Sant Miguel de Balansat (15km). On entering the outskirts of the town take the first left turn and follow this for 1.3km to a right fork signed 'Es Portixol'. This is followed for 2km to a left turn on a bend signed 'Cafe Ca n Sulavetas & Supermarket'. Stay on the main road, climbing through a series of hairpin bends, then continue for 1.2km to where the road bends left and starts to descend steeply. A narrow track goes straight on at this point, and is signed 'No Entry'. Drive down this past a large unfinished building on stilts in the trees on the right, and park opposite the large white villa of Casa Alba Mar. On the right here is a surfaced area in the trees, and leaving the centre of the far side of this is a track (cairned) that bends left and heads towards the sea. This is followed for 5 minutes out onto a headland with an impressive inlet on the right; below here is the Sector Sol. Continuing down to the left for a couple of hundred metres is an area of limestone pavement with a large dead tree near the cliff edge. This is directly above the Sector Sombre.

The SECTOR SOL only has two routes at the moment, though the cliff top is spattered with old bolt sleeves. Both of the routes start from hanging belays on the lip of a substantial roof, reached by abseil, and then make their separate ways back to the cliff top. The grades of these are not known, though they do not look too hard.

The SECTOR SOMBRE is better developed at present. From the large dead tree on the cliff top, a short descent down an open groove should locate chains on the left (looking out). Use these to make a 20m abseil to the base of the face. The routes are described briefly from left to right, though it is worth bearing in mind that, as in other areas on the island, more routes may appear between the ones that already exist.

Sol Y Sombre

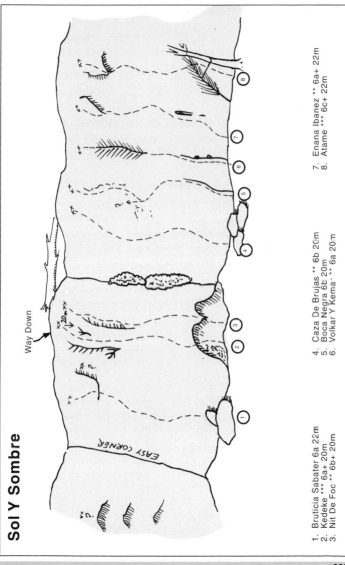

EASY CORNER

Way Down

1. Bruticia Sabater 6a 22m
2. Kedeke *** 6a+ 20m
3. Nit De Foc ** 6b+ 20m

4. Caza De Brujas ** 6b 20m
5. Boca Negra 6c 20m
6. Volkar Y Kema *** 6a 20m

7. Enana Ibanez ** 6a+ 22m
8. Atame *** 6c+ 22m

1. BRUTICIA SABATER 6a 22m

At present the most left-hand route climbs an area of slabby rock around to the left of the landing point from the abseil. Start from flakes and climb the sustained face (harder than it looks) until a pull over a bulge gains the lower-off.

Note: *Across the easy open gully to the left of this route is a bulging buttress with lower-off chains on its crest, but no other fixed gear as yet.*

2. KEDEKE *** 6a+ 20m

This route reclimbs the line of the abseil. From a conglomerate cave pull through the bulges to gain ledges then climb the bulging wall on tiny sharp holds to the easier rib above. Continue up this, cursing the bushes on the way.

3. NIT DE FOC ** 6b+ 20m

The pale hanging groove to the right is entered easily and then climbed with increasing difficulty to a tough finale up a hanging rib.

To the right is a corner choked with cabbages and other exotic vegetables, and just beyond this is a dark slab with bolts up it.

4. CAZA DE BRUJAS ** 6b 20m

The line up the slabby wall starts from a pile of blocks.

To the right are two thin crack systems.

5. BOCA NEGRA 6b 20m

The left-hand crack gives good climbing until it is necessary to swing left and pull over a bulge on a rickety hold to easier terrain. From here to the cliff top is straightforward, but there is no fixed gear and some of the rock is rather suspect. What are the locals playing at?

6. VOLKAR Y KEMAR ** 6a 20m

The right-hand crack is altogether a more edifying business. Climb easily to a deep pocket then follow the thinner crack to a deep groove where things ease again. More pleasant climbing leads to the chains.

Just to the right is a fine vertical face with two good climbs on it.

7. ENANA IBANEZ ** 6a+ 22m

Climb up and right with difficulty to a tufa then back left onto easier rock. Up this to the left corner of an overhang, then make a beefy pull over this final obstacle.

8. ATAME *** 6c+ 22m

Excellent sustained climbing on sharp holds. Start behind the tied-back tree and climb the wall trending slightly leftwards to good holds. Continue up the rib above then swing right and power through the capping bulges to gain a short easy slab.

PENYAL DE S'AGUILA

An area of impressive coastal scenery with a lot of rock, though little of it has been developed. This is the prominent rocky headland that can be seen from both Sector Sol y Sombre and Egagrapolis Tree. At present there are only four bolt lines here, and on these much of the fixed gear is rather rusty. There is plenty of scope for new routes, both traditional and modern, and the area contains many fine crack-lines and impressive overhangs in cliffs that rise to at least 100m.

Access

Follow the instructions for Sector Sol y Sombre but bear left at the 'No entry' sign. Follow the road as it weaves downhill until it eventually arrives at an extensive flat open area with some ruined buildings. Leave the car here and follow the road down to the right (looking out to sea), around two more bends, until at the final bend before the sea it is possible to descend a short awkward gully. At this point there is a large boulder of conglomerate rock. On the front face of this is ES VERITAT QUE PAREIX MONTSERRAT, 7c, though at present the bolts do not instil confidence. Traversing to the right (looking out to sea) for a couple of hundred metres there is a series of ledges well above the water line and capped by an impressive series of roofs. Here there are two bolt-protected cracks and a smoother face. One of the cracks is FRIDAY EVENING FEVER 5 (I guess the right one; what do you think?). The face route is ROSEGON 6b.

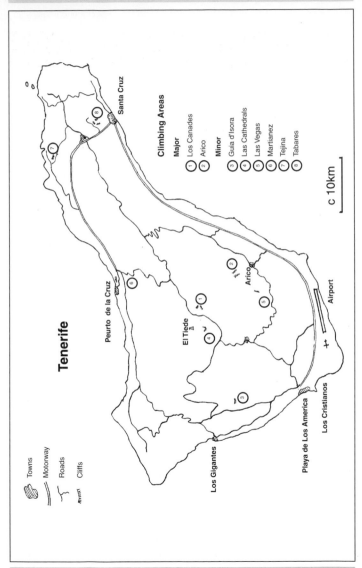

Tenerife

Peurto de la Cruz

Santa Cruz

Los Gigantes

Playa de Los America

Los Cristianos

El Tiede

Arico

Airport

Towns
Motorway
Roads
Cliffs

Climbing Areas

Major
1 Los Canades
2 Arico

Minor
3 Guia d'Isora
4 Las Cathedrals
5 Las Vegas
6 Martianez
7 Tejina
8 Tabares

c 10km

Introduction

When I first visited Tenerife in 1991 I was acting on promising information in a Spanish climbing magazine. After two weeks on the island I felt there was enough climbing here for a short visit, and so I included brief notes in the back of *Andalucian Rock Climbs*. In the event, the place has proved far more popular than I could ever have expected, and so this expanded information given here should provide enough detailed notes for a week or two's cragging for most normal mortals.

In reality Tenerife is not an ideal climbing venue – the cliffs are generally not of an international quality and they are well scattered around the island, thus entailing quite lot of driving. Mallorca and mainland Spain have more to offer the inveterate hot rocker, but (and it's a big but) the winter weather on Tenerife is quite superb, whereas in the Mediterranean it can be unsettled. If you come to Tenerife to explore the island's amazing geology, go on a dolphin safari, hike up the 12,000ft El Tiede, try your hand at wind surfing, and perhaps do some gorge walking as well as some cragging, you should come away well pleased with your holiday. On the other hand you may spend the whole of your holiday in the Lower Gorge at Arico and still love the place. People's reaction to Tenerife tends run the whole gamut from 'The place is paradise' to 'I thought it was a dump', so maybe you will have to go and make your own mind up.

Tenerife is the largest of the Canary Islands, and the whole group is sometimes known as 'the islands of eternal spring', because of their year-round equable climate. With the north-east trade winds keeping the whole island group warm in the winter and cool in the summer, the temperature varies between 20 and 30°C. As the island are only 400 miles north of the tropics it is perhaps understandable why the place is so pleasant, and swimming in the Atlantic at Christmas can be a lot more enjoyable than you might ever have imagined.

The central feature of the island is the volcanic cone of El Tiede, which rises to over 12,000ft and is the highest peak in all of Spain. In winter it is often snow-covered and can present a respectable challenge, though a cable car runs up to over 11,000ft when the summit is free of ice. There is a high-altitude refuge close to the normal route up and down the mountain, and a visit to the top is a memorable experience, with stunning views in excess of 100 miles and sulphurous vents belching out scalding steam. The journey up to the base of the volcano is enjoyable in itself as the road rises from sea level to 8000ft, passing through a series of distinctive climatic zones, from tourists at sea level, through bananas, cacti, pine trees, and semi-desert to the snow line.

By far the busiest time in all of the Canary Islands is the Christmas period, so if you intend to go and meet Santa Claus on the beach be sure to book early! Compared to mainland Spain and the Balearics (where winter is the low season) the cost of accommodation in the winter here is expensive, though it is still possible to get a four-person apartment for £160 in the high season. Avoid these times and you could save a packet.

It is most likely that any package deal will end up unloading you in one of the concrete complexes that run from the airport all the way round the coast to Los Gigantes. All of these are pleasant enough, though Playa de Las Americas is just a bit too 'hip' for most climbers, with discos and bars buzzing well into the early hours. From any of these resorts the two main climbing areas can be reached in about an hour's drive. Because of the amount of driving involved a hire car is an essential (see the notes in the Mallorca section of the guide for a UK contact number for Premier Car Hire).

Camping is a possibility, though it will by force have to be of the wild variety, and finding water can be a problem. There are a couple of discreet spots at Arico that are used on a regular basis, though if you have a hire car, sleeping out is probably as easy an option as any.

The vast majority of the climbing described here is of the 'sport' variety, though I have included brief notes on the island main trad route area for those who want a bit of adventure thrown in. Enjoy your stay.

LAS CANADAS

Character

Las Canadas remains the premier climbing destination on Tenerife at the present time, and it is well worth a visit, perhaps as much for its truly astounding setting as for the quality of the climbing. The cliffs are a pale pyroclastic rock that looks rather soft and loose from a distance. On closer acquaintance it becomes obvious that nothing could be further from the truth: the raw material is hard and rough with a preponderance of pinch grips, pockets and incut edges, all in all, a marvellous climbing medium.

The altitude of the area (2100m) is inclined to cause a bit of puffing and blowing on the first couple of visits, but on the plus side the air is crystal clear, the views are magnificent and you can get a tan in a third of the time it takes on the coast (and if you are blessed with fair northern skin don't forget the sun-block). The area looks rather small from the car park, though in reality is extensive, with over 100 routes at present and lots on undeveloped rock still to go at.

The locals have developed a strange habit of drilling pockets across the undersides of most of the more impressive roofs to give hard, gymnastic problems – being ideal for chimpanzees who do not value their tendons. For more normal mortals there is also plenty to do here.

Access

The cliffs are located inside the *caldera,* or old crater, that encircles the volcano of El Tiede and which is the central feature of the whole island. The rim of the crater is reached by any one of several access routes from the coast and the approach is well signed (see map, Crag Locations). Pick your route and then join the convoy of small white hire cars and the occasional ultra-slow fruit lorry, and zig-zag uphill for approximately one hour to reach the Boca de Tauce at about 6500ft. Follow the road northwards via lava flows, basalt plateaus, volcanic peaks and arid deserts (for about 3km!) until it rises through an area of strange blue rocks, a product of hydrothermal alteration as the signs inform you. Just past these the road flattens out and there is a sign on the right for Los Roques. Drive down the narrow road on the right just past the sign and park by the small quaint house squeezed between the lava flows. The nearest rocks are 30 seconds away.

Las Canadas - Sectors

1 Sector Psiquiatrico
2 Sector Aureola
3 Sector Sexta Dimension
4 Sector Fraggel Rock
5 Sector Rainbow
6 Sector Chumino
7 Sector Guira

N

El Tiede

The Coast

Las Canadas - Overview

1 Sector Psiquiatrico
2 Sector Aureola
3 Sector Sexta Dimension
4 Sector Fraggel Rock
5 Sector Rainbow
6 Sector Chumino
7 Sector Guiri

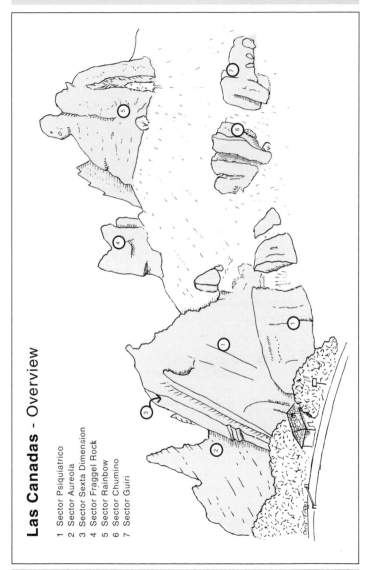

Geography

Las Canadas (the canyons) is a complex maze of towers and canyons scattered around a domed hill. The local climbers have divided the area into a series of 'Sectors' for ease of identification, and I have used the same divisions. Each sector is described briefly, with short notes on individual routes. This, associated with plan views and normal diagrams where appropriate, should ease the location of your target route or area. The sectors are described in a clockwise manner starting from the car park by the small ICONA (roughly equivalent to our National Trust) house (see map). From the car park the easy slabs that stand in front of the SECTOR PSIQUIATRICO are visible just behind the lava piles, and to the left of these is the high tower of the main part of this sector. Left again are the minarets and spires of the SECTOR AUREOLA, and hidden behind here is the extensive north east-facing SECTOR SEXTA DIMENSION. Up the hill to the right is the isolated tower of FRAGGEL ROCK, and above and right of this again is the high red wall of the SECTOR RAINBOW. Down to the right and much nearer the car park are the smaller towers that are the SECTORS CHUMINO on the left and GUIRI on the right.

Note: I have come across three separate topos to Las Canadas and they show considerable differences in several respects, especially in names and grades of many of the climbs! I have attempted to correlate these topos along with information from magazines and from local climbers, and the present best effort is presented here for your information. Best of luck.

SECTOR PSIQUIATRICO

This is the area closest to the car park and it contains many good climbs across a broad sprectrum of grades. Much of the sector faces south. The area starts with the broad slabs close to the car park, then there are some short but sharp overhangs behind the slabs, and just across the bay is the high south-facing wall that is the showpiece of this area.

The extensive slabby area in front of the car park has only two short named routes, and these are located in the gully that splits the area neatly in half. The right-hand triangular set of slabs is very easy angled and can be climbed anywhere at Grade 2 and 3. In the gully that separates the two sections there are the previously mentioned pair of minuscule climbs.

GAFITAS 6b 6m

On the right wall (looking up) of the gully is this short leaning wall, passing two chain link bolts.

TECHOS DE LOS BRAZOS CRUZADOS 6b+ 6m

The steep pocketed prow opposite the previous climb passing a solitary bolt.

The left-hand section of the slabs contains little in the way of fixed gear, but has a selection of worthwhile lower-grade climbs that can easily be done with a small rack of wires and are ideal for beginners or for grabbing a few ticks at the end of the day. None of the lines have names, though I include short descriptions here for those who want them (at least you will be able to tick off then!). There are twin bolts on the highest point of the slab useful for belaying, top roping or for using as abseil anchors. From right to left the lines are:

CRACK 2 12m
The straightforward crack and corner which starts 8m up the gully from the right toe of the slab.

CORNER 3 15m
The crack that starts at the right-hand toe of the slabs leads into a deeper corner then joins the previous line. Finish easily out right or direct with more difficulty.

RIB * 4 15m
The smooth rib has a solitary runner in the form of a hangerless bolt. Hook a wire over and try to avoid falling off!

GROOVE * 3+ 15m
The Interesting central shallow groove is climbed passing a bulge.

FLAKE 5 15m
In the left wall of the groove is a short curving flake with a bolt runner just above it. This protects the tricky crux sequence, the start and finish being much easier.

CRACK 3 12m
The crack on the right side of the rounded rib that bounds the left side of the face is pleasant enough.

TWIN CRACKS 4 12m
The parallel cracks in the front of the rib at the left side of the face have a tricky start but ease as height is gained.

Passing round to the left of the main slabs, a short scramble between the cliff and the encroaching lava reaches another slabby wall, though this one is shorter and is north facing. There are no recorded routes here, though some obvious easy possibilities present themselves to anyone who is interested. Further to the left, in the back right corner of the bay, is a series of overhangs crossed by five short but tough outings, ideal for bumpy boys (and girls) who want to escape the sun.

COITUS INTERRUPTUS 7a 10m

The right-hand line crosses a small roof low down then heads up the tilted pocked wall. Don't loose your concentration at the crucial moment. Small bolts protect.

CARDERO 7a+ 10m

Starting in the same place, traverse along the lip of the hanging slab on the left to ledges.

To the left a roof runs along the length of the face and, passing round the right side of this, is

BIOBLAST 7b+ 10m

Climb round the right side of the roof passing an hourglass shaped pillar and the overhang above with difficulty.

MAXIMUN * 7b+ 10m

Central line over the roof is the best on the wall. Start to the right of the pocket in the lower wall then pass the roofs by powerful pocket pulling.

The solitary bolt to the left may protect a direct start to the previous route, or an indirect start to the next one.

ANDRES, PRUEBALA OTRA VEZ * 8a 10m

The series of drilled and 'arrowed' pockets trend left across the widest part of the roof. Not one for those with tendon troubles.

The area in the back of the bay is described as a bivouac on the local topo, though from the scattering of 'debris' it looks like Servicio would be a more apt description. Above the right side of the back of the bay and to the right of a large prow is an innocuous looking line that is supposedly 7c. Considering its diminutive size it must be a tough one.

The left side of the bay is a fine high wall split by a series of thin diagonal cracks and home to an excellent selection of climbs. Just to make things even better the wall faces just west of south and so is almost always catching the sun. High on the right side of the wall is a large boulder with a prominent sharp arête and this is reached by scrambling up the gully. There are two short offerings here:

1. KUCABAMOKO 5+ 6m

The right-hand face of the boulder.

2. EN ESTE ANGULITO PERDI EL PITO 7a 6m

The arête of the boulder gives a route that is almost as long as its name.

On the right side of the main face and to the right of a large flake there are two routes protected by rather old bolts and sharing a lower-off.

3. ANMARILLO 6c 10m
Straight up the smooth red face on the far right.

4. ENEQUELEBRE 7a+ 10m
Climb up the 'blank' lower wall almost into the base of the open gully then trend steeply right to join the previous climb.

5. BITELCHUS * 6c 12m
The flat wall just right of the bush gives a sustained and pleasant pitch.

6. FOLLADA A MEDIAS * 6a 15m
Left again and just to the right of a large flake is a hole. Climb leftwards out of this then press on straight up the wall.

The next two climbs start from atop the large flake. Clip the first bolt before you fall off!

7. LOS ULTIMOS DIAS DEL MESIAS ** 6a 15m
The vague slanting crack-line gives a pumpy and worthwhile little pitch.

8. LA MISION DEL PEREGRINO * 6c 22m
Climb the wall to the right of the flake crack to ledges then step left and climb the more technical upper arête and a final bulge. Good positions, though feeling rather escapable.

9. DIEDRO BAVARESA ** 5+ 30m
The slanting flake and open groove give a good strenuous pitch. From the ledges above the groove move left to a belay then either abseil off or top out and scramble down the back of the tower. Carry a rack of Friends, though several of the bolts on the previous route can be clipped if required.

10. NO TEESKAKEES * 6b 22m
The rather hacked face to the left of the arête has a steep lower section past a flake and pockety bulge leading to an easier crack and a final baffling sequence on sloping holds. Escaping right onto the arête is taboo at the grade. Large single bolt lower-off.

To the left is the first of three diagonal cracks. This is:

11. VIA DEL CESAR *** 6c+ 22m
An imperial route. Climb the steep lower wall to the prominent large pockets then swing left to a big bolt in the base of the groove. Extemporise up this (crux) then follow the still awkward crack past a poor peg to a lower-off in the left wall of the

Las Canadas - Sector Psiquiatrico

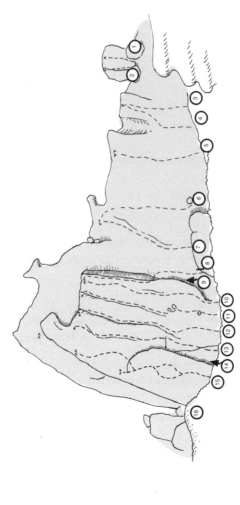

1. Kucabamoko 5+ 6m
2. En Este Angulito Perdi El Pito 7a 6m
3. Anmarillo 6c 10m
4. Enequelebre 7a+ 10m
5. Bitelchus * 6c 12m
6. Follada A Medias * 6a 15m
7. Los Ultimos Dias Del Mesias ** 6a 15m

8. La Mision Del Peregrino * 6c 22m
9. Diedro Bavaresa ** 5+ 30m
10. No Teeskakees* 6b 22m
11. Via Del Cesar ** 6c+ 22m
12. Transilvania ** 6c 24m
13. Cuajada De Pus *** 6b+ 22m
14. Waterloo * 5 12m

15. Hanky Panky * 7a 12m
16. Diedro *** 4 30m

gully above.

12. TRANSILVANIA ** 6c 24m
The groove line to the left is reached up the awkward wall using pockets and followed by good, but rather ungainly, climbing to a tricky final section. The bolts are quite spaced so a couple of small Rocks might not go amiss.

13. CUAJADA DE PUS *** 6b+ 22m
The left-hand and least defined crack-line is reached by climbing straight up the wall just to the right of a prominent flake crack. Once reached the ragged crack gives excellent sustained climbing – just keep going. The lower-off bolts are on the left at the top.

14. WATERLOO * 5 12m
The right-facing flake just left of the bushes is followed (no fixed gear) as it curves over to the left to reach lower-off bolts located just short of the arête.

The smooth face to the left of the flake of WATERLOO is climbed by:

15. HANKY PANKY * 7a 12m
The crux involves a mild run-out to the reach the third bolt. Doing this section on the right is worth 7b, and stepping out right below the lower-off and climbing the upper section of the face by a short loop is the full tick, being worth ** 7c (18m).

Around to the left of the main face is an eye-catching slabby groove line, the classical:

16. DIEDRO *** 4 30m
Follow the crack in the back of the groove (leave it till late in the day if you want to do the route in the sun) to *in situ* belays just below the top of the groove, then climb deviously to the top of the tower, absorb the marvellous view and scramble down the back to escape.

In front of the deep groove is a tall square boulder, home to one of the island's shorter offerings, a 7a boulder problem containing a single bolt just above the crux.

To the left of the deep groove is a wide slabby wall that faces the volcano, and that is home to four climbs.

OJO DEL DIABLO * 7a 25m
Climb the slab and tough overlap on the right of the face, continue up the slab above and tackle the bulging headwall direct. Pegs and bolts protect.

PLACA DEL OMBRA * 6a 25m
Behind the shallow hanging corner (bolts to the right) and the crack-line up the

smooth slab. Carry some wires.

AID A1 20m
The wall, roof and slab to the left. Remember the days!

YONONONO ** 5 28m
The crack that bounds the left side of the face gives a pitch that is well worth seeking out if you climb at the grade. Carry a rack of wires. A steep start up the scarred crack leads to bulges. Step left and pull through a bulge (peg) then follow the crack-line all the way to the top of the tower. Scramble off the back.

The final route in this sector is located a short distance to the right of the gully that leads up to FRAGGEL ROCK.

AL LORO AL LORO QUE VIENE EL MORO 6b+ tackles a bulging wall but had been debolted when I last visited the area.

SECTOR AUREOLA
A complex area of towers and bays to the north of the SECTOR PSIQUIATRICO, and easily reached by passing round the left side of the face and scrambling over blocks and lava. Several of the spires would make good objectives for traditional-style summit-bagging routes; double ropes and a few old slings to abseil from would appear to make sense. The sector is bound on the right by an open gully that gives an access route up to FRAGGEL ROCK, and the first four routes are located on the red leaning wall to the left of the gully and above some rather wiry bushes. The area faces south-west and so gets plenty of afternoon sun. The most right-hand route is:

SUICIDETE 7c 10m
An easy scoop to ledges and then the impressive roof above.

1. CHAIN BICICLETA * 7b+ 12m
The fierce hanging corner with bolts in its right wall.

GUSTAVO REPORTERO 7? 12m
The flying arête on the left looks highly improbable.

PONSELO 7a 12m
The narrow front face of the buttress over a series of bulges.

To the left is a deep narrow ravine with a route on its shady left wall.

DANDO BOTITOS 6c 12m
Follow the old bolts through the bulges.

Las Canadas -
Sector Aureola

1 Chain Bicicleta * 7b+ 12m
2 Placa De Bazochi ** 6a18m
3 El Camion De
   La Basura *6c 22m
4 Una Puta Rara ** 6c+ 12m
5 Guiripolla ** 6c 15m
6 Overkill * 7b 15m
7 Espolon Del Sol ** 6c 18m

N

The narrow front face to the left of the ravine has an unnamed and ungraded climb over the prow then on up the steep wall on jugs.

Around to the left is a north-facing slabby wall bounded on the left by a corner crack. It is home to a couple of worthwhile and delicate offerings:

2. PLACA DE BAZOCHI ** 6a 18m

The right-hand line has good sustained moves up the slab and a tricky roof at the top. Move left to the lower-offs.

PEOR ** 6b 18m

The left-hand line has a sketchy central section and an awkward bulge above.

DIEDRO ** 5 22m

The peg-scarred corner in the angle of the bay is good; the drawback is that you have to place your own kit.

To the left is a wide striated wall with a large perched flake in its centre. This is home to three climbs.

AUREOLA 6c 12m

The right-hand line follows a thin crack that trends right and is protected by rather ancient bolts.

REY DEL POLLO FRITO * 7a 12m

Immediately to the left is this route, 'the king of fried chicken', protected by chain-link bolts. It pulls through a stubborn bulge to reach a shiny new lower-off on the prominent ledge system.

3. EL CAMION DE LA BASURA * 6c 22m

Climb easy rock to a point just left of the perched flake then follow the green bolts with a jig to the left at the third clip. Not as rubbish a route as the name might suggest.

Just around the arête to the left is a hanging groove tackled by:

LA QUILLA * 6c+ 15m

Pull into the hanging crack and climb this until it is possible to get out onto the face on the right. Up this to the top.

TECHO GORDO DE PETETE * 7c 15m

The orange leaning wall to the left is climbed (surprise, surprise) on a series of drilled finger pockets.

The rest of the routes in the Sector Aureola are located on the convoluted west-

facing walls across the opposite side of the bush-filled bay. The first of these starts in the back left corner of the bay, where a short scramble up a slab leads to the base of a rounded buttress, with two bolt lines on it. One of the local climbers has done a girdle traverse of this whole wall (DECADENCIA FISCAC 6c), and this fact explains the existence of occasional single bolts in the middle of nowhere. Further up the gully from the rounded buttress is a solitary route, which presumably climbs the impressive spire via the scoops and roof: CONSUMIR PREFERENTEMENTE 6b+.

LA PUTA RARA Y SU HIJA ** 7a 12m

The right-hand line on the rounded tower climbs the thin rightward-trending crack and the wall above on pockets. Also known as MIERDILLA DE HISTORIA on some topos.

4. UNA PUTA RARA ** 6c+ 12m

The left-hand line. Closely spaced chain-link bolts protect this sustained pitch.

The next two routes start at the very base of the gully used to get to the previous pair of climbs and climb the tower directly above this point. They share both the starting moves and the lower-off station.

TAKE A BIT ** 6c 15m

Bridge the lower crack then tackle the right side of the tower which sports nice new bolts. Steep and satisfying.

RAYA KAYAC ** 6c 15m

The hanging crack up the front of the tower – another route worth seeking out.

To the left is a buttress rising above a large white block. There are three routes here, though the topo only shows two.

An UNNAMED ROUTE trends right up a ramp then climbs the steep left wall of an open groove and over a small overlap to two large rings. It looks about 6a/b and worthwhile.

LA CARA DEL MONO ** 6c 15m

Start from the block and climb the front of pillar, via pockets and a final sizeable bulge, to twin bolts.

5. GUIRIPOLLA ** 6c 15m

From the block climb the bulging rib heading for the right side of the large overhang near the top of the cliff, and exit to the right.

SHIT * 7a 15m

Despite the name the line through the large notch in the overhang to the left proves both hard and worthwhile.

To the left is a corner that could offer a good traditional climb, then the wall swings round and a band of bulges are crossed by two innocuous looking climbs:

6. OVERKILL * 7b 15m
The right-hand line sports some 'odd' holds and requires some radical moves.

SANITARIUM * 7c 15m
The left-hand line offers more of the same, only harder.

To the left is a rounded hollow with a route escaping out of its top left corner.

AUREOLA NO ME TOQUES LA PIROLA * 6c+ 18m
A good route after a rather gripping start. Climb into the scoop then trend left to clip the first (crap) bolt. Pull through the roof, crux, on a chipped hold and clip a good bolt (not before time), then continue more easily and more safely to the top.

7. ESPOLON DEL SOL ** 6c 18m
The arête immediately left of an easy gully (low-grade trad route there for the taking) gives an intriguing pitch, alternately delicate and strenuous. Just remember, it's not all over until it's over.

Around to the left the lava has run up against the foot of the cliff and there is a broad slabby rib:

PAY LA PENA 6a 10m
Start from a small flat area and climb the lower section and a short steepening to a lower-off in an open groove above.

TE QUIERO ZORRA * 6a 10m
The final route lurks in the back of a bush-filled gully and climbs the enjoyably juggy left wall using a steep crack-line.

SECTOR SEXTA DIMENSION

A long sector which has scarcely been developed up to the present day. It is shady and cool in the winter, requiring track suits and a warm top, but would make a great summer venue. It can be reached by walking past the sectors described above and crossing a small col; or, more easily, by walking along the road from the car park, past the barrier and then around a loop to arrive at the right edge of the sector. Less than 10 minutes from the car.

The right side of the sector is fronted by a broad flat sandy area with scattered

Mike Appleton on Zazusa (6c+), Egagropalis Tree, Ibiza

Climber on Cuajada de Pus (6b+), Las Canadas, Tenerife

El Tiede (12,200 feet) sparkles in the distance

fire circles. Tucked away in the right corner of this is:

PAULO LAUDELINO CUBINO 7c 6m
A tiny route on the far right side of the sector. Two bolts protect a wild-looking dyno to easy ground.

Past an area of slabby rock and an isolated block of lava is a bay behind a huge boulder.

ME HELEN LOS PIES 6a 12m
An orange pockety wall just to the right of an easy break leads to ledges below a giant roof.

NO REPERCUTE * 6b 12m
The striated wall 3m right of the corner, and the bulging arête above. Good.

MIERDA 6a+ 18m
Start up the gully on the left side of the face and continue up the open bridging groove above; an odd pitch.

Around to the left is huge projecting beak of an overhang, the Techo de Madrid, which is most easily reached by scrambling up the awkward corner on the right and traversing out to the left. The flat ledge here would form an ideal bivi-spot, as long as you don't sleep walk. There are three routes over the huge roof and all involve using improved holds to a greater or lesser extent.

HUMAN INSECECTICIDE 7c 10m
The line of neatly drilled finger pockets on the right, protected(?) by the worst set of bolts you are ever likely to meet anywhere!

COMIC * 7c+ 15m
The central line across the great roof.

SUBWAY ** 8a+ 18m
Crosses the roof at its widest point; simianly spectacular.

Continuing around to the left there is a small conical tower in the back of the bay, home to two climbs. An easy break on the left gives an access route up from here to Fraggel Rock.

LAS PUTIEDADES DE LULU 6b 10m
The right-trending line.

HAYA O NO HAYA. AQUI ESTA EL RAYA 6b 10m
The left-trending line starting in the same place.

Continuing leftwards past a lot of excellent but undeveloped rock (and three unidentified routes, possibly of traditional style: CANALON PENETRANTE 5+, AMISTADES PELIGROSES 5+ AND TECHO DE ROSAL 6a), the cliff increases in size to a spectacular north-east-facing prow capped by a smooth wall:

SABRA-SATILA **** 7a 45m

The finest route on the island? A majestic pitch started by scrambling up the right and then spiralling out onto the spectacular wall on the left, before blasting up the centre of this. Don't forget the double ropes.

Across the gully is a wide wall crying out to be developed, and on the far left side, 100m or so up the bank, is the last offering in this area:

LINEA MAGICA * 6a+ 25m

Climb the pale streak then continue in the same line to ledges and bolt belays.

FRAGGEL ROCK

The conspicuous tower of Fraggel Rock has a good collection of climbs across a broad range of grades, and offers superlative views and photographic opportunities. Situated a steep 10 minutes from the car, Fraggel is an isolated tower with routes on all sides, though as is usual, the sunny faces have seen the best development. The climbs are described in clockwise fashion starting at the top right corner of the wall that faces the car park.

BANANAS * 7c 12m

Monkey up the smooth yellow wall on the right edge of the face, passing a prominent patch of red rock 'en route'.

DUDO * 7b+ 12m

Starting under the overlap to the left and following the curving line of bolts left then right is this sustained little trip.

MAJESTIX is the bolt line starting in the same place but trending leftwards. The grade is unknown, though it looks hard.

To the left the wall is undercut by a series of substantial overhangs, and three climbs find their ways through these.

MUSSI * 6c 15m

Straight through the right side of the roofs, passing twinned bolts early on, to gain large elongated pockets, then following easier rock to the right of the arête.

BOBO * 6a 15m

Climb the slabby right side of the arête started by trending left through the overhangs. The lower-off is hidden around the corner.

CUSSI * 6b 15m
The prow of the cliff facing the volcano starts over an overhang with a tricky first clip. Spectacular positions.

INDERCISIONES ** 6a+ 18m
From the previous route follow ledges around the corner. Pull through the bulges in the centre of the north face then follow the line leftwards to the apex of the tower.

EIGERBAND ** 6b 18m
The north-east arête of Fraggel is most easily reached by crossing the col behind the tower (to the right of BANANAS). Cross the initial large roof rightwards then sprint up the pale wall and steep arête above.

Behind Fraggel is a small wall facing the tower, which is home to three quick ticks.

PUTA PICOLETA 6a 10m
The left-hand line has three bolt runners.

CERO A LA IZQUIERDA 6a+ 10m
The central line with three bolt runners.

CALLEJON OSCURO 6b 6m
The minuscule right-hand line, with two bolt runners.

SECTOR RAINBOW
The highest (in terms of altitude) face in the area is this impressive red wall. At present there are only five routes here, though there is plenty of scope for more. The wall is reached in a steep 15 minutes from the car, though it perhaps makes sense to visit it via one of the other sectors further down the hill.

   The cliff is referred to as the Sector Rambo (big muscles required?) on one topo, the Sector Rainbow (multicoloured rock??) on another, and the Sector Raimbow (???) on a third, so your guess is as good as mine as to its real name. The climbing is steep and exhilarating, though some of the rock feels a little suspect in places. The routes are described from left to right, and none are equipped with convenient lower-offs at present. From the approach slopes the most conspicuous features of the face are the central double-peaked tower, with a bush at is foot, and an open gully on the right, with a large conifer below it.

   To the left of and behind the Rainbow Wall is a fine looking arête climbed by NO HAY TACTO, an excellent looking but rather inaccessible 6c+.

RABAJAS DE ENERO 6a+ 12m
The white wall 10m left of the bush and to the left of the fall line from the left-hand summit leads steeply to ledges with bolt belays.

CHAPITA LEJANA * 7a 25m
The fine arête to the right gives a steep sustained pitch to a ledge with peg belays. Walk off to the left.

TATOPANI ** 6b+ 25m
Start just left of the bush and climb straight up the steep wall and continue up a short blunt arête to ledges. The obvious direct finish is crying out to be climbed. Walk off to the left or abseil from bolts on the right.

RAINBOW *** 6a+ 30m
A great route, well worth the walk up. Start behind the bush and climb straight up the tilted ladder of jugs (sustained jug-pulling) to ledges. Climb the wall behind, then either lower off the last bolt or (better) continue awkwardly to the top of the tower, bring your second up and walk off the back.

BONCHO EN LAS AMERICAS 6b is situated to the right, on the wall behind the large tree. The bolts look rather old and the rock looks a little suspect.

The final two sectors can be seen to the right of the easy slabs by the car park. Although they do not look especially impressive they contain some worthwhile climbs.

SECTOR CHUMINO
A complex tower that appears rather insignificant from the car park but which is home to almost 30 climbs varying in aspect, grade and length. Many of the routes are located in a deep ravine best suited to warmer weather, or to climbers who like to operate in private.

Walk right, passing in front of the area of 'easy slabs' towards the tower with a prominent large hollow in the left side of its front face (Sector Guira), then trend up and left to the tower with a prominent high white slab on its south face, bounded on its right edge by a recent rock fall scar. Opposite the white slab are two tiny routes: GUIR CANTOSA 6a on the left and BOGLUNDER 6b on the right.

The first routes described at the Sector Chumino are on the face around to the right of the fine white slab.

Note: All the climbs are described from right to left, **except** those on the left wall of the central gully.

1. POR AQUI NO PASAS NI DE GUASA 6b 12m

Las Canadas - Sector Chumino & Sector Guiri

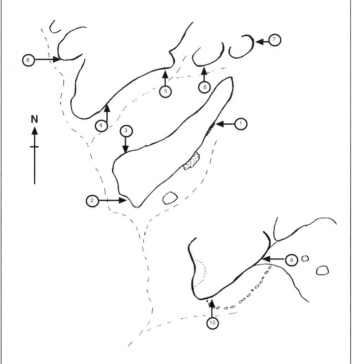

Sector Chumino
1. Por Aqui No Pasas
   Ni De Guasa 6b 12m
2. Placa Kantosa ** 6a 28m
3. Algo Decente ** 6b+ 22m
4. Braguitas Caladas ** 6c+ 22m
5. Maguila Gorila ** 7b+ 22m

6. Me Siento Flex 6b+ 10m
7. Argollita Chachi 6c 6m
8. Metalmilitia * 8a 10m

Sector Guiri
9. Schweinerey * 5+ 12m
10. Pan Bizcochao ** 7a 15m

Start from ledges 6m right of a small built-up bivi-shelter (not recommended) and climb straight up the bulging wall.

ER GALLEGO NO TIENE PELO 6a+ 12m

Start in the same place but trend left to a bolt on the lip of the bulges then continue straight up the rib above.

TOO KISKI LA SOBA 7a 12m

Start from pile of boulders and small battered tree and climb the tough wall above into a hollow near the top of the cliff.

ROCAMADOR 6a 22m

Near the left edge of the wall climb onto a ledge, up a pillar and then the final groove on slightly suspect rock.

The 'fine white slab' is:

2. PLACA KANTOSA ** 6a 28m

Start under an overhang below and left of the fall line from the slab, under a bulging rib. Pull awkwardly out to the right then climb easily to the base of slab. This is much easier than it looks. Exit to the right or left.

ESA CHAPA SOBRA * 5 25m

Around to the left, climb the corner and groove following the line of least resistance.

Around to the left again is the canyon that splits the tower in two. There are a dozen or so routes in this secluded setting, a good place to get away from it all. On the right edge of the canyon the are five routes close together on a fine pocketed wall. The two on the far right are new, and no grades are known, though they look to be about 6c/7a-ish. The central one of the five is:

3. ALGO DECENTE ** 6b+ 22m

Climb straight up the steep pocketed wall to a slab then pass the capping bulge by a tricky pull on a hidden hold.

CHUMINITO PROFUNDO ** 6b+ 22m

The next line to the left. Go up the pocket wall again and pass another bulge to reach the same belays as the previous climb.

EVA NO QUIERA * 7b 22m

The left-hand line trends left up steep rock on poor, spaced pockets linked by dynamic moves.

The next seven routes are on the opposite side of the canyon, described from left to right as it rises steeply up the bank.

VAYA TROMPADA 6b 12m
The left arête (or the wall just to its right?) of the canyon is an unknown quantity.

4. BRAGUITAS CALADAS ** 6c+ 22m
Up the slope and to the right of a crack-line is a line trending left though pocketed bulges to ledges then left again through ever more bulges. Good sport.

MORTALES INGREDIENTES 7? 25m
Starting from the left side of cave is this very steep line, crossing a bevy of bulges to reach the highest point of the wall.

5. MAGUILA GORILA ** 7b+ 22m
The outrageously steep climb just before the wall swings round into a hanging corner, a must for lovers of a swinging time.

MALOS PERROS * 6c 18m
The line up the left wall of the hanging corner (not a route, though it should be) that bounds the right side of the steepest section of the face.

PANZAS DE SANCHO PANZA 6b 10m
A route up the short brown streak to the right of the corner crack.

BOBERIAS SON SOPAS 6b+ 10m
The diagonal line close to the right edge of the wall.

To the right across the top of the gully are two separate small towers, both of which are well spattered with bolts. The first (left-hand) tower has three routes, from left to right:

6. ME SIENTO FLEX 6b+ 10m
Over a prow and up thin diagonal crack.

ADONDE MAGARRO 6b 10m
White bolts protect a climb just left of a brown-streaked groove.

UNNAMED 7a 10m
The smooth bulging rib on the right.

To the right is another small rounded tower with two tiny climbs that are equipped with excellent bolts. This point can also be reached from the front of the sector by walking up the slope to the right of the arrival point.

ARGOLLITA CHUNGA 6b 6m
The left-hand line.

7. ARGOLLITA CHACHI 6c 6m
The line around the arête to the right.

The final three routes in the Sector Chumino are located up the slope to the left of the central gully containing the above climbs. At the top of this is an impressive bulging prow covered in drilled holds (hardly cricket). The stars awarded are for people who enjoy having their tendons stretched to twanging point!

8. METALMILITIA * 8a 10m
The right-hand line over the largest part of the roof.

KIM BASINGER * 7c 10m
The slight less ridiculous line to the left.

EXTASIS 7c 10m
Left again.

EL CAPRICHO DEL NENE 6a 10m
The short arête on the tower to the left.

SECTOR GUIRI

A small tower with half a dozen routes on its south face. The sector is worth a visit for the photogenic nature of these climbs, with the volcano towering in the background, and of course a visit here can easily be combined with routes on the nearby and more extensive Sector Chumino.

Note: The climbs here are described from right to left. Walk right, passing in front of the area of easy slabs to a tower with a prominent large hollow in the left side of its front face and a low walled sandy area around to the right, 5 minutes from the car. How's the altitude affecting you so far? The first routes start up and right of this area from extensive ledges reached by an easy scramble round to the right.

In the back wall of the bay is another contender for Spain's shortest route: two bolts in a 4m high red wall, grade unknown. To the left is a higher wall split centrally by a wide chimney gully that starts 7m above the ledge. In the prow to the right of this are two new stainless steel staples, presumably reached from the gully. No grade known.

To the left of the hanging gully is:

9. SCHWEINEREY * 5+ 12m
A worthwhile pitch, though with only two pieces of fixed kit; carry a couple of slings for spikes if you feel the need.

From just left of the central gully trend left across the wall, passing the first bolt (crux), then follow good holds passing another bolt near the top protecting the final steepening. No fixed belays.

Starting from the 'corral' is:

PALIQUE PALICOSO 6a 18m

Climb the awkward corner (wires?) to a block (or cop out and step in from the right), then step left and clip the first bolt with difficulty. Climb past this, especially thin for the short, then trend left (bolt) and back right to the top of the tower. No fixed belays.

Just to the left is a solitary large bolt in the steep wall that protects either the diagonal groove that leads rightwards into the last route or an unfinished climb directly up the wall.

10. PAN BIZCOCHAO ** 7a 15m

A gift at the Spanish grade, especially as it was initially given 7a+. Climb the crack just right of the arête then layback powerfully through the bulges to gain a rest on the right. Climb the arête then swing back right (tricky clip) before powering over the final bulge. Twin-bolt belay.

Around to the left the side wall of the arête has a worthwhile looking slabby pitch with big beefy 'glue-ins' and a reported grade of 7a+.

PARED TINTO

Twenty minutes along the well-made path that starts at LOS ROQUES is a north-facing cliff on the right-hand side of the path. Here are four well-bolted low-grade routes on rather strange volcanic rock. From right to left these are (my names!):

UNO * 3 30m

Right edge of cliff in two? pitches.

DOS ? 30m

Two metres to the left, possibly two pitches.

TRES ? 30m

Third line from the right, containing bolts and occasional pegs. Second pitch slants left to join next route.

QUATRO ** 4,5 35m

Left-hand line, very well bolted, up odd slippery rock. DON'T be tempted by the pegs in Pitch 3, as very unstable terrain lurks just above.

ARICO

Character

A pleasant open gorge, running north–south and with routes on both sides, thus allowing the sun to be enjoyed or avoided. The place is rather dusty, but this area of Tenerife is semi-desert, so you will have to grin and bear it! The rock is an ignimbrite or welded ash that was ejected from the volcano and was so hot on landing that it fused together into a solid mass, in a similar manner to Oregon's world famous venue, Smith Rock. Gas cavities were trapped in the ash along with various fragments of solid rock, and this has led to the climbs relying heavily on pockets and a remarkable number of 'thread-type' holds. The vast majority of the routes are on smooth open faces, though there are some beetling overhangs and the occasional fine crack-line for a touch of variety. Bolt protection is the norm, apart from a very small number of crack lines, and the routes rarely exceed 22m in height.

Geography

The gorge is divided into Upper and Lower sections, with the car parking just above the top end of the Lower Gorge. The best routes in the Lower Gorge face west and those in the Upper Gorge face east. With a bit of planning it is possible to have a full day on the rock with out getting too fried.

Note: The terms 'left bank' and 'right bank' refer to the sectors when seen **from the normal direction of approach**.

Access

From the coast drive to the small pleasant settlement of Val de Arico (Lomo de Arico on some maps), 35km from Los Cristianos, and turn uphill in the centre of the town on a minor road signed 'Valle de Contador 7km'. Pass round the church, noting the distinctly odd tree, and then follow the road steadily uphill for a couple of kilometres until a double hairpin bend is passed. Take the first right turn after this onto a dirt road which immediately splits into three, and follow the central branch. This rises bumpily past a half-completed building (at least it looks half-completed, despite the fact that it is occupied) and then descends to several parking areas by a white building on the edge of the Lower Gorge. This building has been used in the recent past as a (primitive) climbing hut, especially by German climbers.

Do not block access to the cultivated land here. If you do, you may find your car has been 'moved' on your return!

The Lower Gorge is directly below and is described first. The Upper Gorge is five minutes' walk upstream and is described later.

THE LOWER GORGE

Only developed extensively in recent years the Lower Gorge is home to many steep, hard routes and a small selection of easier fare. Most of the best climbs are on the East Wall and so are in the sun in the afternoon. This may be seen as an important factor if you want to get that all important 'red point', or if your plane leaves tomorrow and you are determined to go home with a proper tropical tan! In the gorge there is some evidence of mining in the past, in the form of spoil heaps and bits of narrow gauge railways, and it has to be admitted that parts of the gorge do have the atmosphere of a quarry. Despite this, much of the climbing is excellent, and half an hour facing that glowing orb high in the southern sky should make up for any shortcomings in the setting.

Access

From the car parking follow a ramp that runs down into the gorge (heading upstream) then double back and descend a tricky little water chute (care required if damp), cross the stream bed and descend stone steps to the gorge bed. The climbs are described in seven separate sectors, firstly down the right bank (looking downstream) and then down the left bank (see diagram for the location of the sectors).

THE RIGHT BANK

All routes here are described from right to left.

SECTOR OSCURO

At the bottom of the stone steps is a small collection of climbs on the right side of the gorge, directly under the rickety looking bridge, a shady setting for cool dudes.

MOSCAS PEGAJOSAS 6c 6m

The tiny shallow groove at the foot of the steps has two bolt runners and a single-bolt lower-off.

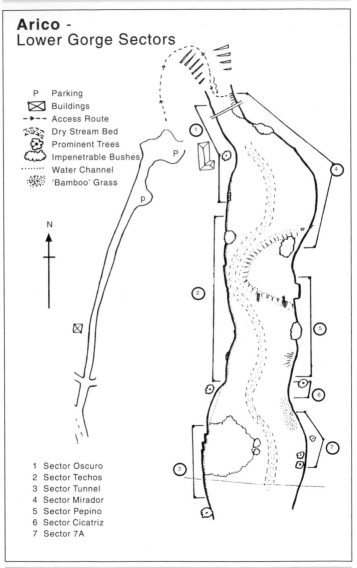

Arico -
Lower Gorge Sectors

P   Parking
⊠   Buildings
-•--   Access Route
Dry Stream Bed
Prominent Trees
Impenetrable Bushes
Water Channel
'Bamboo' Grass

N

1   Sector Oscuro
2   Sector Techos
3   Sector Tunnel
4   Sector Mirador
5   Sector Pepino
6   Sector Cicatriz
7   Sector 7A

ZIPI ? 6m
A thin crack rising above a band of bubbly rock also has two bolt runners.

ZAPE ? 15m
Just to the left a second thin crack is followed onto the wall above.

ANALYSIS FINAL ** 7a+ 22m
The first climb of any substance. Skate up the smooth lower section then head leftwards up the leaning wall above to lower-off right under the bridge. A popular pitch that is always well chalked.

Just left is a new route right under the bridge, climbing bubbly rock and pockets, then more steeply to the lower-off of the previous climb. No name or grade is available.

BLACK DAY * 6c+ 12m
The square pillar and bulging wall 5m left of the fall line from the bridge gives an interesting exercise in 'monkey-up-a-stick' climbing style.

Twenty metres further downstream is another new route, up a bubbly wall, crack and prow. No name or grade is known, though it looks worthwhile and quite tough.

The final two climbs on this sector are situated above three small 'baths' filled with tepid water, perhaps the place to get your laundry done, especially as it's lovely drying weather.

MALDITA SEA MI SEURTE 6c 18m
From the rim of the 'bath' clip the first bolt on the next climb then trend to the right through the bulges and up a slab to a lower-off on the top right corner of the wall.

EL SENOR DE LA BESTIAS * 6b 15m
Make an awkward move to get the first bolt clipped (cheating stone or a shoulder for the short?) then head straight up the steep rib via long reaches. Continue up the arête above with a delicate final move to the belay.

SECTOR TECHOS
A rather uninspiring set of climbs well spaced down the right side of the ravine. They do, however, have the advantage of being in the shade for most of the day.

Opposite where a scree/spoil slope almost closes the gorge is a bolted groove, of unknown grade and name. It appears dirty and vegetated and looks well worth avoiding.

Fifteen metres further downstream is a slightly more worthwhile offering.

LOS FRIKIS DEL MARTIZEZ 6b 22m

An open groove leads via some suspect rock to the final tricky corner with the belays in the right wall.

Fifteen metres further downstream two routes exit from a large cave 8m up. This is reached by awkward dirty climbing. Both routes are a bit of a hassle to strip, and a stout second man is called for.

ATRAPADO EN LA NOCHE * 7a+ 18m

Cross the left side of the roof then continue up the impressive stepped prow above.

VACACION EN CASA * 6c+ 18m

Take a lower line out of the cave to reach a ledge on the left side of the prow, then climb the side wall to the lower-offs.

Twenty metres further downstream and opposite the smooth orange wall of the Sector Pepino are two bolt lines:

SIN PATA PALO 6b 10m

The thin crack gives a short battle with one tricky clip.

To the left is a climb that gets into the prominent cave and exits from this by crossing the large roof; no name or grade known.

The only other routes on the right bank of the gorge are on the SECTOR TUNNEL, which is the blocky wall across the valley for SECTOR 7A (see below) rising above the water channel. There are half a dozen hard routes here, but on our visit to SECTOR TUNNEL all approaches to the area appeared to be blocked by vicious vegetation of impressive proportions. Perhaps an abseil approach would be a good idea. For completeness the routes here are (from right to left, in keeping with the rest of the right bank):

DJ GANLEGO 7a+

ME SOBRAN NEURONAS 7a

CHUMINITO FLAGELOSO 7a

GARIMBA A MEDIAS 6b

and some distance further downstream:

ON THE EDGE 7b+

ESTO ES UN ATRACO ?

THE LEFT BANK

All routes here are described from left to right. The descriptions now tackle the routes on the left bank (looking downstream) of the gorge. The first area on the left is the ever popular:

SECTOR MIRADOR

There is a solitary route right under the bridge at the access point for the Lower Gorge.

TORAN 7a 15m
The thin crack and overhang leads to a lower-off right under the bridge.

Continuing downstream for 100m or so is the main part of this sector, a set of impressive roofs and leaning walls. There are a number of excellent climbs here. The three routes on the far left are reached via a narrow ledge 3m off the ground.

1. SIN EXCESO DE PESO ** 7b 15m
On the far left start at two metal plates bolted to the rock and climb the lower rib to a ledge and the tough leaning face above.

2. JOE PETA * 6c+ 15m
Climb the crack in a corner and the continuation crack above to the belay of the previous route. The bolts are rather spaced so be bold, carry a couple of Friends, or top rope the route!

3. ALFRED J. KWACK ** 7a 15m
Climb the technical lower rib and the tough leaning pocketed wall above. Worth doing for the name alone!

4. BARRIO CONFLICTIVO * 6a+ 25m
The impressive hanging slab is approached up an easy corner crack, and gained by a tricky pull (damn those pigeons). Head left across the slab to a ledge then make a baffling final move to the big beefy belay bolt.

5. COMO MARCA LA LEY ** 6c 25m
Climb the easy crack as for the previous route then traverse out onto the wall (crux) before following pockets to a break. Pull leftwards over the roof and sprint up the final crack on superb finger jams.

6. MAX POTTER ** 6c+ 22m
Pull over the roofs on the right with difficulty and trend left up the wall to a steep hanging slab. Cross this and make a crux lunge round the capping roof to reach the belay bolts.

Arico Lower Gorge- Sector Mirador

1. Sin Exceso De Peso ** 7b 15m
2. Joe Peta * 6c+ 15n
3. Alfred J. Kwack ** 7a 15m
4. Barrio Conflictivo * 6a+ 25m

5. Como Marca La Ley ** 6c 25m
6. Max Potter ** 6c+ 22m
7. El Poder De Un Cono *** 7b+ 25m
8. Aguital ** 7a 15m

9. Techomaster ** 7c 18m
10. El Rompebragas *** 6c 28m
11. La Silla Electrica ** 6c+ 25m
12. Unknown 25m

7. EL PODER DE UN CONO *** 7b+ 25m

Start as for the last climb but head straight up the wall. Pull over the bulge onto a hanging flake then swing right before powering up to ledges. Reach the belay by a detour out to the right.

8. AGUITAL ** 7a 15m

The impressive hanging roof crack is followed by powerful undercutting to a lower-off just around the lip.

9. TECHOMASTER ** 7c 18m

Start to the right of the hanging roof of the previous climb and head up to the roofs before trending leftwards below the lip by sustained strenuous climbing on large but often sloping holds.

10. EL ROMPEBRAGAS *** 6c 28m

Climb up to the band of roofs as for the previous climb then move right and pull over to reach rock of a saner angle. Up this trending leftwards to a lower-off on top of the wall. There may also be a more direct finish to the climb.

11. LA SILLA ELECTRICA ** 6c+ 25m

Use the knotted rope (or follow the new bolts in from the right?) to gain the impressive groove line and follow it as it cuts through bulges in a most impressive fashion.

12. ? ? 25m

To the right is a line starting up the immensely steep side wall and continuing on over roofs galore; it looks way hard!

SECTOR PEPINO

An extensive sector with a fine collection of routes, a good number of which are very hard. For normal mortals there is a small number of more reasonable offerings scattered amongst this patch of 'big boys' territory. The first routes are located at the top of a scree/spoil bank by a projecting railway line, where a large block is jammed under a roof. Three climbs begin from the square recess behind the jammed boulder, and this is reached by a short awkward scramble.

1. CHULO DE TURNO * 7a+ 18m

A bit of a 'one move wonder' – but what a move. Climb the face just to the right of the left arête of the recess to reach the thin diagonal crack that splits the roof and extemporise a way past this to the single belay bolt located in a large semi-detached block!!!

The next two climbs start over the roof at the back of the square recess.

Arico Lower Gorge - Sector Pepino

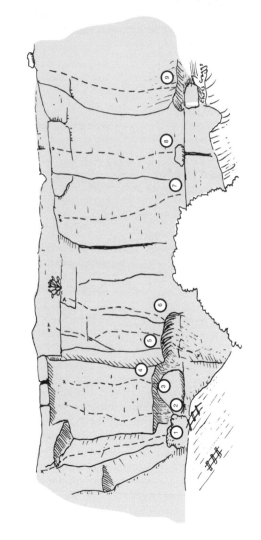

1. Chulo De Turno * 7a+ 18m
2. La Basca Ataca Duro 6c+ 12m
3. Agarramela Bien * 6c 12m

4. Pasion Por El Rudio * 5+ 15m
5. Fantasamagoria ** 6b+ 15m
6. Vado Permanente * 6b 15m

7. Ataud Pa Sies * 7a 18m
8. El Poderio De Javierio * 7a 18m
9. Robert Millar * * 7b+ 18m

2. LA BASCA ATACA DURO 6c+ 12m
Pull over the roof and climb the straightforward wall to a perplexing sequence at the change in angle. Try to clip the belay bolt before you grab it!

3. AGARRAMELA BIEN * 6c 12m
Pull over the right side of the overhang and climb the pockety wall to a tricky bulge. It is very tempting to bridge to the arête on the right here, though the puritanical will press on smartly to the belay.

4. PASION POR EL RUDIO * 5+ 15m
The crack that bounds the recess on the right leads to ledges and the lower-off for the next climb. Gear required.

To the right of and below the large jammed boulder is a bolt belay in a corner to stop your second falling down the unstable slope. Two routes start here:

5. FANTASAMAGORIA ** 6b+ 15m
Climb an awkward arête and slab to the cave then pull over the centre of the roof and follow good jugs up the wall until it is possible to get around the left arête. A short steep wall leads to ledges and the lower-off.

6. VADO PERMANENTE * 6b 15m
Follow the previous climb to the cave then pull over the right side of the bulges and follow the bolt-protected crack (nice idea) to ledges with *in situ* cacti and belay bolts.

To the right is an area of vegetation and then a wall that rises above a horizontal ledge with a conspicuous boulder sat on it. There are two climbs that start off the ledge and they are reached by a short scramble. The left-hand route is:

7. ATAUD PA SIES * 7a 18m
Climb the left-trending line of pockets.

8. EL PODERIO DE JAVIERIO * 7a 18m
Start behind the block and head up the gently leaning wall.

To the right is an impressive red wall rising above a grey scree slope topped by a horizontal cave, whilst around the arête to the right is more impressively steep and smooth rock featuring a prominent curving groove. Further right again is a series of hardly less impressive corners and overhangs. There are many of the islands hardest climbs here, and some of the pitches are rather crowded. The descriptions below and the diagram attempt to sort these out and I apologise in advance if you end up on an 8a instead of a 6b+!

The leaning wall above the cave has two lines on it:

9. ROBERT MILLAR ** 7b+ 18m
The steeply leaning left side of the wall is started from a block and gives a tough pitch.

10. JALA POR EL RESUELLO ** 7c+ 18m
The right-hand climb crosses the roof of the cave and climbs the centre of the wall. It is a notch harder than Bob.

Two climbs are based around the blunt arête that bounds the right side of the wall.

11. VUELO DE TRIPI ** 8a+ 18m
The lower arête to the bolt-on hold, then trend left to climb the left side of the upper arête.

12. SENSACION DE PEPINO ** 7b 18m
Take the lower arête to the bolt-on hold then the right side of the upper section.

The next five climbs start under the smooth orange shield of rock to the right and find their different ways up the impressive rock above.

13. ANIKILATOR ** 7b 22m
Trend left following the curving crack up the lower wall, then continue up the leaning wall and enter the steep sustained groove above.

14. FLYMOUSE * 7c+ 22m
A finish through the bulges to the right of the final corner of the previous route is a tough number.

15. LOMOMASTER ** 7c 28m
The natural line of the wall starts as for the previous two climbs then traverses to the right, following the curving weakness below the headwall, to eventually enter and climb the hanging corner on the right.

16. ARICO POWER ** 8a 22m
Start under the centre of the wall and climb it to the break, then press on up the smooth wall to the left of the final corner of the previous route.

17. Starting in the same place but trending right to climb the smoothest looking rock in the area and the hanging prow above is an unrecorded route. It looks at least 8b.

To the right the sheerest section of the face is bounded by a right-facing flake crack followed by the excellent:

Arico Lower Gorge - Sector Pepino (right side)

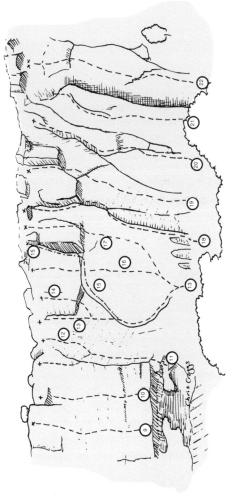

9. Robert Millar ** 7b+ 18m
10. Jala Por El Resuello ** 7c+ 18m
11. Vuelo De Tripi ** 8a+ 18m
12. Sensacion De Pepino ** 7b 18m
13. Anikilator ** 7b 22m

14. Flymouse * 7c+ 22m
15. Lomomaster ** 7c 28m
16. Arico Power ** Éa 22m
17. Unknown
18. Fermentos Lacteos ** 6b+ 22m

19. Ruleta Rosa ** 7c 22m
20. Luna Llena *** 7a+ 22m
21. Bubangos Cream * 8a 22m
22. Putas Zarzes * 6c+ 22m

18. FERMENTOS LACTEOS ** 6b+ 22m
Climb soft grey rock then follow the flake crack around the arête before swinging back left and making a powerful pull into the continuation corner. Finish more easily.

19. RULETA ROSA ** 7c 22m
The orange tilted wall and overhanging groove to the right give a bit of a tussle, even for the talented.

20. LUNA LLENA *** 7a+ 22m
To the right is an impressive flake crack trending right below a bevy of bulges. Climb straight up a subsidiary crack to the flake and attack this with conviction. A gem, but not a route for people who don't like laybacking.

21. BUBANGOS CREAM ** 8a 22m
Starting from a boulder, climb the leaning prow and then press on up the horrendous thin overhanging crack above. Perhaps it is a good idea not to cut your finger nails before trying this one.

22. PUTAS ZARZES * 6c+ 22m
The right wall of a deep corner is climbed following a crack system to a deep horizontal break, then power on through the bulges above.

SECTOR CICATRIZ
Continuing further downstream away from the crowds, the gorge opens out again and there is this sector with four climbs, the first of which starts in a red cave.

PONTE EN POSE * 7a+ 18m
Climb out of the cave and head up the grey leaning wall and final tilted prow.

Further downstream, past prickly pears and other exotic scrub, are three routes, the first of which climbs the wall left of an obvious central arête.

NUNCA MAS * 7a+ 18m
Climb the tilted wall left of the hanging bramble bush and continue over a small overhang to twin lower-offs just below some ledges.

MUCHA FIBRA Y POCA TETA * 7b 18m
The blunt arête is followed to ledges, then the wall above leads to a wire cable lower-off on a level with a giant prickly pear.

LOS CICATRIZ ** 7c+ 18m
The wall to the right again gives quality face-climbing trending to the right to reach a double-bolt lower-off.

SECTOR 7A

To the right is an extensive area of tall 'bamboo' type grass, and the next climbs are reached by walking around the right side of this to reach a series of smart grey walls. This is the final sector on the left bank of the gorge, and if you operate at the appropriate grade the SECTOR 7A is well worth a visit to get away from the crowds. The first route climbs the wall at the far left of the area.

1. BALATE STRON * 7a 28m

Follow a thin crack up the lower wall then head leftward up the head wall passing a small roof 'en route'.

Five metres to the right is a protruding pillar with a crack running up its centre. There are routes to either side of the crack and any keen traditionalist could claim a new route here.

2. CABO CANAVERAL ** 7a 18m

The left-hand line gives interesting climbing.

3. CAVO CANABERAL * 6c+ 18m

The right-hand line leads to the same lower-off in a similar vein.

To the right is an hourglass-shaped pillar, its left side formed by a cave.

4. LA CALBELLA DEL PLACER * 6c 18m

The right arête of the hourglass-shaped pillar leads to a belay right under a giant hanging prickly pear – how did they get to the top of the route to equip it? This is supposed to be the easiest route in the area; but then again, is it?

Right of where the bamboo ends is a red shield split by a thin crack; this is

5. EL REGRESO DEL PATRON ** 7a 22m

The excellent steep wall is sustained and thin; the corner above is not.

The next two climbs start on the wall to the right of an open corner, directly below a horizontal roof near the top of the cliff.

6. SIN MOSKA EN LA TAPIA ** 7a 25m

Trend left up the lower wall following a thin crack and then do battle with the bottom-shaped overhang above (extension wire cable on bolt) and then the easier wall.

7. CHUNGO CHUNGO RAMALASO ** 7a 25m

Start in the same place but swing right and make a couple of perplexing moves up the wall to easier climbing over bulges. Lower off the *in situ* slings around the horizontal tree.

Arico Lower Gorge - Sector 7A

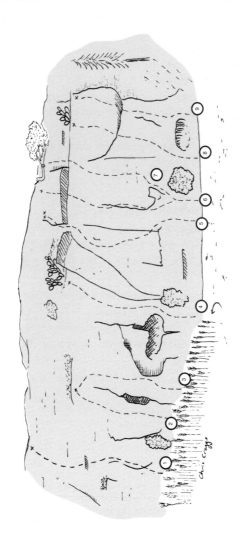

1. Balate Stron * 7a 28m
2. Cabo Canaveral ** 7a 18m
3. Cavo Canaberal * 6c+ 18m

4. La Calbella Del Placer * 6c 18m
5. El Regreso Del Patron ** 7a 22m
6. Sin Moska En La Tapia ** 7a 25m

7. Chungo Chungo Ramalaso ** 7a 25m
8. Lactantes * 7a 18m
9. Alguerto * 6c+ 18m

8. LACTANTES * 7a 18m
Begin just to the left of a cave/hollow and climb the wall trending right, through a bulging section.

9. ALGUERTO * 6c+ 18m
The final offering climbs the arête. Trend right up the lower wall, pull through a bulge and continue up the arête above.

In front of this final area are some large boulders with two short climbs on them:

LA LEGIA DE UN LOCO 7b+ 6m
The short and very sharp right-hand line.

SEMEN RECICLADO 6b+ 6m
The hardly more worthwhile line facing downstream.

THE UPPER GORGE

The Upper Gorge is more open and less imposing than the Lower Gorge and is home to some more amenable routes. A quick walk through the gorge may leave you 'under-whelmed', but get a few of the climbs under your belt and the place will grow on you. The whole area is divided into ten sectors (see diagram on page 251), and the climbs are described up the left bank looking upstream first, and then up the right bank.

From the car park descend into the stream bed and walk uphill for about 5 minutes. The first small collection of routes is on the right side at the SECTOR CORAZON DE METAL (see below). Opposite this is a boulder with a steep face and a bolt belay on top; don't worry, things get better. Continuing upstream a pipe crosses the valley and the first routes on the left bank are 50m beyond this.

THE LEFT BANK
All routes here are described from left to right.

SECTOR PENA DEL LUNES

BOULDER 5 4m
The first route is a one-bolt, one-move wonder. Not the best advert for Arico!

NELSON MANDELE 5+ 6m
The marginally more worthwhile climb just to the right. A two-bolt, two-move wonder.

Twenty metres upstream is a much more worthwhile set of routes starting from a flat ledge reached by a short scramble.

ESPOLON DEL RAMPA * 6a+ 12m
The left edge of the wall gives a pleasant pitch.

PENA DEL LUNES * 6b 12m
Race up the bulging wall just left of the central thin crack.

FISURA DEL PALIZA 6c+ 12m
The thin crack requires the placing of gear; strange indeed.

PLACA DEL FRIKI * 6b+ 12m
The flat wall on the right is climbed past a series of horizontal breaks linked by tricky moves.

NO HAY PIEDA PA LOS GODOS 6c 15m
Climb the thin crack in the wall to the right, then trend left following a line of pockets with difficulty to a lower-off on the left arête.

WIRITO SANTO *** 6c 18m
Around to the right is a grotty corner and in the left wall of this is a line of big bolts. You are unlikely to get lost on this one!

To the right of the corner is a NEW ROUTE up a wall and slab to belay bolts; it then trends right again up to and over a roof. No grade is known but the climb looks good and not too taxing.

SECTOR LOS PINOS

An area well worth a visit, with its central section being formed by a series of smart walls behind an attractive stand of tall pine trees. A small terrace in front of these provides the best camping spot in the gorge. However, the first three routes in the sector are on an isolated buttress 50m downstream from the pine trees. The buttress is distinguished by a line of overhangs across its base.

NEW ROUTE * 6b 12m
Pass the first roof with considerable difficulty then trend right to cross the second band of overhangs before moving right again to reach the lower-off.

NEW ROUTE 6a 12m
Enter the central groove by using a dubious jammed flake, and continue to the roof on more suspect rock. Swing right then pull back left to reach the belay bolt.

ME EMPALO UN PALO 6c+ 12m

Arico - Upper Gorge Sectors

1. Sector Pena Del Lunes
2. Sector Los Pinos
3. Sector Bosque
4. Sector El Luchador
5. Sector Juancho
6. Sector Corazon De Metal
7. Sector Sus Villa
8. Sector Vivac
9. Sector Limbo
10. Sector Tiburon

Cliffs
Broken Ground
Dry River Bed
Paths
Prominent Trees
Prominent Boulders

N

50m

The side wall of the buttress has a small roof and proves to be a tough little cookie.

Fifty metres further upstream and behind the stand of pine trees is the main part of this sector. On the left is a roofed-in cave feature, home to three climbs.

MI ABUELITA LA MALDITA * 6b+ 10m
The steep sharp pocketed wall to the left of the cave.

UF UF * 6c+ 10m
The wall just right of the right edge of the cave is even sharper and steeper.

DISTORSION TOTAL * 5+ 10m
The wall to the right is rather more pleasant – well, at least the holds are larger.

ACEITUNAS 6c 10m
The short steep wall around to the right.

Directly behind the three largest pines is a fine steep slab, home to two good routes:

PAPEO CHACHI ** 6a+ 18m
The left side of the slab and rib above gives excellent sustained climbing.

PAPEO CHUNGO ** 6b 18m
The crack in the centre of the slab and the rib above gives another worthwhile pitch.

Note: Both previous routes used to share a common lower-off at the top of the slab. I have not done the short extensions up the ribs above the respective bolt ladders, so they may be tougher than the grades given here. PAPEO CHUNGO has a fixed maillon attached to the first bolt on the head wall, so it is possible to avoid the final steepening if it proves too much.

To the right and up ledges is a short tilted wall facing in towards the pine trees.

DISTORSION CRANEAL 6c 6m
The left-hand line using some 'constructed' holds.

McNESIO 6a 6m
On the right-hand line Mother Nature has been a bit more generous.

A narrow path continues around an arête to reach a fine wall with a prominent bird-limed hole at 5m. This is climbed by:

CONTROL MENTAL ** 6b+ 18m
Boulder up to the hole then climb the steep wall before trending away to the right to where slabbier moves gain the belay. Well worth seeking out.

PUMIKI EL PRESO * 6c 12m
Continue around the next arête to find a line of green bolts running up a scooped wall and over a roof.

EL PODER CHICA * 6c 12m
Further to the right, just before the cliff disappears into the brush, is flat wall and sharp arête fully equipped with shiny new bolts.

From here there is no way on through the impenetrable brush, even though the Sector Bosque is not far away, so it is necessary to return to the pines and then to the gorge floor.

SECTOR BOSQUE
Opposite SECTOR LIMBO and to the left of some large blocks in the stream bed is the SECTOR BOSQUE, reached by following a narrow path through the trees.

GRADO KENIATA 6b+ 12m
Starting from ledges up on the left. Climb the straightforward lower section then follow the bolts rightwards up the steepening wall above.

MAKI NAVAJA * 6a+ 15m
Start at the point where the path emerges from the trees. Climb an arête then a curving flake on big holds, and finally the wall above.

The next collection of climbs can be reached by following the vague suggestion of a path along the foot of the cliff, past caves and through trees, though it is easier to use another path that starts a little further upstream. The first three climbs start from a comfortable ledge 7m up, most easily reached from the right.

ANARQUIA EN LA PLANETA 7b 10m
The left-hand line.

LA VIUDA DEL BOSQUE 6c 10m
The right-hand line.

LA VIA DEL MEN 7b+ 10m
The route on the pocketed side wall. It is possible to start as for the previous route and to extend the climb, and claim yourself a *.

RELIJATE PRIMO ** 7a+ 18m
An excellent outing up the arête of the wall. The easy square rib leads to more dramatic territory (and a gripper clipper) above. From ledges move right to a final tricky move to the lower-off.

To the right, and behind a large tree, are two routes that climb the same piece of rock.

EL ESCUDO DEL GUERRERO * 7a+ 15m
Plenty of pockets and a bulge thrown in for good measure.

ALUCINA CON MI VERCINA * 6c 15m
An easier variation on the same theme, just to the right.

ALGUIEN PALMO ** 6b 15m
At the point where the regular path meets the cliff face is a steep wall. Jug-pulling through bulges and thinner moves above combine to make a fine climb.

LA PUTA DEL BOSQUE 6b+ 12m
The wall on the right is climbed trending leftwards, and just for a change all the holds are pockets.

SECTOR EL LUCHADOR
The next sector on the left bank is a set of walls situated under a large pine tree on the cliff top, and reached up a steep dusty path leading to good ledges below the wall.

SUPER LOPEZ * 6b 12m
On a square-cut tower trending slightly right to begin with, then bang up the centre of the pillar above.

To the right is a grotty corner (any takers?) and right again is a slab:

EL CONTRATO DEL ZAPATERO ** 6b+ 12m
Climb the slab and the sustained rib above.

EL LUCHADOR ** 6c+ 12m
Climb the lower slab just to the right then step out right onto the face and follow the arête above to the top.

DESEQUILIBRIO GANSO * 7a+ 12m
Climb the wall passing the bulging section by strenuous use of a drilled pocket to a lower-off beneath the rather dangerous looking block overhang at the top of the cliff.

ELEMENTO BARRIADA * 6b+ 12m
Climb the wall trending rightwards, crossing a diagonal crack and continuing up the steeper wall above.

SERVA VIRGEN 6b+ 10m

The steep lower wall leads past three bolts to tape belays on the rim. Abseil off or leave the old karabiner you have been carrying for just such an event.

Further upstream is a fine red face with a diagonal line of pockets running across it from left to right.

COMPRATE UN FRELAX ** 7a+ 18m
Climb the uninspiring corner then cross the steep face on spaced pockets to a break and a final tricky move to the chains.

DOS TALEGOS Y MEDIO * 6c+ 12m
Around the corner to the right climb the bulging wall to the right of a straight crack, passing a pair off 'eyes' to a final slabby section.

SECTOR JUANCHO
Continuing up the stream bed the way ahead is blocked by a series of huge boulders. A small 'tunnel' leads through these and the SECTOR JAUNCHO is located on the left at this point. On the large boulders that effectively block the valley below the centre of the SECTOR JUANCHO are two short climbs.

LA CURVA DEL GATO 6b 6m
The short sharp arête that faces upstream.

LAGARTO JUANCHO 7c 10m
The drilled pockets up the underside of the biggest boulder.

Once through the 'tunnel' a path leads left behind trees to a block on the ground. At this point there are three routes up a steep wall bounded by fine cracks to left and right.

PA LOS POLLOS * 6c 12m
Start at a bolt belay on a ledge and climb the fine sustained crack to twinned lower-offs on the right. The bad news is you will need a rack of Friends.

The wall to the right has three fine climbs for those who enjoy torturous pocket-pulling on 'improved' holds. Good practice for the climbing wall?

MOCO LINE ** 7c+ 12m
The left-hand line proves to be fine and very hard.

PINZATELO BIEN ** 7b+ 12m
The slightly easier and rather better central line.

COMISARIO ANTIDOPING * 7b+ 12m
The least worthwhile route right again.

'OYE FRUDIS' * 6a 12m

Another route to get you ready for back home; carry a rack. Do you think the idea will ever catch on? Fortunately the lower-offs are in place, so there is no need to do battle with the unsavoury territory at the top of the cliff!

ALGUIEN VOLO SOBRE EL CHOZO DEL CUCA ** 8a 15m

This route climbs the steeply overhanging orange prow above the point where the approach path disappears into the trees. Only for the very talented.

DULCE REVOLUTION * 6b+ 12m

A worthwhile climb up the lower wall on the right to the base of a corner and then continuing up the right wall above.

To the right is a massive roof 12m up with a good-looking jamming crack (unclimbed) running up to it. In the right wall of the corner is:

NASIO PA' NA' * 7b+ 12m

Just when you thought it was all over, more harsh pocket-pulling.

Right of the roof is an open groove that could do with a wash and brush up (any takers?), and right again is a wall peppered with a strange collection of paired holes.

SUELTAME GRIFA * 6b 10m

Climb the wall by a series of 'poke its eyes out' moves, past four bolts to a lower-off.

Fifty metres further upstream, to the left of a small 'penicle' and to either side of a corner, are the final two routes.

'AY CHIQUILLA' * 7a+ 10m

The wall on the left requires gear. In all probability the only gear needed is a top rope!

SUMINISTROS CORONAS 6b 10m

The bolted wall on the right past a flake to a lower-off on the lip of the roof.

THE RIGHT BANK

All routes here are described from right to left.

SECTOR CORAZON DE METAL

On the right, 175m upstream from the parking area, is a small sector at the point where an old path zig-zags out of the gorge. It consists of three rounded buttresses separated by two scruffy corners. There are four short routes here.

Dave Spencer pulling the jugs on Rainbow (6a+), Las Canadas, Tenerife

DERECHO 4 6m
The right-hand line has two golden bolts, a covering of dust and creaky holds.

CENTRO 5 10m
The second line follows a tricky shallow crack left of a grotty corner, then trends left to a belay. The lower section is easier away to the right, but that's hardly the point!

IZQUIERDA 5 10m
Pull over a bulge on a block and climb the wall rightwards on poor pockets until better holds lead away to the right to the bolt belay of the previous climb.

CORAZON DE METAL 6a+ 10m
The left-hand route climbs a barrel-shaped buttress via a couple of taxing sequences. Bridging across to the right is most certainly taboo.

SECTOR SUS VILLA

A pleasant sunny sector that is always popular. It essentially takes the form of an open bay with a sharp central arête and a large block in front of the wall to the right.

CASCA LA BASCA A LA LASCA ** 6a+ 15m
The right wall of the recess gives a mildly pumpy pitch on good holds except for the last couple of moves.

BATRIACIO 6b+ 10m
Climb the smooth wall to the left of the blocky corner and the bulge above to a quick 'dyno' for the wire cable belay.

SUS VILLA * 6b 12m
The right side of the arête is agreeably technical, especially if you like pocket-pulling. The slab above is easier.

NO HAY COLEGA SIN TACO 5 10m
Around to the left of the central arête the short wall has generous holds.

EL TERROR DE LAS CHIQUILLAS 5 10m
The left wall of the corner is once again pleasantly unremarkable.

LA VENGANZA DEL GODO 6b+ 12m
Fifty metres further upstream and just left of a prominent tree. Climb the leaning wall to a tatty lower-off in the summit block.

SECTOR VIVAC

Continuing upstream the next sector consists of a spaced series of discrete buttresses. The first one is an orange wall split by a diagonal crack, and is home to three routes:

HONGUITOS PELIGROSOS * 6b+ 12m

The wall on the right has some wobbly holds and the bulges above are passed leftwards to easier ground. Limestone climbers will try to avoid the crucial gnarly jam; gritstone climbers will relish it.

FLIPA FLOPA * 6b 12m

The wall just to the left has a nasty move passing the second bolt and is much easier above.

PETA DE KILO * 6a 12m

A slippery and reachy lower wall on the left leads to juggy bulges climbed trending rightwards to a belay shared with the previous route.

Fifty metres further upstream is the next route, just to the right of the point where a tall pine tree is growing close to the rock at the foot of the cliff.

NO HAY NIVEL * 5+ 12m

A pleasant lower wall, then bulges lead to the lower-off.

Twenty metres further upstream is another attractive red face (not your partner's sunburnt one) steepening as it rises:

NOCHES DE CORAL * 6b 12m

Start on the left in a scoop and follow the green bolts up and right to a steep finale.

The final three routes in the SECTOR VIVAC are to be found another 50 or so metres further upstream. All climb good rock, reached in each case by dirty scrambling.

TODOS CON POLI 6a+ 12m

Start on a ledge and climb a corner crack or the wall immediately to its left to a bulge with the belay on its lip.

TRIPA DE CERDO 6c 12m

Reached by dirty ledges, climb the flat wall and then the bulges.

EL ENANITO IMPOTENTE 6a+ 12m

A short distance to the left a dirty scramble leads to a ledge by a block. Climb the left edge of the flat wall to a lower-off below ledges above.

SECTOR LIMBO

To the left is a short red wall, with many well-chalked pockets and reached by a short scramble up a dusty corner. All the routes are sharp.

DE AQUI PAL LIMBO 7a 10m
The clean wall and blunt rib above the approach path.

Scramble awkwardly leftwards over some large blocks to reach the rest of the climbs. The foot of the wall here is an ace sunbathing spot – just watch the spiky plants.

BERBERECHOS AL NATURAL * 6c+ 10m
A flat wall on small pockets leads to a leaning section and onto a belay shared with the last route.

NO LLEGUES TARDE 7a 10m
Past a nasty looking (and unclimbed) off-width is another smooth pocketed wall.

MADIA LA COCODA 6c 6m
Another (you guessed it) smooth pocketed wall behind the fine tree.

SECTOR TIBURON

Continuing upstream some large boulders block the way. Just past these is an attractive golden wall on the right side of the gorge.

LOS JURONES DE LA OROTAVA * 7a+ 12m
Pass round behind cacti, climb the centre of the leaning wall then the thin groove.

RAPIDO COMO UN TIBURON * 7a 12m
Twenty metres further left, at a prominent hole near the top of the buttress, are two routes. This is the right-hand line, climbing diagonally rightwards across the wall, with a thin move (best done 'rapidly like a shark') to reach the roof, before moving right again to the lower-off.

TRANKI COMO UN BERBERECHO ** 6b+ 12m
Tackle the left side of the wall by a crack through bulges and then the wall above, 'slowly like a cockle'.

The last route on this side of the gorge is some distance further upstream past large boulders and some pine trees.

PICO VENA * 6b 12m
Start from a ledge and climb a prominent beak, and the wall above.

Anyone who has managed to get this far can consider themselves a true Arico aficionado and head for a couple of days on the beach. You deserve it.

Sector De Los Naranjos

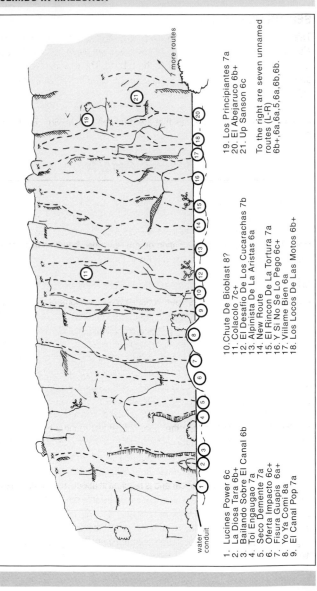

water conduit

1. Lucines Power 6c
2. La Diosa Tara 6b+
3. Bailando Sobre El Canal 6b
4. Toi Engaugao 7a
5. Seco Demente 7a
6. Oferta Impacto 6c+
7. Fisura Guapis 6a+
8. Yo Ya Comi 8a
9. El Canal Pop 7a

10. Chute De Bioblast 8?
11. Colacolo 7c+
12. El Desafio De Los Cucarachas 7b
13. Alpinista De La Aristas 6a
14. New Route
15. El Rincon De La Tortura 7a
16. Y Si No Se Lo Pego 6c+
17. Vilame Bien 6a
18. Los Locos De Las Motos 6b+

19. Los Principiantes 7a
20. El Abejaruco 6b+
21. Up Sanson 6c

To the right are seven unnamed routes (L-R)
6b+,6a,6a,5,6a,6b,6b.

more routes

SECTOR DE LOS NARANJOS

This is the one other area at Arico, which is located 3.5km from the town of Arico, along a recently tarmacked road that takes a left turn off the road to the Upper and Lower Gorges 100m before the first sharp bend. The crag is obvious on the left and is reached in 5 minutes. It is as good (or even better) than the gorge and looses the sun quite early in the morning. All the routes are about 20m long. The climbs are not described – see the topo for illustration.To the right of the topo there are seven unnamed routes that are (from left to right) 6b+, 6a, 6a, 5, 6a, 6b & 6b.

OTHER AREAS

There is a lot of rock on Tenerife and much of it is of climbable quality. Apart from the two main areas of Arico and Las Canadas, I am aware of several other areas that have seen some development, and it is quite possible that there may be many more. The six that I have information on are described briefly in this section in an anticlockwise direction starting at '9:00' with Guia d'Isora.

GUIA D'ISORA

An extensive face which has seen considerable development over recent years, though it would appear that the locals are trying to keep the place quiet. Many of the new routes offer superb long pitches, up to 35m in length. I am grateful to Jon de Montjoy and Hillary Sharp for these updated notes to my original guide.

The cliff consists of a high and broad south-facing wall of excellent red rock overlooking one of the many dry ravines, or *barrancos*, that dissect much of the island. The limited parking for the cliff is reached from the road that runs between Guia d'Isora and Adeje. Two and a half kilometres from Guia, and between two tunnels, are two narrow roads both turning inland. The first one is signed El Jara, and the cliff is located up the other one, hidden just round a bend when heading northbound, opposite a new bus shelter. Follow the road very steeply uphill through the tiny settlement of Acojeja, until stopped by a barrier. Restricted parking is available on the roadside here; have some consideration.

The cliff is visible from the car and is reached in about 15 minutes. Pass through the barrier and after 50m follow an old track that slants down into the dry river bed on the right. From the river bed head straight up the hill opposite to pick up a vague track that slants up to the right through the cacti (occasional cairns) to arrive on the ridge at a stony area about 50m above a prominent 3m high cairn. At this point a well-marked mule track heads up the gorge and passes below all of the cliffs.

The first route climbs a deep roofed-in corner with a hand-crack in its back.

1. POLLO A LA BRASA * 6a+ 25m

From a ledge and follow the sustained corner, through a large roof, to lower-off in the left wall. OK if you like fist-cracks and off-widths.

Forty metres to the right is an attractive slabby rib starting for a ledge above the path:

2. QUE BONITA SUR MIS NINAS * 6a 18m

The rib gives a better and harder pitch than initial appearances might suggest.

Forty metres right is a steep grey pillar:

3. BOY PAL MORO * 6c 15m

A steep and gnarly start leads to marginally easier terrain above.

Further right again and at a higher level is an attractive steep red wall with two prominent cracks splitting it neatly into thirds. Starting near the left edge of the wall is:

4. PETER PUNK ** 6b+ 22m

The lower wall gives fine sustained climbing, though the run-out final section on slightly worrying rock rather spoils the climb.

5. LEFT CRACK ? ? 20m

No fixed gear and grade unknown.

6. BAZUKA PUNK *** 7b+ 22m

The intricate and sustained central pillar gives a pitch of both high quality and high standard, with gradually escalating difficulty.

7. TIRA DE CADENA ** 6b+ 22m

Tenerife's answer to many a gritstone crack-line – slam in the jams and keep truckin'. Now debolted and upgraded from 6a! Carry a rack.

8. DEPARTMENT DE NARCOTICS *** 7a+ 22m

The wall and crack to the right are good.

9. MERCY ** 6c 32m

The open corner and slab above are spoilt by some poor rock. Note the pitch length.

10. EL ENERGAMENO * 7b 12m

The innocuous looking wall left of the blocks proves to be quite mean.

To the right is:

11. ? ? the crack off the top of the blocks.

Guia d'Isora - Left

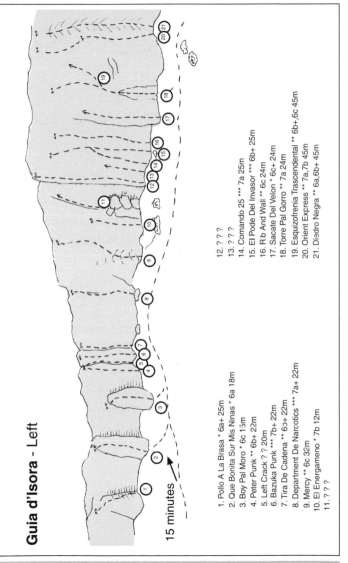

15 minutes

1. Pollo A La Brasa * 6a+ 25m
2. Que Bonita Sur Mis Ninas * 6a 18m
3. Boy Pal Moro * 6c 15m
4. Peter Punk ** 6b+ 22m
5. Left Crack ? ? 20m
6. Bazuka Punk *** 7b+ 22m
7. Tira De Cadena ** 6> + 22m
8. Department De Narcotics *** 7a+ 22m
9. Mercy ** 6c 32m
10. El Energameno * 7b 12m
11. ? ? ?

12. ? ? ?
13. ? ? ?
14. Comando 25 *** 7a 25m
15. El Pode Del Invasor *** 6b+ 25m
16. Rb And Wall ** 6c 24m
17. Sacate Del Velon * 6c+ 24m
18. Torre Pal Gorro ** 7a 24m
19. Esquizofrenia Trascendental ** 6b+,6c 45m
20. Orient Express ** 7a,7b 45m
21. Diedro Negra ** 6a,6b+ 45m

12. ? ? the huge arête.

13. ? ? the wall.

To the right is an attractive broad pillar with two climbs that share an upper section:

14. COMANDO 25 *** 7a 25m
The front face of the pillar gives excellent sustained climbing.

15. EL PODE DEL INVASOR *** 6b+ 25m
To the right the steep pocketed lower wall leads to an enjoyably intricate slab above.

16. RIB AND WALL ** 6c 24m
The next lie to the right.

17. SACATE DEL VELON * 6c+ 24m
The less worthwhile line to the right.

18. TORRE PAL GORRO ** 7a 24m
A good but slightly friable pitch that starts up a prominent rock scar.

19. ESQUIZOFRENIA TRASCENDENTAL ** 6b+,6c 45m
Is the extended right-hand line with the same start.

20. ORIENT EXPRESS ** 7a,7b 45m
The slab and wall left of the big groove.

21. DIEDRO NEGRA ** 6a,6b+ 45m
Excellent but unequipped.

To the right is a huge red wall with a series of bolted crack-lines. No further details known. Round the arête are more bolt lines including:

22. ? ? 40+m
The partly bolted and smart looking groove line.

23. CAFE CALIENTE Y DURO *** 7a+ 32m
The superb pocketed pillar to the right of the groove.

Rounding the next arête is another host of routes including an obvious crack and head wall.

24. BRILLIANT *** 7c 32m
The crack is 7a, the wall above is tougher. The route can just be done on a 70m rope, but great care is required when lowering off.

Right again are two routes that share a lower-off , these are:

25. ? ? 8a? 20m and

26. MANIPULADOR DE ELEMENTOS ** 8a 20m on the right.

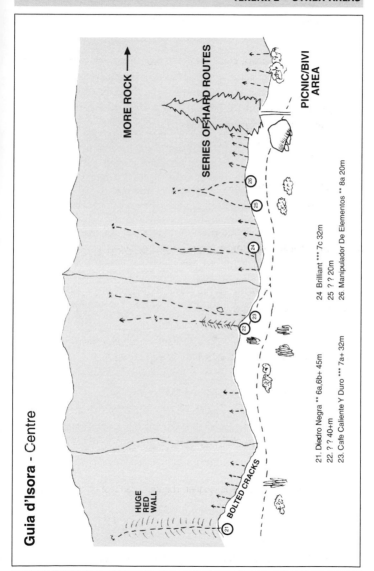

Guia d'Isora - Centre

MORE ROCK →

SERIES OF HARD ROUTES

PICNIC/BIVI AREA

HUGE RED WALL

BOLTED CRACKS

21. Diedro Negra ** 6a,6b+ 45m
22. ? ? 40+m
23. Cafe Caliente Y Duro *** 7a+ 32m

24 Brilliant *** 7c 32m
25 ? ? 20m
26 Manipulador De Elementos ** 8a 20m

To the right is a superb flat picnic/bivi spot, more hard routes and the rocks continue for miles.

LA CATEDRAL

On the final section of the drive to Las Canadas (see section 'Las Canadas', Sectors map) a series of towers and spires away on the left may catch the attention of any mountain climber worth his salt. The most elegant of these is the 120m high Dru-shaped peak of La Catedral, which is home to about a dozen routes set in a very traditional mode. Parking is possible on the roadside just before it begins to rise up towards Las Canadas, and the west face of the peak can be reached by a 20 minute walk across the shimmering ash desert. It is also possible to descend the step loose terrain from the Mirador at the Roques de Garcia to reach the east face, but there is always the problem of the walk back out.

On close acquaintance much of La Catedral is composed of amazing 'Devil's Causeway'-like basalt columns, any one of them being of impressive proportions. A topo available from the climbing shop in Santa Cruz (see appendix) has some rather sketchy topos of the routes here. For completeness I include diagrams and grades of the best looking routes on both faces; positions of stances are approximate. Take a full rack, double ropes, possibly hard hats and definitely some care. Any more detailed descriptions would be gratefully received. Routes are listed from left to right. Descent from the summit is by two long abseils down the south ridge of the mountain.

THE WEST FACE

On the subsidiary tower on the far left side of the face:

1. EL PET 5,3+,4+,4
Reputedly 'loose but good', leading to the col/shoulder.

2. COLLADO DIRECT   6c,5,5+,6b
The face just to the right, bolted but rather spartanly so, also leading to the col/shoulder.

And on the main peak starting from a major ramp/ledge reached by a scramble from the right:

3. VIA SUBIRANA 5,5+
The groove on the far left leading to the col/shoulder.

4. VIA DEL TECHO 5+,A3&5,4+
A left-to-right slanting line to the impressive central roof, then the right side of the tower above.

La Catedral - West Face

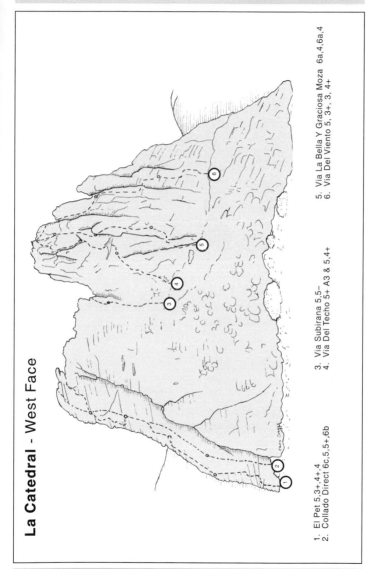

1. El Pet 5, 3+, 4+, 4
2. Collado Direct 6c, 5, 5+, 6b

3. Via Subirana 5, 5–
4. Via Del Techo 5+ A3 & 5, 4+

5. Via La Bella Y Graciosa Moza 6a, 4, 6a, 4
6. Via Del Viento 5, 3+, 3, 4+

5. VIA LA BELLA Y GRACIOSA MOZA 6a,4,6a,4

The central line on the face and reportedly worthwhile; some bolts.

6. VIA DEL VIENTO * 5 100m

I have done this one so you get a full description! An exiting way up the tower. Start up and left of the toe of the buttress below a shallow black corner about 20m up the face.

1. 5 35m Trend right past two fixed pegs to pass a rounded rib awkwardly. Head left into the black groove and climb this to a niche, old bolt runner, and possible stance. Climb the steep crack into a niche (crux) then traverse left over stacked blocks to a stance in the base of an open groove.
2. 3+ 25m Climb the groove pleasantly to easier-angled rock, and climb this to an open bay with a stance on the left below stacked blocks.
3. 3 25m Cross the loose blocks, move left and step into the open groove. Climb this to a stance on the col.
4. 4+ 10m Move right to a thin crack and climb this passing a peg. Move out left 10m on good holds (bolt) and swing round the corner to ledges and peg belay. Scramble to the top.

Descent: Just below the high point (facing the Mirador) are three pegs joined by a wire cable. Abseil 15m off these and move left across a groove to twin bolts. Abseil 28m off these to ledges, then move right (looking out) and scramble out onto the front of the buttress to large twinned ring bolts. Abseil 40m from these to the col behind the tower.

THE EAST FACE

1. VIA BAEZ-ALON 3+,1,4-,3+

Starting from the shoulder between the two faces and following the line of least resistance to the top.

2. LA PLACA ROJA 5,3

A fine variation finish up the red wall. From its top, continue up the arête or traverse right to the regular route.

3. VIA ORIGINAL 4-,2,4,4

A direct line up the buttress and groove to the right.

4. VIA CUIO-ANGUEL 5,A1&4,4+,3

The groove and buttress right again.

LAS VEGAS

Probably the least worthwhile of the developed areas that I have visited. The cliff

La Catedral - East Face

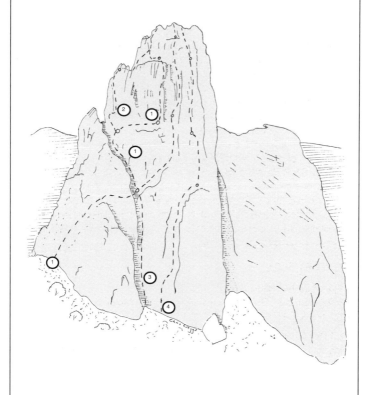

1. Via Baez-Alon 3+,1,4-,3+
2. La Placa Roja 5,3
3. Via Original 4-,2,4,4
4. Via Cuio-Anguel 5,A1&4,4+,3

Las Vegas - Sectors Los Pinus and Los Moco

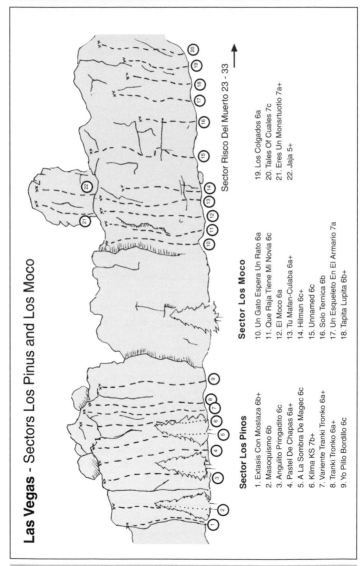

Sector Risco Del Muerto 23 - 33

Sector Los Pinos

1. Extasis Con Mostaza 6b+
2. Masoquismo 6b
3. Angulito Pringadito 6c
4. Pastel De Chapas 6a+
5. A La Sombra De Magec 6c
6. Kilma KS 7b+
7. Variente Tranki Tronko 6a+
8. Tranki Tronko 6a+
9. Yo Pillo Bordillo 6c

Sector Los Moco

10. Un Gato Espera Un Rato 6a
11. Que Raja Tiene Mi Novia 6c
12. El Moco 6a
13. Tu Mafan-Culaba 6a+
14. Hilman 6c+
15. Unnamed 6c
16. Solo Ternica 6b
17. Un Esqueleto En El Armario 7a
18. Tapita Lupita 6b+
19. Los Colgados 6a
20. Tales Of Cuales 7c
21. Eres Un Monsrtuotio 7a+
22. Jaja 5+

is a blocky basalt, and is both dusty and somewhat loose in places, though the cliff is home to about 30 routes. The crag is reached by turning uphill in the centre of Chimiche onto a minor road signed Las Vegas. This followed for 3km until it fizzles out just short of Caesar's Palace. A walled track is followed uphill for about 10 minutes until another track branches down to the left across a narrow dry valley, past orange orchards and up to the left side of the cliff behind some shady trees at the SECTOR LOS PINOS and SECTOR LOS MOCO. The routes here are generally short and from 6a to 6c. Further to the right again is the SECTOR RISCO DEL MUERTO. The topo here is based on a local one, though identification of many of the routes is awkward. Almost all the climbs contain some bolts, but a small subsidiary rack is probably a good idea, just in case. No route descriptions – see the topo.

MARTIANEZ

A recently developed cliff on the northern side of the island in Puerto de la Cruz. Here are a dozen routes (up to 20m) on basalt peppered with gas pockets set just below the road. Like Tejina, the whole area is heavily vegetated with cacti and other exotics. The routes can get rather slick because of the humidity generated by the proximity of the ocean.

Martianez is situated to the east of Puerto de la Cruz, below the coast road. Travelling east along the road there is a right turn to the apartment block of the Edificio Columbus. Just after this there is roadside parking on the left. Walk along the road to just before a tunnel where a path on the right zigzags down the slope to the cliff.

TEJINA

The best developed cliff on the northern side of the island, with 50 closely packed and quite short routes (up to 15m) on a pocketed and cracked basalt. The whole area is much more heavily vegetated than the southern side of the islands, and (perhaps not unexpectedly) it rains a lot more up here than on the south coast. It is probably worth a visit if you are in the area, but is a bit of a trek from the resorts.

Approach the cliff via La Laguna, following signs for Tejina and Teguesta. On the outskirts of Tejina turn uphill (north) by some chalets, and then turn left again to follow the dirt road to parking by a water tank.

TABARES

On the northern side of the island and overlooking the outskirts of Santa Cruz is a valley with a lot of outcropping rock. Unfortunately it is basalt, though there a good number of worthwhile climbs here. The cliffs are accessible from the town of La

Cuesta, which is reached from the motorway (not well signed) between Santa Cruz and La Laguna. Drive uphill through the centre of La Cuesta past several 'No entry' right turns until a minor road turns north in the middle of the town signed 'Valle Tabares 1.7km & Los Campitos'. This is followed for a couple of kilometres, passing a very red bridge, until the road rounds a bend and the cliffs come into view. The cliffs outcrop in a horseshoe around the head of the valley (see diagram), and three areas have been developed at present. They are described in order of popularity, which is also happens to be in reverse order of quality.

Immediately after the bend (care needed) is a right turn down a dirt track that leads to the parking (in an area that masquerades as the local rubbish dump) for the SECTORS TUBERIA and MACROCALMA. For the PARED DE ENFRENTE it is best to continue on the main track, over a very smelly river, and park by the first buildings. A track leads in front of the first house to the cliff edge.

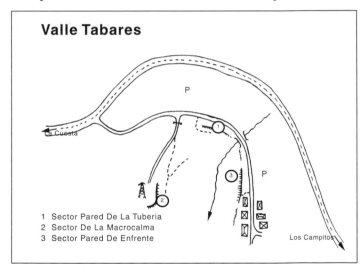

Valle Tabares

1 Sector Pared De La Tuberia
2 Sector De La Macrocalma
3 Sector Pared De Enfrente

SECTOR PARED DE LA TUBERIA

A short sunny cliff of polished rock containing some desperate pitches. If a 10m high, plumb vertical 8a+ is your idea of heaven, look no further. From the parking descend a short slope to locate the crag, which is characterised by the water pipe running along its foot. The routes here are all short and sharp, the Spanish grades feeling especially tough.

On the far left are several very short lines. The first one of any significance is a crack in the back of a recess, which is immediately to the left of a buttress with three bolt runners in it.

PAULIT 5+ 10m
The slippery crack; gear required.

PAPAS CON CARNE 6c 10m
The gymnastic buttress just to the right; three bolts protect.

MAPA 6a+ 10m
The slippery finger-crack just right again. Gear required.

POTAGE DE BERROS 6c+ 10m
The thin crack to the right, protected by three bolts on its right side.

BUTERFINGERS * 7a 10m
The tenuous finger-crack in the groove to the right; gear required.

MARTIN EL LAJA * 8a+ 12m
The 'impossible' blank wall to the right protected by four bolts.

ATOMICA 7b+ 12m
The thin seam to the right has a peg and bolt *in situ*; other gear required.

ALIEN 8a 12m
Another 'impossible' wall climb protected by four bolt runners.

METALLICA 7c 12m
The desperate thin crack line to the right. Three *in situ* pegs protect the most difficult section.

SUICIDAL TENDENCES 7a 12m
The crack just to the right with three bolt runners finishing at the cliff top agave.

ANDORINA 6b 10m
The more reasonable crack to the right; the trouble is, you have to place your own kit.

To the right are two more lines following a bolted crack and arête; no grades known.

SECTOR PARED DE LA MACROCALMA
The tall buttress below the power pylon is home to a series of climbs, many of which are worthwhile. They are up to 22m high and north-east facing, so normally reside in the shade. The cliff is reached down a well-made footpath that branches

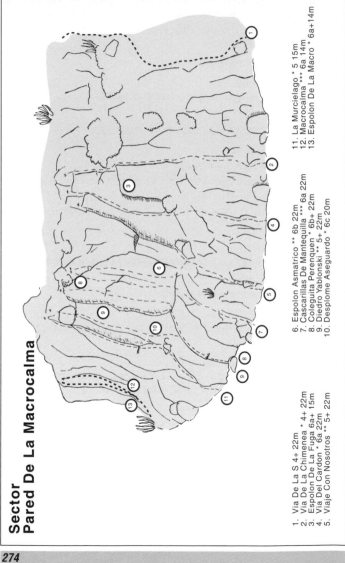

Sector
Pared De La Macrocalma

1. Via De La S 4+ 22m
2. Via De La Chimenea * 4+ 22m
3. Espolon De La Fuga 6a+ 15m
4. Via Del Cardon * 6a 22m
5. Viaje Con Nosotros ** 5+ 22m

6. Espolon Asmatrico ** 6b 22m
7. Cascarillas De Mantequilla *** 6a 22m
8. Coleguita Perenquen * 6b+ 22m
9. Diedro Yablonski ** 5+ 22m
10. Desplome Aseguardo * 6c 20m

11. La Murcielago * 5 15m
12. Macrocalma *** 6a 14m
13. Espolon De La Macro * 6a+14m

left from the side track forking right off the main track. On the far right is a rather nondescript area of rock, but in the centre of the cliff is fine clean facing hanging above more broken rock and bounded by two fine grooves. Around to the left are more good groove and crack lines.

On the far right side of the face is the nondescript line of:

1. VIA DE LA S 4+ 22m
A groove in the lower wall leads past a couple of bolts to a possible stance and easier terrain trending right.

To the left is a huge perched block/flake halfway up the cliff. The right side of this is climbed by:

2. VIA DE LA CHIMENEA * 4+ 22m
Climb the lower groove to a possible stance at the foot of the chimney, then follow it and a blocky crack to the cliff top.

There are three short 'eliminates' based around the actual chimney of the last route.

LA VIA HILTI 6a 10m
The wall immediately right of the chimney, climbed via a thin crack to a lower-off.

PASTA GANSA 7a 10m
The wall just left of the chimney to a lower-off.

3. ESPOLON DE LA FUGA 6a+ 15m
Starts as for VIA DE LA CHIMENEA then steps out left to climb the arête on its left side. The best of the trio.

To the left the most obvious feature of the cliff is a fine hanging face, bound on its right by a long twisting groove line. To the right of this is a crack-line that runs straight up the cliff to the top of the previously mentioned groove:

4. VIA DEL CARDON * 6a 22m
Climb easy terrain to a bush at the foot of the crack (possible stance) then follow the crack, not the bush, past three bolt runners to the cliff top. A supplementary rack is probably a good idea.

The long groove is:

5. VIAJE CON NOSOTROS ** 5+ 22m
Climb a corner crack into the foot of the groove then follow it rightwards past five bolts to the cliff top.

Above the start of the groove proper is a roof and leaning wall with a bolt ladder up it: VIA DEL TECHO A1 20m (it will never catch on).

To the left is the showpiece of the cliff, a fine shield of rock hanging above more broken terrain. I hesitate to suggest that the area is worth a visit for the best of the routes here, but in the words of the lottery, just maybe.

6. ESPOLON ASMATICO ** 6b 22m
Climbs the right arête of the hanging shield. Approach from the left via a thin finger-crack above a cactus; five bolts.

7. CASCARILLAS DE MANTEQUILLA *** 6a 22m
As for previous climb, but cross roof to gain fine central arête. The best route here.

8. COLEGUITA PERENQUEN * 6b+ 22m
The right wall of the deep groove; sustained and fingery.

9. DIEDRO YABLONSKI ** 5+ 22m
The right-hand groove is entered up strenuous juggy wall (clip bolt out to left). Sustained with crux near the top; exit to the right.

10. DESPLOME ASEGUARDO * 6c 20m
The narrow wall between the two grooves.

BUZONES ** 5+ 18m
The left-hand groove is entered from the left. A fine sustained climb.

UNNAMED * 6a 16m
The wall around to the left is approached via finger-crack (two peg runners in wall), and then follow the easier arête above.

11. LA MURCIELARGO * 5 15m
The obvious open groove is approached up the ramp and climbed passing a big jammed block. One awkward move then easier above.

SOPA DE TRIPIS ** 6b+ 15m
The smooth open groove (pegs) is approached up a steep wall.

12. MACROCALMA *** 6a 14m
Steepening groove to right of hand-crack approached up a ramp. Steep and juggy at top.

13. ESPOLON DE LA MACRO * 6a 14m
Hand-crack is approached as for last climb and followed out left.

DIEDRO DEL DESVIRGO * 6a 14m

Final long groove is entered over a small overhang and followed thinly to a final steepening. Can be dirty.

There are also two short routes up and left: ORUMINIKUB 6b+ and FUERA DE COBETURA 6c+.

SECTOR PARED DE ENFRENTE

This is the imposing set of grooves and pillars on the eastern side of the valley (west facing). There is limited roadside parking and the routes are approached from above, by abseil, as almost all of the lower section of the face consists of an unsavoury band of soft red rock and a series of dripping overhangs, although four routes ignore this fact and start from the gorge bed. Running along the cliff top, squeezed between spiky plants and a huge drop, is a wire cable installed in the interests of security. Use it – you know it makes sense. The climbs are of two sorts, fine sustained crack-lines (a rack of Friends required) and the faces between the cracks that are bolt protected. The routes are generally tough, and this, allied to the difficulty of locating specific routes from above, means a circumspect approach is sensible. The place may make an ideal top-roping venue if you don't want to get involved in too much of an epic. The climbs are described briefly from left to right (facing the cliff), and their positions can be located using the diagram, in relation to the clusters of fixed bolts spaced along the cliff top.

1. MAGNUM 44 * 6a+ 25m
The left-hand route is one of the few to run the full height of the basalt. A fine sustained hand-crack. Friends required.

2. DELICIAS TURCAS * 5+ 18m
The next hand-crack to the right, starting from the ledge.

To the right two face routes climb either side of a blunt rib:

3. BUJERITOS * 6c 18m
The left side of the rib; five bolts and a peg protect.

4. OVERKILL * 6b 18m
The right side of the rib; five bolts.

5. PREPARATE 7a 18m
The thin hand-crack is reached from a stance on the right and has two peg runners. Take wires and Friends.

6. FISURA TRANSPARENTE * 6b 18m
The wall to the right starting and finishing up thin cracks. Three bolts in the centre;

Sector Pared Enfrente

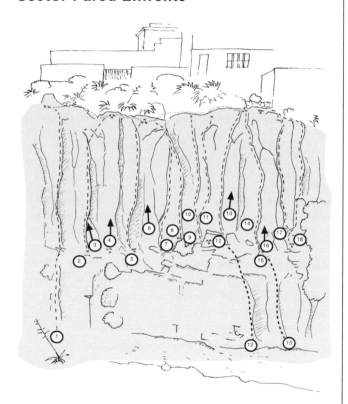

1. Magnum 44 * 6a+ 25m
2. Delicias Turcas * 5+ 18m
3. Bujeritos * 6c 18m
4. Overkill * 6b 18m
5. Preparate 7a 18m
6. Fisura Transparente * 6b 18m
7. Ataud Vacante ** 6a+ 18m
8. Therminator * 7a 28m
9. Autopista Al Inferno ** 7c+ 18m

10. Killer * 6c 18m
11. Extasis Technico * 6c+ 18m
12. Genocidio ** 6a+ 28m
13. Mad-Max * 7b 18m
14. Moc-Moc * 7c 18m
15. Iron Maiden * 6c 28m
16. Bib-Bip 7a 18m
17. Dosis Heavy Metal ** 6a 18m
18. Metalmorfsis * 5+ 18m

wires and Friends for the rest.

7. ATAUD VACANTE ** 6a+ 18m
The hand- and finger-crack directly above the belay.

8. THERMINATOR * 7a 28m
The thin twisting crack contains three peg runners; carry a rack of wires. An optional pitch from the foot of the cliff is there for those who want it.

9. AUTOPISTA AL INFERNO ** 7c 18m
The narrow wall and flared arête to the right is tough; six bolt runners protect.

10. KILLER * 6c 18m
The thin crack just right of the pillar; keep left at the first fork and right at the second.

11. EXTASIS TECHNICO * 6c+ 18m
Start as for the previous climb, but follow the right fork until it bears away left; then leap out onto the face on the right (bolt then peg), then up a crack to the top.

12. GENOCIDIO ** 6a+ 28m
The long fine hand-crack to the right, gained from the bed of the gorge. Carry a rack.

13. MAD-MAX * 7b 18m
The thin face to the right; four bolts protect.

14. MOC-MOC * 7c 18m
The thinner face right again. Three bolts protect the hard section; take gear for the rest.

15. IRON MAIDEN * 6c 28m
The thin hand-crack has an optional start from the gorge bed.

16. BIP-BIP 7a 18m
The face to the right; three bolts protect the hard section.

17. DOSIS HEAVY METAL ** 6a 18m
The fine thin hand-crack; gear required.

18. METALMORFSIS * 5+ 18m
The final route starts up and over a block, then follows a hand-crack.

GRAN CANARIA

Introduction

Several of the other Canary Islands have quality rock climbing, though not of the quantity that is available on Tenerife. The biggest of the other venues is Tamadaba on Gran Canaria. Like Tenerife Gran Canaria is a classical volcanic island, a smooth cone rising from the sea. The highest point of the island is the Pico de Las Nieves (Peak of the Snows) at 1949m, and is easily accessible from the nearby car park. North-west from here is the lesser peak of Tamadaba (1444m) and just north again is a collection of almost 300 sport routes running along a series of terraces overlooking the north-west quadrant of the island. The cliffs are set in the pine trees at an altitude of 1250m, thus alleviating the worst of the heat, though the area can be cloud covered when a northerly wind is blowing over the island. There are ten developed sectors, and the most accessible and well developed four are described here briefly: SECTOR SUPER NOVA, SECTOR GULLICH, SECTOR EL CAMINO and SECTOR CARABALLO.

Details of the routes are set out on the topos on the following pages.

Access

The cliffs are reached from Artenara, which is 12km west of Tejeda. Tejeda can be reached by any one of a series of steep and winding roads that run inland from the eastern side of the island (40km to 50km). From Artenara follow the road north-west for 10km to a right turn into the Zona Recreativa de Tamadaba. The sectors listed are arranged around the head of the Barranco Oscuro, whilst the other developed sectors are around the rim of the promontory of the Llano de Mimbre, just to the west.

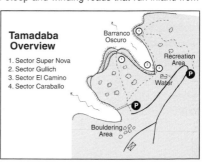

Tamadaba Overview

1. Sector Super Nova
2. Sector Gullich
3. Sector El Camino
4. Sector Caraballo

Barranco Oscuro

Recreation Area

Water

Bouldering Area

Sector Super Nova

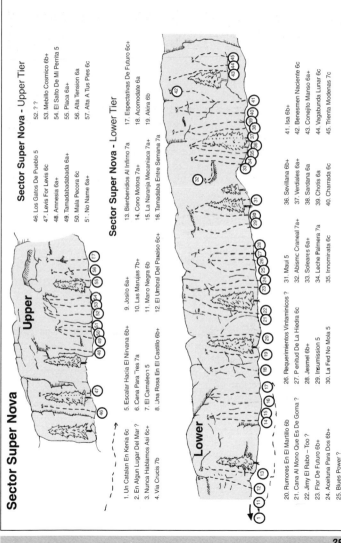

Upper

Lower

Sector Super Nova - Upper Tier

46. Los Gatos De Pueblo 5
47. Levis For Levis 6c
48. Amnesia 6a+
49. Tamadabadabada 6a+
50. Mala Pecora 6c
51. No Name 6a+
52. ? ?
53. Mebillo Cosmico 6b+
54. El Salto De Mi Perrita 5
55. Placa 6a+
56. Alta Tension 6a
57. Alta A Tus Pies 6c

Sector Super Nova - Lower Tier

13. Bienbenidos Al Infirno 7a
14. Cono Motora 7a+
15. La Naranja Mecaniaca 7a+
16. Tamadaba Entre Semana 7a
17. Espectativas De Futuro 6c+
18. Acomodate 6a
19. Akira 6b

1. Un Catalan En Kenia 6c
2. En Algun Lugar Del Mar ?
3. Nunca Hablamos Asi 6c+
4. Via Crucis 7b
5. Escalar Hacia El Nirvana 6b+
6. Cena Para Tres 7a
7. El Camaleon 5
8. Una Rosa En El Castillo 6b+
9. Josito 6a+
10. Las Marujas 7b+
11. Maro Negra 6b
12. El Umbral Del Paraiso 6c+

20. Rumores En El Martillo 6b
21. Cana Al Mono Que Es De Goma ?
22. Jimy El Rabo – Too ?
23. Flor De Futuro 6b+
24. Aceituna Para Dos 6b+
25. Blues Power ?
26. Requerimientos Vintaminicos ?
27. Penitud De La Hiedra 6c
28. Jesmel 6b+
29. Insumission 5
30. La Fed No Mola 5
31. Maui 5
32. Abismc Craneal 7a+
33. Soleares 6a+
34. Leche Palmera 7a
35. Innomirata 6c
36. Sevillana 6b+
37. Verdiales 6a+
38. Sardana 6a
39. Chotis 6a
40. Charrada 6c
41. Isa 6b+
42. Benesmen Naciente 6c
43. Conejito Manso 6a+
44. Vagabunda Lunar 6c
45. Trienta Modenas 7c

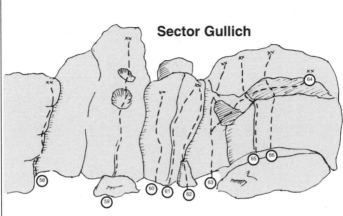

Sector Gullich

58. Patric Wolfgang 6a+
59. No Name 5
60. Sobre – Vivo 6b+

61. Excelsior 7a
62. No Name 6a+
63. Dos Negras Y Un Oso 7b

64. Emiliano Zapata 8b
65. Pasajero Free 7b
66. El Techo Del Gullich 7a

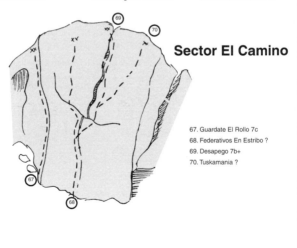

Sector El Camino

67. Guardate El Rollo 7c
68. Federativos En Estribo ?
69. Desapego 7b+
70. Tuskamania ?

Sector Caraballo

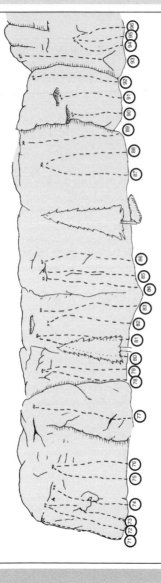

71. Blanca Y Negros 6b+
72. Dracue – La Endemoniaca 5+
73. Graviterapia 5
74. Elena 5
75. Como Se Lama, Pepe? 5
76. K.E.T. 5+
77. Escarbe 5+
78. Hamer To Fall 6b
79. Que Dios Reparte Suerte 6a
80. Contraluces 6b
81. El Ultimo Sociq 6b
82. Slurp 6b

83. Lobotomia 6b+
84. Bailarina 6b
85. Pepusila 5+
86. Somebody To Love 6a
87. Los Guantes Del Papa 6b+
88. Individuo Rono 7a+
89. Panicc En Juencalillo 6a+
90. Calle Urbana Democratica 5

91. Estalactita Humana 6c+
92. Tianaman (no gear) ?
93. Codigo Neuritico 6a
94. Julio, No Me Sanciones 6b
95. Ship Follator 6b
96. Vuelva Usted Manana 6b+
To the right are a further 20 routes, the best of which are Tamaran 7a+, Moneyba 7a, El Polla Boba De Los Patines 7a+, Veulo A Ciegas 7b

LANZAROTE

Introduction

The last volcanic eruptions took place here between 1730 and 1736, and with 300 recognisable craters the place can still be considered geologically active. The island is ringed by miles of basalt cliffs that drop straight into the sea. The scope for traditional climbing, sea cliff traversing and deep water soloing is extensive, though being the Atlantic the sea can be rough (not as rough as the rock however). There are currently four developed sport climbing areas, three of which are described here: Barranco de Teneguime, Jameo de la Puerta Falsa and Cueva de Orzola. The other one is Las Maretas, on the south-western tip of the island, overlooking the sea; it looks well worthwhile (see map). There is topo guide available for perusal in the local climbers' hangout, La Arepera, Bar de Jose in Guatiz.

BARRANCO DE TENEGUIME

A short distance to the north-west of Guatiza is a rocky ravine with the largest collection of climbs on the island along its northern flank. From Guatiza take the minor road towards the cemetery and turn right. This narrow road is followed round a series of bends for 300m, passing over the ravine, until after a long left-hand bend there is a track on the right with limited parking. Follow this up onto the plateau above the ravine, then descend by abseiling or walking round the end of the cliff.

The routes are shoen from left to right and the continuous wall is divided into three sectors: SECTOR LA CARA DEL INDIO, SECTOR JUMANJI and SECTOR EL 34.

The two other developed cliffs are towards the northern tip of the island where a couple of *jameos* (sunken volcanic depressions) contain about 20 routes between them. Both can be visited in a day and are easily reached from the Guatiza to Orzola road. Most of the routes are pretty tough, especially at the second venue.

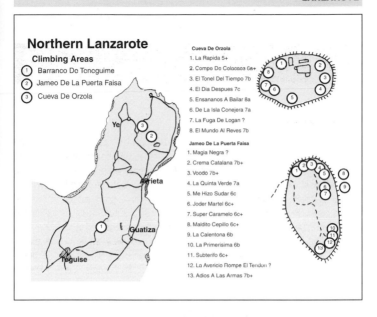

Northern Lanzarote

Climbing Areas

1. Barranco De Toncguime
2. Jameo De La Puerta Faisa
3. Cueva De Orzola

Cueva De Orzola

1. La Rapida 5+
2. Compo Do Colocaos 6a+
3. El Tonel Del Tiempo 7b
4. El Dia Despues 7c
5. Ensananos A Bailar 8a
6. De La Isla Conejera 7a
7. La Fuga De Logan ?
8. El Mundo Al Reves 7b

Jameo De La Puerta Faisa

1. Magia Negra ?
2. Crema Catalana 7b+
3. Voodo 7b+
4. La Quinta Verde 7a
5. Me Hizo Sudar 6c
6. Joder Martel 6c+
7. Super Caramelo 6c+
8. Maldito Cepillo 6c+
9. La Calentona 6b
10. La Primerisima 6b
11. Subterifo 6c+
12. La Avericio Rompe El Tendon ?
13. Adios A Las Armas 7b+

JAMEO DE LA PUERTA FALSA

From the roundabout by the petrol station in Arrieta turn inland and follow the road towards the Mirador del Rio for about 3km to a right turn at a junction signed towards La Cueva de los Verdes. Park down here after 600m and take a short track to reach the descent into the north-west corner of the obvious large hollow. The routes are between 14m and 25m long.

CUEVA DE ORZOLA

The second venue has a small collection of short sharp routes. These are reached by following the approach to the previous cliff, but at the right turn for the Cuevas continue straight on towards Ye. At the high point of the road is a minor right turn towards Orzola. A short distance down here the crag is situated to the right in an obvious open cave.

Barranco De Teneguime -
Access and Routes

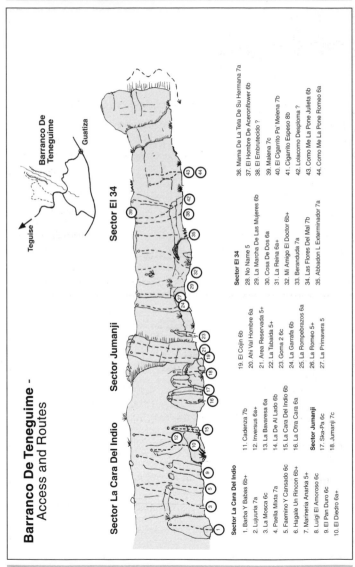

Barranco De Teneguime

Teguise

Guatiza

Sector La Cara Del Indio

Sector Jumanji

Sector El 34

Sector La Cara Del Indio

1. Barba Y Babas 6b+
2. Lujuuria 7a
3. La Mosca 6c
4. Paella Mixta 7a
5. Faemino Y Cansado 6c
6. Hagale Un Rincon 6b+
7. Marineria Anarka 5+
8. Luigi El Amoroso 6c
9. El Pan Duro 6c
10. El Diedro 6a+

11. Cadenza 7b
12. Inversus 6a+
13. La Bavaresa 6a
14. La De Al Lado 6b
15. La Cara Del Indio 6b
16. La Otra Cara 6a

Sector Jumanji

17. Ska-Pa 6b
18. Jumanji 7c

19. El Cojin 6b
20. Ahi Val Hombre 6a
21. Area Reserviada 5+
22. La Tabaida 5+
23. Goma 2 6c
24. La Garrafa 6b
25. La Rompebrazos 6a
26. La Romeo 5+
27. La Primavera 5

Sector El 34

28. No Name 5
29. La Marcha De Las Mujeres 6b
30. Cosa De Dos 6a
31. La Reina 6a+
32. Mi Amigo El Doctor 6b+
33. Beranduda 7a
34. Las Flores Del Mal 7b
35. Abbadon L Exterminador 7a

36. Mama De La Teta De Su Hermana 7a
37. El Hombre De Aceroniflower 6b
38. El Embrutecido ?
39. Malena 7c
40. El Cigarrito Pa' Melena 7b
41. Cigarrito Espeso 8b
42. Lolacomo Desploma ?
43. Como Me La Pone Julieta 6b
44. Como Me La Pone Romeo 6a